MARIA MALIBRAN

MARIA MALIBRAN

Diva of the Romantic Age

by

APRIL FITZLYON

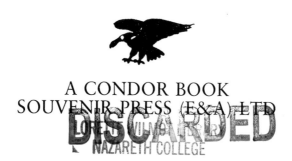

A CONDOR BOOK
SOUVENIR PRESS (E&A) LTD

First published 1987 by Souvenir Press
(Educational & Academic) Ltd,
43 Great Russell Street, London WC1B 3PA
and simultaneously in Canada

ISBN 0 285 65030 0

Phototypeset by Input Typesetting Ltd, London SW19 8DR
Printed in Great Britain by
Billing & Sons Ltd, Worcester

To my friends
Martine and André Le Cesne
who have done so much to help me

PREFACE

Maria Malibran was the saint and martyr of the French Romanticism of the 1830s, a cult figure almost as potent as Elvis Presley or John Lennon today. She was also one of the greatest opera singers of the nineteenth century.

It has not been my intention to write a conventional biography of La Malibran, the singer, or to write a book about opera, but rather to view La Malibran as a product and symbol of French Romanticism, an expression of Romantic attitudes. A large number of conventional biographies of La Malibran, the singer, already exist; the most recent, Howard Bushnell's *Maria Malibran — A Biography of the Singer* (Pennsylvania State University Press, 1979), gives a fully documented account of her career, and there is no need for another. Those who want more factual details than I give about her performances and travels, as well as numerous anecdotes about her, true and false, which are also included in most earlier biographies, will find it satisfactory.

My aim is rather different: I have attempted to show how La Malibran's personality and dramatic style, moulded by her private experiences, made her into the personification of the Romantic movement of her day and influenced her contemporaries, particularly writers, to such an extent that she became a mythical figure. In my opinion, La Malibran left an even greater mark on French life and literature than she did on operatic history.

I have also tried to show La Malibran as a prototype of the woman dramatic artist who becomes a great star and is, as a result, confronted with various problems inherent in that state: the tensions between private and public life — Yeats' 'perfection of the life or of the work'; the actress's problem of identity; the dramatic artist's relationship with her public; and the actress's position in society. All these problems — except, perhaps, the last — still face women on the stage today.

It is never easy to discover the truth about someone who became a legend in her own lifetime; it is almost impossible to do so about someone who became a cult figure — the numerous hagiographies have by now almost totally obscured reality. However, as a result of my research, using much unpublished material, my account of La Malibran's personal life differs considerably from those in other biographies. I cannot claim that my account presents the whole truth — no biographer can ever claim that — but I believe it to be nearer the truth than earlier accounts are, and I think it helps to explain various aspects of her life and art.

If I have described in what may seem excessive detail La Malibran's death in Manchester and subsequent events there, this is because the whole story has never been fully told before, and because both at the time and ever since, the City of Manchester has been very unfairly criticised in continental publications in connection with those events. I felt that, after 150 years, it was time that the record should be put straight.

As many of the names in this book may be unfamiliar to English readers, the index is also a brief biographical dictionary, giving the dates, nationality, and title to fame of everyone mentioned. All translations are my own, unless otherwise stated.

Acknowledgements

First and foremost, I would like to thank Martine and André Le Cesne (Madame Le Cesne is La Malibran's great-great-great niece). They put their family archives at my disposal, and gave me every help and encouragement while I was writing this book. Jacques-Paul Viardot, La Malibran's great nephew, also put his archives at my disposal, and his friendship and knowledge of his family history have been of very great assistance to me in many ways.

Monsieur P. Raspé, Bibliothécaire at the Bibliothèque du Conservatoire Royale, Brussels, was extremely kind and helpful to me when I was in Belgium, and since.

I would like to thank the staff of the following libraries: the British Library, the London Library, the Theatre Museum, Victoria and Albert Museum, Central Music Library, Westminster, Chiswick Library (London Borough of Hounslow), Manchester Central Library and Local History Library; Bibliothèque Nationale, Paris, Bibliothèque de l'Opéra, Bibliothèque de l'Arsenal; Bibliothèque Royale Albert 1er, Brussels, Bibliothèque du Conservatoire Royale.

The following have kindly allowed me to reproduce pictures in their collections: The Royal Library, Windsor Castle, by gracious permission of Her Majesty The Queen, the British Library, the Victoria and Albert Museum, the Theatre Museum, the Royal College of Music; Le Cesne Collection, Paris, Monsieur Robert Maupoil, Paris, Bibliothèque Nationale, Paris, Bibliothèque Royale Albert 1er, Brussels, Bibliothèque du Conservatoire Royale, Brussels; J-A. Carlotti, Lyon; Anthony Gasson, London.

The quotation from Tito Gobbi's *My Life* is reproduced by kind permission of Miss Ida Cook, Signor Gobbi's literary collaborator.

The following have been very helpful to me in various ways: John Bignell (photographer), Marie Broussais, the late Martin Cooper, Colonel Victor Houart, Mrs Kloegman, Dr Edward Larkin, Raphael Nadal, Alexander Schouvaloff, Rivers Scott, Professor Patrick Waddington, Richard Walker, John Watts.

Finally, I would like to express my gratitude to Tessa Harrow of Souvenir Press, a wonderful editor, who has spared no time or trouble in the production of this book.

CONTENTS

LIST OF ILLUSTRATIONS

La Malibran, 'the prima donna whom thousands have worshipped, who was looked upon as the goddess of song during her brief existence.'

The Manchester Guardian, 1st October, 1836

Rossini, on the singers of his day:
'The most remarkable was Madame Pasta; Madame Colbran was the foremost; but Madame Malibran was unique.'

'She was an adorable woman, a great artist, wonderfully gifted both as to voice and as to intelligence, an exceptional human being, and very cultivated; at the same time, her nature was original, almost eccentric.'

Gilbert Duprez, the French tenor, who often partnered her

'A day will come when people reading La Malibran's life will think they are reading a legend; so much of it was incredible, so much fantasy was mixed with reality, so much poetry with prose, so much that took place in daylight was so extraordinary that it was like what one usually only sees behind the footlights. La Malibran acted her life and lived her parts.'

Her friend, the critic Henri Blaze de Bury

'It is, perhaps, a fact unique in history, that there should be such a cult for the memory of a great artist.'

F. J. Fétis, in his funeral oration
for La Malibran, January, 1837

PROLOGUE

Humanity has always needed and created cult figures. Societies have either worshipped many gods or, if they were monotheistic, have tended to treat certain human beings — saints or kings or heroes — as if they were semi-divine. In Christendom the Church for many centuries had a virtual monopoly of cult figures — saints. But with the decline of religion and the secularisation of society, particularly after the French and Russian revolutions, the veneration of saints began to diminish, sometimes as a result of active repression by the state; new, secular saints began to emerge. People in every epoch adapt cults and cult figures to their own specific needs.

All such figures must, by definition, be exceptional. Christian saints, according to history or legend, were outstandingly holy, wise, devout or brave; martyrs were remarkable by the manner of their deaths; often, miracles were attributed to them. Secular saints, too, must be exceptional: brave, or beautiful, or talented or skilled in some way. They must be somehow isolated, for they must stand out from the crowd; and there must be some element of risk or danger in their way of life, which highlights their particular form of courage or skill. Modern cult figures are usually people who perform difficult or dangerous feats before large audiences — certain types of sportsmen, solo instrumentalists, pop musicians, solo ballet dancers — and thus give the public the thrills it craves. A lone figure facing a large audience is essentially heroic, and therefore cult figures often come from the theatre.

The origin of the theatre in most civilisations was religious, and the ritual of a theatrical performance is akin to a religious ceremony. The actors in their costumes, set apart from the audience — like priests in their vestments, remote from the congregation — perform a mystery: they take on other characters, portray emotions which are not their own, become possessed by alien spirits; they hoodwink the audience into believing that it is witnessing real events, real emotions. This is mystery, magic; and it is both fascinating and disturbing. Actors hold up a mirror to us, and show us things which we do not always wish to see. At the same time, they represent us; they do things on the stage which we would like to do, but cannot, or dare not do. Often people identify with actors and actresses, or they desire them. They are mediums, sex symbols, exorcists, dreams, a source of catharsis.

As theatre people play to large audiences and attract wide publicity, it is hardly surprising that, from time to time, one of them should capture the public's imagination in some special way, possessing talents, personality, physical appearance and life-style that exactly match the mood of the moment. Such people become trend-setters, models of perfection, ideals. They exert a more powerful spell than their fellow performers; and, particularly if they die young, a cult is born.

It is born for the performer's own generation, and no other. People a little older or younger are impervious to the spell. But on their exact contemporaries such stars make a mark which can never be effaced. They can move audiences to frenzy, to ecstasy, to hysteria, simply by their presence. They need not even perform; they only have to be seen. Everything they do, on and off the stage, becomes significant. The smallest details of their private lives are of interest, for stars must be seen not only to be extraordinary, but also to be ordinary, so that ordinary people can identify with them. They must live in the limelight, yet remain somehow mysterious: for they have become minor gods and goddesses, not quite human, and not quite divine.

Gradually, however, these stars become possessed by their public, which demands more and more of them. It heaps on them honours, flattery, money, love; but, having created them, considers that it owns them. As a result, the great star, the cult figure, rarely knows who or what he or she is. The distinction between reality and illusion becomes blurred, and the strain of being both private person and public fantasy sometimes proves too great. For the star is required not only to bear all the desires, dreams and frustrations of the crowd, but also to expiate them. He or she becomes a scape-goat. Only the gods have the secret of eternal youth; so the victim must be sacrificed, to be reborn as a god or goddess, forever young, to preserve that generation's youth. What we love, we kill. The public deifies its victims, but first it drives them to the altar. Once the sacrifice is made, the apotheosis begins.

*   *   *

It may seem incongruous that an opera singer such as Maria Malibran could become a cult figure. Opera has now become a minority and élitist taste, a museum art, which does not reflect contemporary life or ideas. Few operas are now being written, and fewer still have popular appeal. But, at the beginning of the nineteenth century, opera was immensely popular with a huge public from all classes of society; moreover, opera and ballet were the only theatrical arts to cross frontiers and gain an international audience. Opera was the nineteenth century equivalent of the cinema: brash, violent or sentimental; appreciated mainly by young people; often based on contemporary novels; a source of hit tunes; a magnificent spectacle; an escapist dream world.

What the public wanted above all was novelty; there had to be two or three new operas every season. Old operas — those more than two or three years old — were revived only if they were really exceptional. They were not written to last, although some of them have done so. If an opera was successful, people would go to see it over and over again, as they do some films; after the first few performances the plot ceased to matter very much, since everyone knew it already. What mattered was the singers, the great stars; they had their fans and detractors, and what the audience relished was how they sang, how they would surmount the vocal difficulties, how they would improvise, how they would act.

Singers were the absolute rulers of early nineteenth century opera. They were much more important than the composer and, unlike him, they earned enormous sums. They were much more important than conductors, who were then only just beginning to emerge and had not yet become stars; and, if there was a producer or director, which was not always the case, they were much more important than him, too. Singers could make or break an opera, and fill or empty a theatre. They aroused violent passions, and their fans were dedicated.

But, unlike their modern equivalents, they had no help from the media — they were only just beginning to be boosted in the press — and they had to make their way by sheer merit. They were not created by a director or a producer, nor were they beautified and publicised by the camera, nor amplified by a microphone. They rarely had business managers or agents. Female stars could sometimes advance their careers by sleeping with a composer or an impresario; but protection without great talent would not take them very far. They had to reach the top by their own efforts alone, by their musical and dramatic gifts. We can judge, from the music which composers wrote for them, that they were extremely accomplished; and, for the big stars, the rewards were enormous. It was the only more or less honourable profession in which a woman at that time could earn a great deal of money.

Maria Malibran was not necessarily the greatest singer of her day, but she was the singer who supremely captured its imagination, and those who were lucky enough to hear her in the theatre, or to meet her, never forgot her. Memoirs and letters of the period, newspapers, novels and poems contain more references to her than to any other performer, and almost all the references are flattering. Her early, tragic death completed her apotheosis, and her cult still continues, after a century and a half.

PART I

NEW YORK

1

The future Maria Malibran was born in Paris, at 3 rue de Condé, on 24th March, 1808, the daughter — according to her birth certificate — of Manuel Rodriguez Garcia and of Maria Joackim Siches [*sic*] 'his wife'. The child's names were registered in the French form: Marie Félicité; but she was always to use the Spanish form: Maria Felicia.*

As will be seen, not all the details on her birth certificate were quite correct; but the gist of it was true. She was the daughter of a Spanish couple who called themselves Garcia, and who had only arrived in Paris a few months earlier. Both her parents were singers and actors; her father was soon to reach the very top of his profession, and has left a mark on musical history.

Maria's father, Manuel de el Pópulo Vicente Rodriguez — to give him all the names on his baptismal certificate, for he added Garcia to his names later† — was born in Seville on 21st January, 1775. His mother was Mariana de Aguilar Martinez; his father was Jeronimo Rodriguez Torrentera. Manuel sometimes used the name Rodriguez, but he did not use his mother's name, as most Spaniards do.

Manuel never knew his father; he believed, or told his children that he believed his father to have been a gypsy, and used to say that he was born in a district of Seville where only gypsies lived.¹‡ this may have been true, or it may just have been good publicity, for Garcia was to make Spanish gypsy music popular outside Spain, and he liked to cultivate the wild outlaw image, so popular with the

* Her name is often given as Maria Felicità, but this is incorrect. (Birth certificate: 1278 (2ème arrondissement) 24th March, 1808.)
† In 1842, after his death, his son Manuel Patricio had the 'second name' — Garcia — added to his father's baptismal certificate, presumably in order to make the family's use of that name official.
‡ He was born at 35, calle del Fourento, and baptised in the church of Santa Maria Magdalena. (Baptismal certificate G. No 004382, Book 32, Folio: 192.)

Romantics. But people who knew him sometimes supposed that he and Jewish or Moorish blood;² there was, apparently, something exotic, un-European, about him, and he transmitted his slightly un-European features to both his daughters.

Manuel's mother died when he was six, and he then entered the famous choir school of Seville Cathedral, where he received an excellent musical education. When he left the school he was well-trained as a singer of church music, and he soon became a prolific composer, and also played the guitar. He first appeared on the stage in Cadiz at the age of seventeen under the name of Garcia, which he was to give to his descendants and which has not yet died out.

Garcia's musical gifts were not his only assets. He was good-looking, with curly hair, excellent teeth and a fine figure. Goya's portrait of him* shows a rather self-assured young man, with a plump, still boyish face, reflective eyes and a sensual mouth. In later portraits the face is thinner and harder, and the eyes — no longer reflective, but very dark and piercing — are his most striking feature. In character Garcia was passionate, exuberant and enterprising, a man of great energy and many talents; 'he could do anything, from cooking to writing an opera.'³ His fiery, passionate acting, his fine tenor voice and his virtuoso technique enchanted the public; only the discriminating noticed that he often lacked taste. On stage, singing his own music and accompanying himself on the guitar, he was always sure of applause.

Off stage, it was a different matter. Garcia was an extremely difficult man, hot-tempered, domineering and aggressive. Theatre directors did not find him easy to deal with, and composers and other singers treated him with caution. Even as a very young man he was feared, and his potentialities for violence were recognised. There were persistent, but unconfirmed, rumours that he had killed a man in Spain; this may not have been true but, given his character, it was not impossible.

Garcia's stage career is well known. He appeared with ever-increasing success in Madrid as a tenor (sometimes taking baritone parts), and as a composer of *tonadillas* and operettes, which were just becoming popular in Spain. He was an excellent actor, much

---

* Now in the Museum of Fine Arts, Boston, Mass., USA. There is some controversy about the date of this portrait, but it must have been painted before Garcia left Spain in 1807.

influenced by his friend Maiquez,* the leading Spanish actor of the day. In 1807 he left Spain for Paris, where he rapidly rose to prominence in the operatic world, thanks to his exceptional gifts and to his friendship with Ferdinando Paer, Napoleon's favourite composer and *Maître de chapelle*. Six weeks before his daughter's birth Garcia had made his first appearance at the Théâtre Italien in Paer's *Griselda*, and from then on he was recognised as one of the leading tenors in Europe.

His private affairs are considerably less well known than his public career; he and his children and grandchildren saw to that. At the age of twenty-three he was already married to his first wife, Manuela de Morales, who was a second-rate professional singer and actress, best-known for dancing the bolero.[4] At first she ranked higher in the Madrid opera company than her still inexperienced husband; but Garcia did not take subordinate roles for long. He was soon playing leading parts opposite a young singer, Joaquina Briones. She was twenty-two years old,† had been a widow since the age of twenty, and came from a theatrical family — her sister was also in the opera company. Briones was their stage name, their real name being Sitches.

Garcia's love-affair with the young widow soon became an open scandal in Madrid, particularly because his wife was a member of the same company. Garcia sometimes appeared on the stage 'like a sultan in his harem'[5] with both his wife and his mistress. There were allusions to the scandal in the press, and complaints were made to the theatrical authorities, who were reluctant to take action, fearing 'an act of untoward temerity' on Garcia's part.[6]

On 17th March, 1805, Joaquina gave birth in Madrid to Manuel Garcia's son, Manuel Patricio, the first of their three outstandingly gifted children. He was to become a great teacher of singing; Jenny Lind was one of his pupils. Born in the year of the Battle of Trafalgar,

---

* Maiquez spent three years (1799–1802) in France, where he became the disciple and friend of the French actor, Talma. Talma had been brought up in England; as a result, when he went to France he introduced many reforms into the French theatre. Maiquez's whole style of acting changed after his visit to France; his performance of *Othello* (Madrid, 1st January, 1802) caused a sensation, and opened a new epoch in the Spanish theatre. Garcia's performances of Rossini's *Otello*, which were later to be famous, probably owed a great deal to Maiquez and, indirectly, to Talma.

† Born on 26th July, 1780, in Madrid.

Manuel Patricio was to die a hundred and one years later in Edwardian London, only eight years before the First World War. Sargent painted his portrait, and Dame Rebecca West, who died in 1983, remembered being taken to see him when she was a child.

Manuel Patricio's baptismal certificate describes him as 'the legitimate son of Manuel Rodriguez and Joaquina Sitches';[7] but he was illegitimate, the product of a bigamous marriage. His parents had apparently gone through a marriage ceremony, but the church authorities had not made the connection with Garcia's marriage to Manuela de Morales. How and where Garcia had married his first wife is not known; but there was no divorce in Spain, and Garcia knew that his second marriage was bigamous. According to his younger daughter, Joaquina 'sacrificed her good name for years by passing herself off as his mistress in order to conceal the crime of bigamy which he had committed'.[8] As the Garcia children knew the truth about their parents' marriage and were aware that their mother — Catholic and superstitious — suffered on that score, their concern when they grew up for their own 'good names' is understandable. As for Garcia himself, he 'believed neither in God nor in the devil',[9] and there is no reason to suppose that his bigamous state worried him.

In after years a number of myths about the Garcias' past were circulated by their children and grandchildren in an attempt to cover up the matrimonial irregularities which, like myths, were to be such a speciality of this family. It was alleged, for example, that Joaquina was 'of noble birth', and had originally been destined for a convent; she was taken for one last visit to the theatre before taking the veil, saw Garcia on the stage, fell in love with him and married him.[10] No mention was ever made of her first marriage, and her stage career in Spain was glossed over, although she did later appear on the stage in France and America. Manuel Patricio used to say that he was born in Zafra, in Catalonia, although his baptismal certificate clearly states that he was born in Madrid.[11]

Joaquina's life with Garcia was very difficult; she was 'ill-treated, knocked about, brutalised by him'.[12] But she remained loyal to him although, according to her younger daughter, she shed many tears in secret. She was not well-educated, but was a talented singer and actress and, when young, lively and vivacious. She was full of common sense, tact and courage; as she grew older, after 'all the harsh trials of a tortured life',[13] she had wisdom and dignity. She was a peace-maker by nature, and succeeded in keeping the family together, despite Garcia's violent temperament. Her children all loved and respected her and, in her old age, so did the Russian novelist Ivan Turgenev.

In the spring of 1807 Garcia left Spain with both his wives.[14] He may have hoped to obtain a divorce in France, for between 1792–1803 divorce had become relatively easy there; but by the time he reached France the laws had been tightened up again. He probably left because of his matrimonial complications, and also because he found Spain too provincial for a man of his ambitions.

Two of Garcia's children — at least — remained behind in Spain: Manuel Patricio, who was left with his maternal grandparents; and a daughter, Josepha. It is not at present known exactly when or where Josepha was born; her mother's name was Manuela Aguirre.[15] Josepha used the surname Rodriguez; Aguirre may have been one of Manuela de Morales' names, but Garcia's first wife does not appear to have had any children. When Josepha later joined her father in France, he passed her off as his niece, although many people knew their true relationship. Josepha, like all Garcia's children, later became a singer, under her married name: Ruiz Garcia.

What happened when Garcia and his two wives crossed the Franco-Spanish frontier in the spring of 1807 is not clear. Garcia and Joaquina arrived in Paris that summer, and Manuela de Morales was back in Madrid in April, 1808, and was taken on again for one season at the Coliseo de la Cruz; after that she disappeared from the theatrical records, and from history. Manuel Garcia and Joaquina never returned to Spain. Their daughter, Maria Felicia, was born about nine months after their arrival in Paris.

2

Maria Garcia's childhood, like her family background, was unconventional. From the age of three, when her parents took her from Paris to Naples, she was to be a traveller, a nomad; she was never really to belong to any country. Although Spanish, she was never to visit Spain. Born in France, she spoke Spanish at home, and French and Italian outside it. She was a good linguist, and later learned English well; but she never spoke any language perfectly. She was always to be rootless.

In Naples, where she spent four years, she had her first music lessons, from Hérold and Panseron, who were both very young and were visiting Italy at the time. In Naples, too, she made her first precocious appearance on the stage, at the age of five or six, in a child's part. This first encounter with the public boded well for the future; even when she suddenly refused to sing and walked off the stage, saying she had sung like a dog and wouldn't sing any more, the audience applauded.[1]

In 1814, when he was nine years old, Manuel Patricio came to Naples to rejoin his parents, whom he could not remember, and his sister, whom he had never seen. His relations with his father were always to be very strained, but he and his sister became firm friends and allies.

Naples in the early nineteenth century was the equivalent of Hollywood a hundred years later. It was a very important operatic centre, and opera was then the only international show business. The city was full of stars: Garcia; Isabella Colbran, Rossini's first wife; and Rossini himself, then in his early twenties, among many others. There were tycoons, such as the impresario Domenico Barbaia. And all these people had their hangers-on: aspiring composers, hopeful librettists, starlets, middle-men, sharks, fans, and people keen to earn an honest or dishonest penny. It was a corrupt and permissive society; Maria learned early in life to have no respect for the theatrical profession. The Garcia children mingled with the crowd, learned the ways of the theatre world, and probably picked up a good deal of information about stagecraft, music, acting and theatrical intrigues which would be useful to them later, as would their father's important friends.

So far, the theatre appears to have been the children's only nursery and school; Maria had no real childhood with other children of her own age, which is perhaps why she liked dolls and games so much when she grew up. Instead of playing, she watched her father, on and off the stage, with a mixture of fascination and fear. She was used to the idea that he was a great star, and that he could transform himself at will into any persona he chose. She was used to seeing him transformed physically, by make-up and costumes. She was used to him being one character on stage, and a quite different character off it. From a very early age she began to confuse reality and fiction; for her, the frontier between the two was always to be blurred.

In 1815 in Naples Garcia created the part of Norfolk in Rossini's *Elisabetta, regina d'Inghilterra*, and from then on Garcia and, later, both his daughters, were to be prominent exponents of Rossini's music. After the fall of Garcia's patron, Murat, King of Naples, in 1815, the Garcias and Rossini moved to Rome. There Garcia appeared in the first performance of Rossini's *Il barbiere di Siviglia*, in the part of Almaviva which Rossini had written specially for him, and which he was later to perform frequently in Paris, London and New York. Both his daughters were to be notable Rosinas in the same opera.

Maria's mother did not allow her to attend the first night of *Il barbiere*. But the day after that memorable fiasco (for which Garcia was in part responsible) she went with her father to console the composer, as he recalled many years later. As soon as she came in she ran up to Rossini, burst into tears, and put her arms around his neck, saying:

'Ah, if Mama had only sent me to the theatre last night!'
'And what would you have done?'
'Oh, while they were hissing your beautiful music, I should have shouted with all my strength: "You are all snakes; go back to the wild places and understand the music of the bears, the only sort that you deserve." '
'She really would have been capable of doing just that,' Rossini added, 'for she was a little demon. Then she said to me: "Don't be sad; listen: when I am grown up, I'll sing *Il*

barbiere everywhere, but (tapping her foot) never at Rome, even if the Pope on both knees begs me to." '[2]

In fact, she was to sing *Il barbiere* in Rome sixteen years later.

In 1816 the Garcias recrossed Europe, still in chaos after the Napoleonic wars, and returned to Paris. Maria was a pale, skinny, hyperactive eight-year-old, too much prone to climbing on roofs and other dangerous things of that kind, highly-strung, with large dark eyes, and little education. It was decided to remedy this, and she was sent to a convent school in Hammersmith,* probably in 1819 when Garcia was appearing in London. She remained at the convent for about two years.[3] There she learned to speak English well, and to write it badly; unlike her father, she became and remained a practising Catholic. At school, Maria became used to the English way of life, and later, when she grew up, she always felt quite at home in England.

In 1821 Joaquina Garcia, who had been appearing in small parts at the Théâtre Italien in Paris, had to abandon them. On 18th July of that year she gave birth to the Garcias' third and last child, a daughter. Pauline Garcia was eventually to become, under her married name, the immensely distinguished singer Pauline Viardot, the inspiration of many composers and writers, and the Egeria of the Russian novelist, Ivan Turgenev.[4]

This late addition to the family must have caused complications at the time. Garcia was forty-six and his wife forty-one when Pauline was born; Manuel Patricio was sixteen, and Maria thirteen. But the new baby was welcomed by everyone, and Garcia in particular adored this child of his middle age. Cruel and even violent with his two elder children, he never ill-treated Pauline, and she reciprocated his adoration. Her siblings did not resent this; they were always on good terms with their younger sister.

---

* The convent in Hammersmith was probably the one run by the Benedictine Nuns of Dunkirk (on the site of the present Sacred Heart Girls' School) from 1795–1863. They were an English order which had gone to France to escape Cromwell, and returned to England because of the French Revolution. Their school in Hammersmith flourished, and was attended by girls from the best English Catholic families — why they accepted Maria Garcia, the daughter of actors, is something of a mystery. The nuns left Hammersmith for Teignmouth in 1863. (See: *A History of the Benedictine Nuns of Dunkirk*, ed. by the Community, with a preface by D. B. Wyndham Lewis, London, 1958.)

As soon as it was possible, though by modern standards long before that, Garcia began to train Maria's voice; she was about fourteen or fifteen. When Maria and Manuel Patricio had been small children Garcia had allowed them to sing little songs of his own composition at parties; but as soon as he began to train their voices seriously, all that ceased, and they were only allowed to sing exercises in private. Dedicated to her vocation to become a great singer, Maria led the life of a novice, with no contact with the outside world.

At first she seemed to have little aptitude for music; her voice was slow to develop, and she did not appear to have a good ear. Probably only someone as experienced as her father could have discerned her potentialities. Manuel Patricio had even less aptitude for the stage, and no desire to become a singer; Garcia took no notice of his son's wishes, and forced him to study singing; but he concentrated most of his formidable energy on Maria.

All accounts agree[5] that Garcia was not only an extremely hard task-master, but actually ill-treated his children,* and that they both endured torments while he was teaching them. There were many jokes about it, in Paris and in London, but it was not a joking matter. On one occasion, a friend who happened to witness a scene between Maria and her father, had to intervene;[6] Garcia frequently hit his son and daughter, sometimes in public; people passing his house could hear Maria's agonised cries coming from it.[7] Even by the standards of that time, Garcia's treatment of his children went well beyond what was considered permissible. Joaquina tried, without much success, to keep the peace.

Although Maria suffered cruelly from her father, and was terrified of him, she was extremely ambitious and competitive, and she

* Except the account by his younger daughter, Pauline, who was only eleven when Garcia died and cannot have had very clear memories of her siblings' childhood. She hero-worshipped her father. In an interview which she gave to the *Musical Courier* sixty-two years after her sister's death (12th January, 1898) it was stated: 'Madame Viardot resents vigorously the calumny that gained ground, she does not know how, as to her father's cruelty and brutality. The story even is told that Malibran acted the terror of Desdemona through the sense of actual fright with which her father inspired her. Such a condition of things, says Madame Viardot, is absolutely impossible. He was impatient, impetuous, easily aroused, severe with mistakes and stupidity ... Spanish, but never brutal or cruel, as reports would make him.' But Pauline Viardot was being disingenuous (see p. 38).

submitted to his iron discipline because she realised that it was the way to stardom. Garcia understood her; he would taunt her by saying that she would never be anything but a member of the chorus; this spurred her on to ever greater efforts. She had great will-power and courage, but these were always at odds with her fragile physique.

Sometimes the stress was too much for her. At this time she began to have 'fainting fits', when 'one would have thought she was dead'.[8] These 'fainting fits' were to recur throughout her life, particularly when she was under stress, and particularly when the stress was connected with her father. They clearly had more psychological and medical significance than was realised at the time.

Garcia seems to have had an uncanny power over his daughter. She said that when he looked at her he had such an influence on her that he could, if he wished, have made her throw herself from a fifth floor window into the street without hurting herself.[9] She was terrified of him, but at the same time fascinated by him. She always remembered her childhood as deeply unhappy because of him; yet, at the same time, she was bound to him by some close affinity, which perhaps went beyond the bounds of a normal father-daughter relationship. Their contemporaries sensed this, and it was rumoured that Garcia had an incestuous passion for his daughter.*

But, although her father was at least 'a tyrant and a ruffian', if not worse, he was 'a first-rate teacher of his art';[10] and eventually the painful lessons began to bear fruit. Garcia allowed his daughter to appear at small private concerts and, in 1824, when the family moved from Paris to London, where Garcia had an engagement as principal tenor at the King's Theatre, Maria was taken on there, too, in the chorus.

She had a remarkable voice; she was really a mezzo-soprano, but Garcia had given her a range of three octaves, and she could sing soprano parts as well. He had taught her superb technique, and she was already an excellent actress, and was to become a great one. Her father had also given her some of his own bad taste; she gradually corrected this, but the flamboyant side to her character, also inherited from Garcia, was to lead her to commit occasional errors of taste throughout her career. She began to appear in some private and public concerts in London, but attracted little attention; she was sixteen years old.

Her chance came the following year, when the great prima donna

* See pp. 122–124.

Giuditta Pasta, who had been playing opposite Garcia at the King's Theatre, had to return to Paris. The directors of the theatre were left with only one prima donna, who was ill. It had been a bad season, and not least of the directors' troubles had been Garcia's difficult and cantankerous behaviour; but at this juncture, when he proposed that his daughter should take a major role, the directors had little alternative but to accept. It was decided at very short notice to put on *Il barbiere di Siviglia*, with Garcia as Almaviva and Maria as Rosina. Garcia had probably been coaching her for weeks, and she had known the music since childhood;* but it was still quite a feat for a seventeen-year-old, who had never appeared in the theatre before, to prepare for it in two or three days.

Maria Garcia made her début on 11th June, 1825. Because the opera had been announced at the last moment, not all the critics were present; those who were there realised that, although very young and inexperienced, she had great potential, and she pleased the public. The *Times* critic, reviewing her second performance on 14th June, said:

> She is a very agreeable young lady. Her figure is good — her features rather expressive than handsome — her action free yet modest. Her voice is pleasing, but not yet of extensive power. She, however, manages it with infinite skill.[11]

The directors of the King's Theatre promptly engaged her for the rest of the season; her father, acting on her behalf, drove a hard bargain with them.

Later that season Maria appeared in a small part in Meyerbeer's *Il crociato in Egitto*, with Velluti. Velluti was almost the last of the castrati, at least so far as the stage was concerned. As no castrato had been heard in London for some twenty-five years, his appearance aroused a great deal of curiosity, and much unkind comment. But Velluti was an excellent artist and, despite the fact that some people looked on him as a freak, and thought his voice sounded 'like a peacock's scream or a superannuated lady scolding her servants,'[12] he gradually won over the London public and spent some years

---

* Rossini remembered her singing *Una voce poco fa* when she visited him the morning after the first night of *Il barbiere*, in Rome in 1816. She was then only eight years old; but after attending only a few rehearsals of the opera she had, said Rossini, 'remembered nearly all the pieces'. Michotte, *An Evening at Rossini's*, p. 126.

here. He foretold that Maria would have a brilliant career, but recommended that she should not sing in public too much until her powers had matured. Garcia took no notice of this advice.

At the end of the 1825 season Garcia did not renew his contract with the King's Theatre, nor did he allow his daughter to do so; as she was in love with a member of the orchestra, or thought she was, she would have liked to stay in London. Garcia had other plans; for some time he had been contemplating a most audacious enterprise: the introduction of Italian opera to the New World. At the end of the London season he took Maria on a tour of the English provinces: Manchester, York and Liverpool, where he charged extremely high fees for his daughter's appearances. After that, on 1st October, 1825, Garcia and all his family, together with a scratch company of second-rate singers, embarked in Liverpool for New York, which they reached thirty-seven days later.

3

In New York the Garcias were awaited with enormous interest. News of their projected tour had preceded them and had been a topic of New York conversation for some time. When the Italian opera company landed in America, while Garcia tried to get an orchestra and chorus together, which was not easy, and rehearsed his company, a mounting fever of excitement, fanned by the press, gripped New Yorkers. No one really knew what to expect of Italian opera; a few people had seen it in Europe, and they were only too ready to instruct their less well-informed compatriots. A flood of letters and articles appeared in the newspapers.

There were articles on '. . . *Italian music*, a style seldom heard in this country, and less understood than any other';[1] and articles on how to behave at the opera, and what to wear. Ladies, it was suggested, should pay 'more attention to the dressing of the hair and bust', and gentlemen were reminded that they should not keep their hats on throughout the performance.[2] Unfortunate rumours had been circulating about the nature of the new entertainment, which had adversely affected advance booking. A long article reassured those who had feared '. . . that on our stage, too, dancing in all the extremes of the French ballet was to accompany the music. This is an error. There will be no dancing — nothing that the most fastidious delicacy can take offence at . . .'[3]

The Garcias themselves were also given considerable advance publicity. They were described as 'some of the most distinguished artists of Europe;[4] in fact, Garcia was already past his prime, his daughter was a promising debutante of seventeen, his son had never appeared on any stage, his wife had retired, and the rest of the company was either old or inexperienced. Maria was said to be the equal of Pasta, and to prove this the high fees she had earned at the York Festival were quoted. She was far from being the equal of Pasta at that time, although she was to be later; but the Americans thought that, if she was expensive, she must be good.

While the company was preparing for the first performance —

having to do all sorts of things they would never have done in Europe, such as painting scenery — Garcia received a visit from Lorenzo da Ponte.[5] It is said that when the old man — he was seventy-six — announced that he was the librettist of Mozart's *Don Giovanni*, Garcia effusively embraced him, singing the drinking song from that opera as he did so. What is more certain is that da Ponte who, after a very chequered career in Europe, had gone to America to escape his creditors, was of great assistance to the Garcias. He had taken on, single-handed, the mission of introducing Italian culture, language and literature to the New World; he was made the first professor of Italian at Columbia College (later University) in 1825. He did much to arouse American interest in Italian opera, and helped to make Garcia's first performances in New York a success.

The company's New York season opened at the Park Theatre on 29th November, 1825, with a performance of *Il barbiere di Siviglia*. Garcia played the part of Almaviva; Maria was Rosina; Manuel Patricio was Figaro — his first appearance on the stage; Joaquina took the small part of Bertha. As the first performance in the New World of Italian opera in Italian, it was a landmark in theatrical history. New Yorkers sensed that it would be a great occasion,[6] and the large and distinguished audience, which included Joseph Bonaparte (ex-king of Spain), and the young Fenimore Cooper with his friend the poet Fitz-Greene Halleck, was not disappointed. On the whole, the performance was received with extravagant, if ill-informed, enthusiasm. New Yorkers understood at once that Garcia and his daughter were very accomplished artists, but did not at first realise that the rest of the company and the orchestra were barely adequate. Rossini's music was generally much liked, although one critic, to da Ponte's fury, described it as 'monstrous'.[7]

This performance made history for another reason: it marked the emergence of Maria Garcia as a star. She conquered New York on that first night, and was to reign supreme there as long as she remained in America. From now on she began to eclipse her father; he was still highly praised, but not as much as she was, and Americans soon became critical of him. Maria had, of course, advantages which her father could not offer: her youth, her looks, her sex; but it is clear that, in crossing the Atlantic, she had matured and had ceased to be a pupil. From that first night her star status was firmly established, and for ever.

Da Ponte, who probably knew more about Italian opera than anyone else in the New World at that time — he had, after all,

worked with Mozart, Salieri and other composers and great singers
of an earlier epoch in Vienna and London — described Maria Garcia
as 'incomparable', and later paid her a graceful compliment in one
of his poems.[8] He was the first of many poets of distinction to
celebrate her; American poets of less distinction soon followed suit.[9]

In New York Maria Garcia's gifts as an actress were soon recognised; and her versatility — her ability to play comedy and tragedy
with equal success — was often to be commented on as the season
progressed. At the age of seventeen she already possessed all the
qualities for which she was later to be celebrated in Europe.

It was not difficult for the Signorina, as the Americans always
called her, to become a star in New York; she had no competitors,
and Americans had no standards of comparison. An inexperienced
prima donna faced an inexperienced audience. In New York she was
not only to gain the experience she so badly needed, but was always
to be supported by a sympathetic and responsive public, which she
had no difficulty in handling.

Thus, at the very beginning of her career, Maria Garcia learned
to look on the public with some contempt, for she knew it to be
ignorant; but she also thought of it as friendly, easily won over, clay
in her hands. 'Here they are already half mad about Italian opera,'
she wrote to Pasta some three months after her arrival in America,
'and I, as you can imagine, am the Heroine!!! How lovely to be in
a country where they don't understand a thing!!'[10]

＊　＊　＊

After the success of *Il barbiere*, Garcia put on an opera of his own,
which was not a great success; Rossini's serious operas, *Tancredi*
and *Otello*, fared much better. *Otello*, in particular, aroused great
enthusiasm; in Europe it had been considered one of Garcia's
greatest parts, and the fact that Edmund Kean appeared in Shakespeare's *Othello* the day after the first performance of the opera
increased public interest.[11]

England's greatest tragic actor of the Romantic school was, in
1826, nearing the end of his short, brilliant and sensational career.
His health was ruined by drink and debauchery, his memory was
failing, a scandalous law-suit had alienated him from the British
public, the press, and most of his friends. He had left England in
1825 to escape the outcry against him; but news of his misdemea-
nours had preceded him across the Atlantic. On a previous American

tour (1820) he had created a scandal in Boston; in December, 1825, he had revisited that city with disastrous results. The Boston Riot, in which the theatre was wrecked and many people narrowly escaped death, had, perhaps, turned American opinion outside Boston more in his favour, however, and he was peacefully received in New York.

Garcia, on leaving the stage at the end of his first American performance of *Otello*, found Kean waiting in the wings to congratulate him. This was a sensational compliment, for it was well known that Kean could not tolerate any competition, and was disliked by his colleagues in the theatre for that reason. Othello was one of Kean's greatest parts; praise from him was therefore praise indeed. Garcia politely responded by taking his whole company to see Kean's performance the next evening.

Although by then Kean was a wreck of a man, some of his amazing power and originality remained. His style of acting — passionate, fiercely individual, unrestrained — was the antithesis of the classical school. Maria may have seen him in England when she was a child; but now that she herself was a maturing artist he made a great impression on her. 'I have earned as much applause as if I were *Kean*,' she was soon to write with pride,[12] and her own Romantic style of acting — passionate, fiercely individual, unrestrained — probably owed something to Kean. In so far as she was influenced at all, she was always more influenced by actors — of all types — than by singers.*

At that first performance of *Otello*, Garcia as the Moor and his daughter as Desdemona produced in the audience 'sensations of sublimity and terror beyond which no imagination can reach.'[13] In fact, the sensations of terror were not only in the audience. Writing to Pasta on the eve of the third performance of *Otello*, Maria said that if Pasta were to care for her a little, she would 'die happy tonight, for, to tell the truth, Papa frightens me when he kills me.'[14]

---

* It is known that La Malibran admired Talma, Kean, Harriet Smithson, Mademoiselle Mars, Marie Dorval, Deburau and many other actors and actresses; the only singers whom she is known to have admired wholeheartedly were Pasta, Nourrit and Lablache.

4

New Yorkers, as they applauded Garcia and his company in the theatre, could have had no idea of the family tensions behind the scenes which often heightened the tension on the stage.

Garcia's cruelty to his son and elder daughter had in no way diminished, despite Maria's successes in London and New York. Although, in London, she had already earned considerable sums of money, her father always controlled it. She realised that the only way she could escape him, his cruelty and, perhaps, his amorous attentions, and gain her independence, was to marry and leave the theatre.

In London, she had seemed to be on the verge of a love affair with an orchestral player at the King's Theatre. This did not suit Garcia at all, since the success of his American trip depended on having his daughter as prima donna. He could not risk an American season without her, and he had nipped this romance in the bud.

How real Maria's love for the orchestral player was, it is difficult to say. Her letters at this time show her to have been childish and emotionally immature. Deprived of companions of her own age, she had an adolescent crush on Giuditta Pasta, who had been playing opposite her father in London. Pasta neither reciprocated nor encouraged this, and did not reply to Maria's letters. As Maria referred to Pasta as her 'bride', and said she would like to 'eat' her, Pasta's reticence is understandable.[1]

On the voyage to America Garcia's cruelty to his children had continued unabated. Passengers, watching the company rehearse on deck, were shocked by the 'brutal manner in which Garcia sometimes treated the singers, but especially his son and daughter.' On one occasion he 'suddenly struck his son a blow with his fist so violent that the youth dropped on the deck as if shot.'[2] Robert Dale Owen, a passenger on the ship, recalled that

> One evening after a rehearsal at which he [Garcia] had been so violent that his daughter seemed in mortal fear of him, she and

I sat down, on a sofa on deck, to a game of chess. At first she appeared as lively and bright as usual; but, ere the game ended she turned deadly pale, her head sunk on my shoulder, and had I not caught her in my arms she must have fallen to the floor. I carried her down to the cabin quite insensible; and it was some time before she recovered.[3]

On the voyage a Captain McDonald of the RE, a young and handsome British officer, fell in love with Maria. Since she was 'a most interesting girl, simple, frank, bright as could be, charming in conversation, a general favourite,'[4] this was not surprising; but it was not something which Garcia could tolerate, especially as the Captain was not rich. So this romance also came to nothing.

In New York Garcia is said to have prevented another nascent romance between his daughter and the poet Fitz-Greene Halleck. By this time Maria was becoming desperate; she herself made advances to a certain W. Rogers, someone connected with the opera company; he rebuffed them.[5] It seemed that she could find no escape from her father, at home or on the stage.

In the theatre, the whole Garcia family was obliged to act out parts which only exacerbated the violent disagreements and tensions of their home life. For example, in Rossini's *Il barbiere* Garcia played his daughter's lover, which he may, in fact, have been, or have wished to be. His son, in full adolescent revolt against his father, as Figaro had to play his father's friend and accomplice. Maria, whose only desire was to escape her father, on stage had to pretend to be in love with him; in addition, as Rosina, she had to plot her escape from the strict tutelage of the elderly Dr Bartolo, just when, in real life, she was plotting to escape from her father. Even Joaquina, in the small part of Bertha, in her one important aria had to sing of the pains of growing old, yet still feeling love — feelings which, at the age of forty-five, she was probably experiencing in real life. If she suspected that the rival in her husband's affections was their daughter, her anguish must have been powerful indeed.

But *Il barbiere* was a comic opera, not to be taken too seriously. In *Otello*, in which Garcia played the title-role and Maria was Desdemona, the situation was more frightening; and Maria, as we have seen, was frightened. There are several anecdotes about these New York performances of *Otello* which are probably apocryphal, or at any rate distorted; the accounts are all by people writing long after the events, who could only have been told about them by

Maria herself, and the stories did not get into the American press. All the same, the gist of them — that Maria feared her father might really kill her in the last act — was true.

In one version, Garcia gave his daughter six days to learn the part of Desdemona, and threatened that, if she did not acquit herself to his satisfaction at the first performance, he would really strike her with the dagger* in the last scene. Her fear made her play the part with genuine fear, and as Garcia raised the dagger she was so terrified that she bit his hand and actually drew blood. This version seems quite in keeping with what we know of Garcia's character.⁶

Another version of the story is that after a family row between father and daughter, which had raged all day, and which Joaquina had vainly tried to calm, a performance of *Otello* took place in the evening. In the final scene, when Garcia/Otello approached Maria/Desdemona to kill her, Maria suddenly saw that her father was holding a real dagger instead of the usual stage prop. Terrified, she lost her self-control and screamed in Spanish: 'Papa! Papa! For God's sake don't kill me!' This story ends with an anticlimax: the stage dagger was broken, which is why Garcia had to use a real one.⁷

Otello is a story of jealousy, and Garcia had every reason to feel jealous. He felt the jealousy of a master whose pupil had outstripped him, and the jealousy of a father whose daughter had suddenly become nubile, and whom he feared to lose to another man. Maria, like Desdemona, was terrified. The audience, knowing nothing of these tensions, merely applauded what it believed to be the actors' ability to portray imaginary feelings. From those early New York performances of *Otello* onwards, the part of Desdemona always had a special, personal significance for Maria. Perhaps, because of this, she moved the public profoundly whenever she performed it.

* In Rossini's opera Desdemona is stabbed, not suffocated as in Shakespeare's play.

Early in 1826 Maria at last found a possible means of escaping from her father, in the shape of a middle-aged business man, Eugène Malibran. This unlikely candidate proved to be more responsive than W. Rogers, but he was not immediately won over by the young prima donna's advances. There can be no doubt that at first Maria took the initiative, and that Malibran reacted with caution.

François Eugène Malibran was half-French, through his father, and half-Spanish, through his mother. Born in Paris on 15th November, 1781, he and one of his brothers had gone to Spain in 1808, the year of Maria's birth, as suppliers of meat to Napoleon's armies. After the French defeat in Spain Malibran had emigrated to America, becoming an American citizen in 1818. In New York he was a merchant and banker, dealing principally in sugar and molasses from Cuba, where two of his brothers were living.[1]

By the spring of 1826, some three or four months after the Garcias' arrival in America, the question of a marriage between Eugène Malibran and Maria Garcia was already being discussed — or rather, was being fought out — in the Garcia household. Reasonable discussion with Garcia was never easy at the best of times, and the question of his daughter's marriage roused him to such fury that Joaquina was hard put to it to keep the peace. It must be admitted that there was some reason for Garcia's disapproval, for Maria was a mere seventeen, whereas Malibran was forty-five, only six years younger than Garcia himself. In addition, Garcia's company was not doing well financially and, without his daughter, who alone drew the public, he would not be able to continue to put on operas. Malibran, however, was reported to be rich.

An intelligent forty-five-year-old bachelor does not take on a volatile teenager without some misgivings, and Malibran was not blind to the problems involved. But Maria set out to seduce him, and in the end she was successful. Although her principal reason for wanting to marry was to escape her father, she obviously thought

Malibran a congenial person, and was, or imagined she was, in love with him.

There were clandestine meetings, and Maria's letters — written in French — clearly prove that there is no truth in the allegations later made that Garcia forced her to marry Malibran against her will[2] — quite the reverse. 'Ducky, you're a darling; little love, you're an angel, I love you!' she told him, and went on in her own peculiar style:

> Tell me, little puss, don't you love me? Oh! Yes you do, I can see you do; I'd like to have a little gold lacrimatory to catch your sweet tears in, and I'd like to swallow them in great gulps, and then scent myself with the perfume of your breath. What a lot of nonsense all at once! Never mind, that doesn't change the keen and eager feelings of my boiling heart.[3]

Malibran did not, apparently, melt immediately to these blandishments. In another long letter, in which the consummate actress, rather than the young girl, is easily discerned, Maria wrote: 'I can't believe that your heart is indifferent to my advances, for I try every moment of the day to make you understand my tender feelings, with which no one else has been able to inspire me.'[4]

Still Malibran hesitated. He put down his thoughts on paper, perhaps in order to clarify his mind before an interview with Maria's parents:

> Age: Such a great difference between us.
> Fortune: which, like the reputation which I enjoy, has doubtless been exaggerated — lack of certainty of succeeding in business so long as one is involved in it. Misfortunes which may occur — on the other hand, the hope of complete success, above all if Cuba remains calm.
> My reputation: Perhaps made flattering by some friend who has too good an opinion of me.
> Obstacles: Shown up by the above, to which must be added those which her parents may make.

At this juncture, Malibran suddenly became less rational, and wrote a sentence which turned out to be true: '*Tout à elle pour la vie.*' Then he became more practical again:

> Talents: which give her the right to aspire to a great future — which will enable her to be independent of everyone — she

does not value herself at her true worth, or rather her modesty reduces the riches which she possesses, happy character, amiability — inestimable — she doesn't know herself.

After all these eminently sensible notes, Malibran suddenly showed a more human side to his nature, and added a few lines inspired by an all too human feeling: jealousy.

Marriage which was to have taken place in London. Name of the person and his status — what nationality — was he rich or poor? How long did he court her?[5]

This curious document is important, since it is the only one, written by Malibran himself, which has so far been found; no letters from him have yet come to light.

The notes show him to have been a decent middle-aged man, perfectly aware of all the dangers which such a marriage could — and did — entail, and not prepared to embark on it lightly. It gives the lie to all the myths and legends about Malibran, spread later by his wife and her friends, which portrayed him as avaricious and unscrupulous, and painted a picture of Maria as his innocent victim. However, a decent middle-aged businessman is not glamorous, and Malibran's true image could never have captured the public imagination, as his wife's did. In all operas, middle-aged or elderly husbands are ridiculous, if not downright villainous; and Malibran, by marrying Maria, was, for the rest of his life and for long after it, to be typecast as in an opera. In fact, all the evidence shows that Maria seduced him in order to gain her independence, that he genuinely fell in love with her, and ultimately became her victim.

Some sort of an agreement was reached between Malibran and Maria's parents, in which money played a part. The details are not clear, but it seems that Malibran offered to pay Garcia $50,000 (or 100,000 francs) in compensation for the loss of his prima donna, and that Garcia offered a dowry of $25,000, which he certainly did not have, and could not have paid.[6] Garcia did, however, obtain some concessions from both Malibran and Maria: she was to perform with the opera company until the end of the season, and to appear under her maiden name.

On 22nd March, 1826, a civil marriage ceremony between Eugène Malibran and Maria Garcia took place before the French Consul in New York; and on 23rd March, the day before her eighteenth birthday, a Roman Catholic marriage ceremony was performed by Father Peter Malou at St Peter's Church.[7]

Afterwards, Malibran collected the letters which Maria had written to him before their marriage, and tied them together with a label: '*Petits billets de Maria avant notre mariage.*' He was prudent to do so; these letters, and his own notes, constitute the only evidence of what really happened between them before their marriage.[8]

Garcia did not want his influential friends in Europe to know that he had been defeated by his teenage daughter, or that the whole of his American tour was in jeopardy as a result, so in public he put on a brave face. He wrote to Giuditta Pasta to tell her that his daughter had married, and was retiring from the stage 'because her husband does not wish her to follow this career; and, to tell the truth, it's a pity, because she would have made an excellent little prima donna. However, as he's rich he does well to take her out of this labyrinth.'[9]

The Malibrans' honeymoon was short; Maria appeared in Rossini's *Il turco in Italia* two days before her marriage, and in *Il barbiere* nine days after it. The press which, at that time, had not yet acquired its insatiable curiosity about the private lives of public people, discreetly noted that this was her first appearance 'since she has entered into the silken bands of matrimony (light may they prove, and happy and enduring) . . .' The audience greeted her with such applause and wavings of handkerchiefs* that Maria 'almost sank beneath her emotions.'[10]

Maria Malibran was now only partly liberated from her father. At home she was as free as any wife was at that time — Malibran was never a heavy-handed husband — and she lived in a pleasant house.† At about this time she wrote — in English — to a friend in London: 'My husband, Mr Malibran, is what we call a perfect Gentleman, and so much so as never to make me repent of having married him, such a worthy gentleman.'[11] But in the theatre her father still reigned supreme, and his word was law. He still murdered her in *Otello*, courted her in *Il barbiere* and, when *Don Giovanni* was added to the repertoire, tried to seduce her as Zerlina. But, although she wanted to retire from the stage, she kept her word and continued to appear in the theatre. Despite what she had suffered

---

* At that time only men applauded; ladies waved their handkerchiefs.
† 36, Liberty Street, at the corner of Broom Street.

from her father, she was deeply attached to the rest of her family, and always did all she could to help them.

But it was a strain. During a performance of Rossini's *La cenerentola* Maria, who had seemed indisposed at the beginning of the performance, fainted on stage. Manuel Patricio was so affected by his sister's plight that he, too, was unable to continue singing, and the performance was abruptly terminated.[12] Maria's 'fainting fits' were almost always the result of clashes with her father and, on this occasion, too, there had probably been some scene between Garcia and his two elder children.

By now, after four months of opera performances twice a week, American interest was beginning to fall off. Garcia complained, as he always did, of '. . . the difficult position I am placed in by the management here and the difficulties I meet with at every step';[13] but his frequent indispositions annoyed the public, and he was rapidly losing popularity. A small band of devoted enthusiasts regularly attended the opera; but New York was then too small and provincial a city to support a permanent opera company.

In an attempt to save the situation new operas by Rossini were introduced, but *Il barbiere* was the only one that never failed to please. An opera by Garcia himself, *La figlia dell'aria*, was especially written for New York; New Yorkers did not appreciate the compliment. They felt that '. . . to be stunned with the trumpets, kettle-drums and cymbals of the Signor Garcia [. . .] is taxing our indulgence too much.'[14]

The situation was temporarily saved by Lorenzo da Ponte, who '. . . had an extremely keen desire' to see what he always referred to as 'his' *Don Giovanni* again.[15] On the first night da Ponte, who had not seen 'his' opera for some thirty-five years, was both deeply moved and exhilarated: his American pupils and friends who had not, perhaps, fully understood or believed his past glory, could now see for themselves.

Don Giovanni was a success, thanks to Mozart, da Ponte and Maria Malibran. 'This magnificent piece, so striking, both in its music and in its poetry, has made a great impression,' wrote one critic, 'and the star of Rossini pales before this brighter star.'[16] Da Ponte's libretto was recognised to be 'so much beyond anything we have before had at the opera that it gives an additional zest to the entertainment.'[17] As to the singers, the *Albion* considered that 'the only person who can be praised without any exception is Mlle Garcia . . .',[18] and the rest of the press agreed. Garcia himself, as the

Don, was not universally liked, although in the past it had been considered one of his greatest parts.

Don Giovanni temporarily saved the situation for Garcia, and Zingarelli's *Giulietta e Romeo*,* the last opera to be added to the repertoire, was a modest success. After a short summer recess Garcia announced a new season at the Park Theatre, which began on 29th August, and seemed set to continue till Christmas. But then suddenly he announced that the opera would close for good on 30th September; no reason was given. There were rumours that he was going to Philadelphia, that a fund was to be organised for the establishment of a permanent opera in New York, that something was going to be done — but nothing was done. After a farewell performance of *Il barbiere*, Garcia, his wife, his son and his small daughter Pauline, with one or two other singers, sailed for Vera Cruz.[19] It has been suggested that Garcia so much disliked his son-in-law that Joaquina persuaded him to leave New York before he committed some act of violence. Garcia had decided to try his luck in Mexico, where he could speak Spanish. Maria Malibran remained behind in New York with her husband.

* La Malibran was to be famous for her performances in three different operas based on *Romeo and Juliet*: Zingarelli's *Giulietta e Romeo* (1796); Vaccai's *Giulietta e Romeo* (1825); and Bellini's *I Capuleti e i Montecchi* (1830). She usually played Romeo in all three operas.

6

Separated from her family for the first time, freed from her father's attentions and tutelage, Maria Malibran began to lead the normal life of a young married woman — a life of leisure, which she had never known before. She was charming and high-spirited, and had plenty of American friends; since she had left the stage and married Malibran the stigma of being an actress was no longer attached to her. The Malibrans entertained; and probably at those soirées the hostess sang. Although singing had been her profession, it was also her pleasure; all her life she was to sing generously just for her friends. She also took to singing in the choir of Grace Church* on Sundays; and her magnificent and magnificently trained voice must have sounded incongruous amongst the amateur voices in that austere Protestant setting.

Her Catholic confessor, Father Malou, viewed these activities with misgiving. Fearing that she might be contemplating leaving the Church of Rome, he wrote to remonstrate with her about taking such a step, the thought of which made him 'shudder'.[1] Her reply to the good priest must have been sharp, for the bishop himself next intervened.[2] But it is clear that the bishop was less worried about Madame Malibran's soul — which anyway did not appear to be in great danger — than jealous of the fact that she had only sung once in St Patrick's Cathedral.[3]

This life of ease lasted only about three months. Malibran's fears about his business and about the situation in Cuba were all too soon realised, and he sank more and more deeply into debt. His wife's potential value as a prima donna was difficult to realise without an opera company; but she secured an engagement to give a few performances in English ballad operas at the Bowery Theatre. She probably did not mind going back to the stage for a limited period

* In the 1820s Grace Church was on the south-east corner of Rector Street and the southern end of Broadway. It had a cupola, topped with a cross.

— it was the only life she had known, and her father was no longer there — and she was eager to help her husband.

The Bowery Theatre, the largest in New York, had only recently been completed; it held about 3,000 people. Unlike the other theatres, in which smoky oil lamps gave off noxious fumes and went out if there was a draught, it was lit by gas.[4] English ballad operas and other popular entertainments were given there, designed to appeal to a wide low-brow public, very different from the audience which had patronised the Italian opera.

Maria was engaged to sing at a fee of $600 per night — said to be the highest fee ever paid at that time to any performing artist in America.[5] Thus, Maria Malibran, always to be a very expensive star, at the age of eighteen was already receiving higher fees than such experienced and distinguished artists as Kean and Macready. She was aware of this, and of her own worth. 'I well know,' she told her mother, 'that I have done more than any other foreigner will ever do.'[6]

She appeared in Braham's *The Devil's Bridge* (in the breeches part of Count Belino) and in Arne's *Love in a Village*. In these ballad operas, with spoken dialogue, she had to sing and act in English for the first time, and she was almost solely responsible for the music, since most of the other parts were spoken, or very indifferently sung. According to da Ponte, the rest of the company was 'a troop of dogs'.[7] It was the first time she had ever appeared on the stage without her father's coaching and supervision, and ballad operas were an art form of which she had no experience.

The result was a resounding popular success; despite the high prices, the huge theatre was packed. The Signorina received an ovation, and it was thought that her slight foreign accent gave her English diction 'a romantic fascination'.[8] This appears to be the first time that the adjective 'romantic' was applied in print to the future goddess of Romanticism. Maria Malibran's success in English opera with an inferior company was greater than her success had been in Italian opera with a relatively good company; Italian music was not, Americans considered, 'germane' to their 'infant taste'.[9]

Maria was able to write to her mother: 'My début has been the most *fashionable* that has been seen, the fullest and the biggest success. . . . Anyway, last night it was *Love in a Village* for the first time, and they were even happier.' Eugène, she told her mother, was 'delighted'.[10]

She gave ten performances, and earned at least $6,000; but it was not enough to solve her husband's problems. Therefore, in June, 1827, Maria decided to go to Philadelphia, without him, and to give some concerts there.

The letters which she wrote to her husband while she was in Philadelphia give us some idea of the nature of their relationship at that time. She wrote to him frequently, sometimes twice a day. Her letters were long, playful and affectionate; and, as all her letters were to be throughout her life, they were original and spontaneous, expressing her immediate mood. She wrote to her husband in French, with many mistakes, and with many words in Spanish, Italian and English.

After her first concert in Philadelphia, Maria got up early to go to Mass; but she wrote to her *cher petit chou* beforehand, at half-past five in the morning, to tell him of her success. As she planned to give another concert in Philadelphia, she asked her husband to send her some music and costumes. Eugène Malibran must have had a busy time looking for 'the bodice for Rosina White gros de Naples [. . .] trimmings in white satin which you'll find in the box where the old woman's costume is, they are with some black velvet and paillettes, the costume for Tancredi [. . .] Don't forget to send me the white feathers which are in a white box. It must be no sooner said, than done.'[11]

In a letter written the next day, after describing a complicated practical joke she and some friends had played on another member of the party, she turned to more intimate matters: 'Go on telling me that you're fond of me and try to raise . . . your head . . . and so far as furniture goes, all we need . . . is a cradle (do you get me?) [. . .] Come on, kiss me; goodness, there's only a *sheet of paper* between us, and I can't kiss you.' She signed this letter: 'Your wife who loves you.'[12]

By the next day, her mood had changed and she was in one of those black depressions to which she was always to be prone. She had decided — wrongly — that her concert had not been a success, and everything annoyed her, especially the Philadelphians, since she had to remain dressed '*all day*, from the morning onwards', in order to receive their calls. She had been taken to see 'the *prison*, and the *Water works*, and *Museum*', which had not amused her.

'I've got the *blue devils* horribly today,' she told her husband, 'my nerves are on edge in an ill-omened way. I'd really like to hang myself . . . round *your neck* . . . but nothing doing.' Then, in a final paragraph, she revealed the cause of her depression: 'I must finish, for I feel like crying. Tell me if there aren't some letters from *Papa* and *Maman*, they say he has arrived in New York, for *God's sake*, tell me.'[13]

Having so recently acquired her freedom, the thought that her father might reappear terrified her. At the same time, she missed her mother and her siblings. She begged them to write to her; but, she told her mother, 'I don't dare ask Papa, because I'm afraid that he won't write, and if he does . . .'[14] Her attitude to her father was still a combination of fear and fascination.

When she returned to New York, she found that the rumours were false; her parents were still in Mexico. But her husband's financial situation had further deteriorated. Seven judgements, totalling $25,000, were pronounced against him on 10th August, 1827; he offered to pay his debts at 80 cents to the dollar[15] – but how was he to do it?*

It was not possible for Maria Malibran regularly to earn large sums in America where there was, as yet, no steady audience for music. It was therefore decided that she would return to Europe, where she could be sure of finding work, in order to help pay off her husband's debts; it was also decided that he would join her in Europe as soon as he could.

In order to finance her journey, Maria obtained an engagement for six more performances at the Bowery Theatre. Then, on 29th October, 1827, she gave a farewell benefit concert.

It was a memorable occasion, such as New York had never

---

* It is often stated that Eugène Malibran went bankrupt, and his wife, in a letter to him, refers to his 'bankruptcy' (letter of 2nd August, 1828, Teneo, p. 469). But, according to Bushnell (p. 40) New York had no bankruptcy law. It is also often stated that Eugène Malibran was briefly imprisoned for debt (for example, Hogarth, II, 409). The anonymous author of 'Madame Malibran's Marriage' (*Temple Bar*, Vol. 65, May–August, 1882, pp. 38–43) repeats this allegation. He recounts that Malibran bought linen to the value of $50,000 just before his marriage, for which he did not pay; when his creditor tried to reclaim the linen, he was told that Garcia had taken it with him to Mexico. There seems no way of verifying this story, but it is possible that Malibran gave the linen to Garcia in lieu of the sum which he had promised him as compensation for the loss of his prima donna. However, it is clear that, long after their marriage, La Malibran considered that her husband still owed Garcia money (see p. 87).

previously witnessed, and people still remembered it, and the Signorina, thirty or forty years later.[16]

An enormous and brilliant audience assembled; it was estimated that the receipts were $2,220 — an unprecedented sum. The programme was extremely long, a mixture of very diverse pieces, including: extracts from Boieldieu's *Jean de Paris* (in English); *Una voce poco fa* from *Il barbiere* (in Italian); an aria from *Der Freischütz* (in German); and songs in Spanish and French.

The first part of the programme did not go well at all. One report said bluntly that the Signorina appeared to be 'extremely ill';[17] another said, more tactfully, that she was 'struggling with feelings that ill-suited the mimicry of acting [. . .] her whole manner was indicative of the strongest emotions. The audience entered fully into these feelings.'[18]

At the end of the concert the Signorina came to the front of the stage, and sat down at her harp in order to accompany herself in a farewell song* which she had composed especially for the occasion. But her emotion was too much for her; she abandoned her harp,

---

* La Malibran's farewell song to New York; words by Arthur F. Keane:

> Away o'er the blue waves of ocean,
> I go to my own native shores;
> Yet this bosom will glow with devotion,
> To the clime and the scenes it adores.
> Round memory's shrine fondly lingers
> The joy that has twined here a spell;
> And the harp that vibrates to these fingers
> Sighs in sadness the tones of farewell!
>   Farewell! Farewell!
> Sighs in sadness the tones of farewell.
>
> Where Italy's bright skies are shining,
> And France, sunny France, spreads her bloom,
> This heart will look back with repining,
> And its pleasure be saddened with gloom.
> Deep thrilling emotions are breaking,
> While my thoughts on remembrances dwell;
> And my voice, as these visions are waking,
> Breathes in sadness the notes of farewell!
>   Farewell! Farewell!
> Breathes in sadness the notes of farewell!

(Odell, *Annals of the New York Stage*, Vol. III, 330–1).

someone struck a few chords on the piano, and she sang a couple of verses. The words were hardly inspired, but the performance was, and the effect on the audience was overwhelming. In spite of the singer's youth, the eerie repetition, to a slow and measured accompaniment, of the word 'farewell' filled the audience with sadness, and a strange sense of secret foreboding. People seem to have realised that evening that Maria Malibran was not just a very good singer, but a being somehow set apart from the rest of humanity, and that hers was to be a tragic destiny.[19]

New Yorkers said farewell to their Signorina with affection and regret. They realised that they had been privileged to have such an artist with them for two years, and they valued her not only as a singer, but as a person. 'Perhaps there never was an instance of a public actor making so deep an impression on private affections.'[20] They foresaw, as perhaps Eugène Malibran did not, that wicked, decadent Europe and the theatrical profession would hold many dangers for such a young and attractive woman; and they sensed that there was something 'peculiarly interesting in the history and destinies of this lady'.[21]

Two years in New York had given Maria Malibran inestimable advantages: varied theatrical experience; the experience of being a star, with no competition, in a small and friendly world. She had been isolated from other top performers — except Kean — and had therefore evolved an original style of her own. Although in after years Maria looked on New York as the scene of what she liked to think of as the greatest tragedy of her life — her marriage to Eugène Malibran — when she left America her parting from her husband was, if not a tragedy, at least a sorrow.

On 1st November, 1827, Maria Malibran sailed for France. Her husband came to see her off, but the parting was unsatisfactory, for reasons which she explained in her first letter, written at

40° longitude, half way, 1827.

My good little friend, my dear little pet. I must apologise to you thousands and thousands of times. On the cruel day of our separation, my heart had not the strength to say anything. I left without telling you so many things which I wanted to say, but the restraint which I imposed on myself so as not to grieve you prevented me from saying anything which might have made you unhappy.

So far, she told him, they had had a good wind, but she had been sea-sick all the time, except on the day when she was writing. Magnanimously, she asked after him.

> Tell me, dear friend, how do you spend your time? What are you doing? First, you think about me, then you dream about me, and then you talk about me with your friends, that's all very good, but I want to hear that you are looking after yourself, I want to know where you are living, and I want to insist that you have a good time.

Her letter ended abruptly: 'I feel rather sick, and so I'll stop until the first moment when I feel better.' That moment came only on 20th November, and did not last long; the weather had changed, the wind was against them, and everyone was ill.[22]

The combination of sea-sickness and the rapidly increasing distance between her and her husband made Maria think of him with real affection. 'I really need to see you now,' she told him, 'that's natural, but it's one of those needs which is not for *show*, but for you yourself, for your good little heart.' Then, in one of her disconcerting outbursts of frankness, she defined her feelings for him:

> . . . it is hard to be separated from people *one loves*, from you. *Pauvre ami*, I assure you that I've never loved you with passion, as I've already told you, but since I'm no longer with you, your good qualities appear so vividly in my mind, that I see I made a mistake in believing that I only loved you *faithfully*. I feel sick, dear friend, I'll leave you for a bit . . .[23]

It is doubtful if these words — too little, and too late — were much consolation to Eugène Malibran, left behind with his debts in New York, while his attractive young wife headed for fame and fortune without him. But she did, at that time, love him faithfully, if not passionately. She told him that she had rebuffed the advances which two passengers had made to her, and assured her husband that, even if the angels in heaven were to come to tempt her, she would resist, like Saint Anthony. Even if she should have an inclination to succumb to temptation, she told her husband, '*you would be there*, and the Eternal Father would be there too,' to restrain her.[24]

On 28th November, 1827, twenty-eight days after leaving New York, Maria Malibran arrived in France.

She was nineteen years old.

She had already experienced an unhappy childhood, great cruelty, possibly incest; she had married a man old enough to be her father; and she had become a star. Yet, as her letters show, she was still immature. She had no experience of leading an independent life, and, indeed, no experience of ordinary life; but her life was never to be ordinary.

PART II

PARIS

INTRODUCTION

Les romantiques ou frénétiques, comme on voudra . . .
Delacroix, *Journal*

Like all good musicians and actresses, Maria Malibran's sense of timing was impeccable; she arrived in Paris at precisely the right moment to fulfil her destiny. Had she come a little earlier, no one would have appreciated her; had she come slightly later, she would have missed certain crucial events, and her legend would not be as perfect and complete as it is. She landed in France just when the French Romantic upsurge was gaining its final momentum, and she was to be in Paris during those heady months which preceded the events of 1830.

That year was to mark a turning point in French political, social and artistic life. The July Revolution removed the ageing and reactionary king, Charles X, from the throne, and put the more liberal and younger Louis-Philippe in his place. Although Louis-Philippe was moderate and intelligent, and had the makings of an enlightened and civilised monarch, he ultimately failed to please anyone. He was disliked by the Legitimists, the aristocracy, the Bonapartists, the bourgeoisie whom he sought to emulate, the liberals, and the working classes. But, when he first came to the throne, he seemed preferable to his predecessor, and his accession was greeted as the dawning of a new and hopeful epoch.

In the arts, too, revolution was in the air. Young Frenchmen were already strongly attracted to ideas from England and Germany, whose Romantic movements of a slightly earlier period were influencing thought and art all over Europe. But it was Shakespeare, whose works the French were only just discovering, who proved to be the greatest revelation; his works were at least as vital in the formation of the French Romanticism of the 1830s as writers of the Romantic movement itself, such as Goethe, Byron and Walter Scott. A company of English actors had visited Paris in 1822, but had attracted little attention; they had arrived too early. In 1827, however, a company headed by Charles Kemble and Harriet Smithson performed *Hamlet* and *Romeo and Juliet*, and created a profound impression. Berlioz spoke for his whole generation when he wrote: 'Shakespeare, happening on me unexpectedly, left me thunderstruck. His flash of lightning which, with sublime thunder, opened up for me the heaven of art, illuminated its remotest depths.'[1] Another revelation — Beethoven's symphonies — struck Paris at about the same time (1828). 'The shock it gave me,' wrote Berlioz, 'was almost comparable to that given me by Shakespeare.'[2] Weber's *Der Freischütz*, given in Paris in a very garbled version (*Robin des Bois*, 1824), nevertheless revealed a new world of opera to the French; it contained almost every Romantic element which they admired and were seeking in art at that time.

In the famous battle for *Hernani* (25th February, 1830, some four months before the July Revolution), Victor Hugo and his young supporters won a major, if temporary, victory in the theatre against the French Classical tradition. In his preface to *Hernani* Hugo launched a second Romantic manifesto, shorter, less turgid and more to the point than his flatulent but seminal preface to *Cromwell* (1827). In it he wrote: 'Young people, let us be of good cheer! However difficult people may try to make the present for us, the future will be bright. Romanticism, so often ill-defined, is, all things considered, [...] nothing but liberalism in literature. [...] Freedom in Art, freedom in Society, that is the dual aim ...'

In the febrile weeks preceding the July Revolution, such words had a potent effect; and the publicity which *Hernani* and its stormy first night attracted spread the Romantic message far beyond the confines of literary coteries in Paris.

Despite the influence of *Hernani*, in reality the various ideas and attitudes which shaped the Romantic Movement had been germinating in intellectuals' and artists' minds for years all over Europe. In France in 1830, thanks to a number of highly gifted men and women, these ideas coalesced into a definable movement, and began to reach the attention of a wide public. The production of *Hernani* at the Théâtre Français was, on the face of it, a rebellion against the rules and traditions of the French Classical drama; it was a battle between youth and age and also, in those tense weeks before revolution broke out, a political gesture. In no time at all, young people in the provinces who had never been to the Théâtre Français or thought about the Three Unities, were infected by the same spirit and rallied, each in his own way, to Hugo's battle-cry: 'Freedom in Art, freedom in Society'. Some read the poetry of Lamartine, Hugo or Vigny, and found that it expressed what they themselves were thinking and feeling; others turned to politics; still others merely let their hair grow long and wore eccentric, usually mediaeval, clothes. What had begun as an intellectual movement was rapidly becoming a fashion. Young people all over France found that they shared the same ideals, attitudes and tastes, and that these were not the ideals, attitudes and tastes of their parents. The generation which was growing up in the 1820s admired the same writers, listened to the same music, wore the same clothes, and wished to disassociate itself from the immediate past. A youth culture was exploding, and the time was ripe for it.

In the 1830s, as in the 1960s, the first post-war generation was coming to maturity; they were the children of those who had lived through the French Revolution and the Napoleonic wars. 'During the wars of the Empire,' wrote Musset, 'while husbands and brothers were in Germany, anxious mothers had given birth to a generation which was passionate, pale, highly-strung. Conceived between two battles, brought up in school to the rolling of drums, thousands of children looked at each other with eyes of despair, while flexing their puny muscles. From time to time their blood-stained fathers arrived, lifted them up to their gold-bedecked chests, then put them on the ground again, and mounted their horses.'[3]

These children were now growing up in the usual untidy aftermath of major wars: a disillusioning and boring peace. They, of course, blamed their parents; and, inevitably, the latter's standards of morality, social attitudes and politics were found wanting. New leaders were sought.

During the previous forty years the French had become accustomed to the cult of great men, of heroes. But, by the 1830s, men of action were out of fashion, since there was now much less for them to do. France in the 1830s, like England in the 1960s, had lost an empire; young people no longer had military outlets for their energies, and they turned, perhaps reluctantly, to the peace-time activities of art, music, literature, the theatre. The new heroes were writers and artists of all kinds, who could express the feelings of the post-war generation and, with the sixth sense of artists, define the new epoch which seemed to be dawning.

Never had writers, poets in particular, been held in such high esteem or wielded so much influence. Goethe, who was still writing, and Byron, who had died six years earlier, had created a whole new ethos all over Europe. Sir Walter Scott, whose influence outside England was second only to Byron's, was still alive. In France, the ageing Chateaubriand, sixty-two years old in 1830, was the father and inspiration of the new Romanticism; while Benjamin Constant, who died in 1830, formed a living link between the events of that year and Madame de Staël (1766–1817), whose writings had helped to precipitate them.

Of the Romantics of 1830, Stendhal, a transitional and rogue figure, was the eldest; he was forty-seven, had served under Napoleon, and had not yet written *La Chartreuse de Parme*; *Le Rouge et le noir* appeared in 1830. Lamartine was forty; Alfred de Vigny and Balzac were in their early thirties. But by far the largest and most precocious group, who were to make the final Romantic breakthrough which their elders had prepared, were those born after 1800 and so under thirty, none of whom could more than dimly remember the Napoleonic era. It was an exceptionally gifted generation, and only the most important can be named here: Victor Hugo, for a time the acknowledged leader was, with Dumas, the eldest, at twenty-eight; then came Berlioz and Mérimée, twenty-seven; George Sand and Saint-Beuve, twenty-four; Gérard de Nerval was, like Maria Malibran, twenty-two; and the two youngest of this group, Alfred de Musset and Théophile Gautier, were twenty and nineteen respectively.

It was a talented generation not only in France, but in the rest of Europe, too. Amongst the foreigners in the same age-group who came to Paris in or around 1830, and who were to help to make it for a time the artistic capital of the world, were: Liszt, nineteen in that year; Chopin, who was twenty; Mendelssohn, twenty-one; Bellini, twenty-nine; the Polish poet, Adam Mickiewicz, thirty-two, and the German poet, Heinrich Heine, who was thirty-three. Marie Taglioni, who was to become the personification of Romanticism in ballet, as Maria Malibran was to personify it in opera, was twenty-six.

The new attitudes — all of which have at some point been labelled Romantic — were extremely disparate, sometimes contradictory. Nostalgia for a remote past — mediaeval, gothic — was coupled with a belief in a rosy future. A taste for violence and cruelty, particularly in the graphic arts and the theatre, went hand in hand with a gentle, elegiac sensibility. Reality was a horror from which the Romantics tried to escape at all costs, either through their imagination, or by isolating themselves in their private dreams. Some Romantics were frenetic, others withdrawn. Melancholy was the prevailing mood, reflected in a fashion for dark and muted colours.

A revival of interest in Christianity coincided with the growth of humanism and rationalism. Minority and bogus religions, odd sects, fringe medicine and sciences all flourished. Mystery was the vogue; the occult, the supernatural and the macabre had vast appeal; dreams and strange sensations were sought after, often with the help of drugs. The beauties of nature, the wilder the better, were suddenly perceived, and extolled. Everything exotic and foreign was valued; Spain, Italy and the Middle East had just been discovered by many Frenchmen as a result of the Napoleonic wars, and were considered particularly attractive. Gypsies, bandits, anyone living without the law and people living far removed from normal urban society, were thought to have the secret of 'real' life, and were much admired. Tears, fainting-fits, and ill-health became fashionable; a robust and healthy physique was a positive disadvantage, a pale, unhealthy complexion *de rigueur*. An unspecified, but possibly mortal illness excited interest, even envy; and early death was the crowning glory. Suicide was a status symbol, albeit a posthumous one. Indeed, an obsession with death was one of the most powerful forces of the period, and is reflected in much of its art, literature and music; a generation which, unlike that of its parents, had not known violent death in war, was fascinated by it.

The individual, and individualism, now reigned supreme; and within each individual every contradiction was valid, just as, in the Romantic theatre, tragedy and comedy were no longer to be separated. Passions, good or bad, but preferably violent and mixed, were to be expressed, not controlled. Restraint, like the Classical tradition which had advocated it, was out of fashion. Freedom of the individual was the order of the day, and the heart, rather than the head, was suddenly the sole arbiter of people's actions. Some individuals were more individual than others: artists, poets, musicians, were mages, who could see into their own and other people's hearts, and into the future, and could interpret what they saw to others.

For centuries the hired servants of the rich and powerful, artists of all kinds were breaking free and gaining a new status. They now resented patrons who controlled them, although they were happy to take their money, provided no strings were attached. In reality, most of the great patrons had disappeared with the *ancien régime*, and the new universal patron — the bourgeoisie, dubbed 'grocers' by the Romantics — was the hated enemy of all Romantics, most of whom came from a middle-class background themselves. Artists were now 'free', but often much more impoverished than they had been in the past. Some championed aestheticism, art for art's sake; others withdrew into their ivory towers; still others turned to committed art, art with a purpose or a message, art for the people. Attempts were made by artists, as in 1968, to form an alliance with the workers. Some women began to realise that they, too, were oppressed, and that they, too, might win their freedom; and some artists supported them. Many, particularly musicians, influenced by the ideas of Saint-Simon, believed that they had a special mission to serve humanity and raise it to a higher level. All artists had a new sense of their own importance; and the public gradually began to take them at their own evaluation.

Suddenly, every young man and woman dreamed of becoming an artist, or at least of acting out real artists' ideas. Horrified parents looked on, as their sons' hair grew longer, their daughters starved themselves and grew pale, and their life-styles became ever more eccentric. Bank clerks' children refused to follow in their parents' footsteps, and instead suffered from *ennui, le mal de siècle,* and spent their time writing poetry. Parents blamed the Romantic writers whose works their children so avidly read; and the parents were right. Literature was, to the 1830s, what pop music was to the 1960s — on the young its effect was intoxicating. Every young man imagined himself to be Werther or René, Chatterton or Obermann; every girl saw herself as Indiana or Lélia.

Real artists were living through a transitional period. The social and political changes brought about by the French Revolution and the Napoleonic wars affected everyone's lives; but they had a particularly radical effect on the lives of performing artists, and on their relationship with the public. The decline of court and aristocratic patronage made it essential for musicians and actors to appeal to a wider and more democratic audience, however much they might despise the bourgeoisie, if they wanted to make a living; and the new curiosity about the individual made the public look on artists as people, whose private lives were of interest and were beginning to become news. The modern obsession with show business people was in the process of being born.

In the world of opera — always a microcosm of the bigger world — these changes began to be profoundly felt in the 1820s. Audiences were beginning to tire of the heroes and heroines of classical antiquity, and wanted something which would reflect contemporary life. This did not always please the various censorships of the time, who saw the theatre as a potential medium for disseminating subversive ideas. In Paris in 1830 Rossini reigned supreme; he was not a true Romantic, and his operas did not often reflect modern life; but no other contemporary composer could equal his ability to write sparkling music for the human voice. He was soon to be challenged by truly Romantic composers, such as Bellini and Donizetti. At the same time Auber, with *La Muette de Portici* (sometimes called *Masaniello*) produced a work which, although set in Naples in the seventeenth century, was interpreted by audiences when it was first produced in 1828 as having a contemporary political significance, and in 1830 it sparked off the revolution in Belgium. But, by 1830, anything which could be even remotely interpreted as advocating 'Freedom in Art, freedom in Society' inflamed the young.

There are almost as many definitions of Romanticism as there were manifestations of it, and none are really satisfactory. Paul Valéry considered that, to attempt to define it, one must have lost all sense of intellectual discipline, and one cannot but agree with him. In retrospect it can be seen as an intellectual movement, a literary revolt, an artistic style, something which can be discussed, annotated, theorised about; but those who were young in 1830 were trying to create a new world for themselves, an experience which later generations can never fully recapture. To them, Romanticism was the spirit of the times, *their* time, *le mal de siècle*, a revolution, a revelation, a fashion, a pose, an attitude. It was the spirit of the youth of one particular generation, and of no other. This so-called second Romantic movement did not last long — about ten years at the most — but so long as it survived it was intoxicating. Its artistic, social and political legacy was vast, and still shapes much of our lives today.

Maria Malibran, born, like the other Romantics, in France during the crucial Napoleonic years, arrived in Paris in 1827 when the movement was reaching its peak. She knew virtually no one, and had probably scarcely even heard of Romanticism. She had been, until then, entirely cut off from people of her own generation, and had been living in what was then a provincial city — New York; she can have had little idea of the theories, attitudes and fashions which accompanied the movement in France. Yet, by 1830, she was not only on very friendly terms with most of the leading Romantics, but she herself had become identified with Romanticism. It would be easy to assume that, young as she was, she was influenced by the very brilliant artists and intellectuals whom she met in France. In fact, the opposite seems to have been the case; it was not the French

Romantics who influenced La Malibran, but she who influenced them. She was to make the Romantic ideal come alive; both on and off the stage she was to live what others only wrote or dreamed about.

1

'You want to know what my impression of Paris is?' wrote Maria to her husband, a month after her arrival in France. 'You shall hear it straight away. First of all: pretty hats, bonnets, etc. beautiful dresses etc. Pretty jewellery in the shops which I never look at for fear of temptation.' She did not, at first, like Paris as much as New York; she found Parisians too insincere and snobbish: 'The ladies prettily dressed in a pretty negligée, negligently prepared for an hour beforehand . . .'[1]

Maria went to stay with her husband's married sister, Madame Chastelain, and her family. At first this was a great success, and they were very friendly. 'What pleasure that gives me!' she told her husband. 'Absolutely all I need is you for it to be *nex* [sic] *plus ultra*.'[2]

At the same time, she was welcomed by old friends of her family in the theatrical world, and was reunited with her brother, who had also arrived in Paris. Society ladies, particularly Countess Merlin, who was of Spanish origin and had had singing lessons from Maria's father, and Countess Meroni, took her up and did all they could to launch her. Musicians, such as Rossini, Paer, Boieldieu and Cherubini, realised her vast potential as an artist, and watched her performances in private houses with intense interest; but at first they were cautious, since they had not yet heard her sing in the theatre.

Only a month after her arrival in Paris Maria was able to tell her husband that she had sung at the Duchess de Berry's house:

I was all the rage. Mme Pizaroni [Mme Pisaroni, an excellent singer, who took part in the same concert] has a great deal of talent. But she is ugly, very ugly and makes faces while she sings. As I am slightly passable and don't make faces, that alone could assure my success, but don't worry, that wasn't it. Later I sang at the house of Countess Merlin, who had a splendid gathering, and where I had all the success to which I could aspire. People talk of nothing but my method, my voice, my way of singing, people say I'm a worthy successor to Madame *Pasta*, and they say I have many advantages over her. You'll say: there you are, overcome by flattery, and you let yourself be seduced by praise. Set your mind at rest, my friend. Those are *Ladies*, and I don't say that there weren't any gentlemen. But when Rossini, when Mme Rossini, who has never paid a compliment in her life, comes with open arms to embrace me in front of a great many people, to pay me a thousand compliments [. . .] that's a reason for me to believe something, besides, don't be afraid of me becoming proud as a result and that I shall consider myself something big in my little private self.[3]

Maria was in no way exaggerating; she was indeed 'all the rage', and an opportunity to prove herself in the theatre soon came. A benefit performance was announced at the Opéra for Galli, a favourite singer and an old friend of the Garcias; Maria was invited to take part. It was to be an all-star affair: Madame Pisaroni may have been ugly — it is said that at her début a murmur of fright spread through the audience when it saw her face — but she was a first-class contralto of great experience. Maria was to sing Semiramide to her Arsace in Rossini's *Semiramide*. Actors from the English company then in Paris were next to give two acts of *Romeo and Juliet* with Harriet Smithson (later Berlioz's wife) as Juliet. The evening was to end with one act of *Il barbiere* with Henriette Sontag.

It is said that the first time Maria Malibran heard Henriette Sontag sing, she burst into tears, saying: 'My God! Why does she sing so beautifully!'[4] Her distress was understandable, for Sontag was an outstanding singer. Coming from America, Maria had not realised how high European standards could be.

Henriette Sontag was the only serious rival Maria was ever to encounter, for Pasta, ten years older, represented an earlier generation and a different style of performance. The rivalry between La Malibran and Sontag was to be intense, and to arouse violent emotions amongst audiences. Coming as it did at the outset of Maria's career, this rivalry was very beneficial to her; she was anyway extremely competitive, and Sontag spurred her on to ever greater achievements.

Henriette Sontag was born in Coblentz in 1806, and was thus two years older than Maria. She, too, came from a theatrical family; but she was even more precocious, having first appeared on the stage at the age of six, and at fifteen she was called on to replace an indisposed prima donna at the theatre in Prague, then directed by Weber. She later moved to Vienna, and appeared both in German and Italian opera. Her voice was a high soprano, and her technique was impeccable; she lacked only dramatic power. Weber chose her as his first Euryanthe (1823); she sang the soprano parts at the first performances of Beethoven's 9th Symphony and *Mass in D*; she was a notable Agathe in *Der Freischütz*. She went to Paris for the first time in 1826, had a great success there, and returned in January, 1828, just after Maria's arrival.

All this was certainly quite enough to make Maria weep; but it was not all. Sontag was an extremely beautiful woman; she was very well-built, had delicate features, and was a ravishing blonde with auburn tints in her hair — the very personification of Nordic beauty. She was also the personification of the Nordic spirit, and of nascent German nationalism, through her association with Weber and his operas. Sweet, feminine, and seemingly rather prim, she excelled in works 'of a light and placid style'.⁵ Those who liked her thought her ladylike; those who disliked her thought her genteel, mechanical and predictable. She reminded one critic of 'an English nursery-maid'.⁶ She was, in fact, very popular in England and in Germany, but the French Romantics were scathing about her.

The benefit for Galli, on 14th January, 1828, was a great occasion; the Opéra was filled with a distinguished audience, and a number of rival claques. Everyone was keen to hear Garcia's daughter for the first time; everyone was keen to hear Sontag again; and the English actors were then at the height of fashion. Rossini, the director of the Opéra, and Laurent, the director of the Théâtre Italien, both attended, and watched Maria's performance with professional eyes: Rossini had known her since she was a baby, and she was to sing his music. Throughout the performance Rossini and Laurent were both secretly calculating how much they would have to offer her in order to secure her for the season.

In the first act of *Semiramide* Maria was extremely nervous,* and by the end of the act the audience had still not made up its mind

---

* Throughout her career, and despite her success, La Malibran always suffered from stage-fright on first nights. Many great actors and actresses suffer similarly, and some even consider it a necessary evil, since it makes the adrenalin flow, and puts the artist into a state of heightened sensibility which enables him or her to 'get into' the part. (See André Villiers, *La Psychologie du comédien*, pp. 171–181.)

about her. She was coldly received at the beginning of the second act; but, realising that at that moment her whole future was at stake, she recovered her nerve and began to sing really well. Then, sensing that the audience was beginning to be won over, she became ever more brilliant and daring. 'The audience was conquered,' said Fétis, 'and passed from the most disdainful coldness to the most immoderate enthusiasm.'[7] By the end of the performance the audience was delirious; objective judgement was suspended; people were overcome with that mass hysteria which very occasionally breaks out in the theatre when a great star first emerges. In one evening Maria had ceased to be Garcia's daughter, and had become La Malibran. Next day her name – her husband's name — was on everyone's lips. She was still only nineteen years old.

The critics were almost unanimous in their praise. Only Fétis, an old friend of her family, pointed out her defects in an avuncular way, said she had much to learn, and that her singing was 'absolutely devoid of taste and method.'[8] But no one listened to him except, perhaps, Maria herself. The public mind was already made up: La Malibran was a great star, and whatever critics might say about her, then or in the future, it had little effect on public opinion.

What was it about La Malibran's performance that night — and on so many subsequent nights — that so excited the audience? What kind of a singer was she? Now, a century and a half after her death, it is almost impossible to answer that question. We know a few facts: that she had a splendid, but not perfect, mezzo-soprano voice with a very wide range; that her father's schooling had given her excellent technique, and the ability to improvise with great skill; that she could take both soprano and mezzo-soprano parts; that she was a remarkable dramatic actress, equally great in comedy and tragedy. Her sister Pauline Viardot had all these qualities, yet never generated the same excitement; and other great singers of the epoch — La Pasta, Isabella Colbran, Henriette Sontag, Mme Schröder-Devrient, the young Giulia Grisi — possessed some, if not all, of the same qualities; yet they never thrilled the public to quite the same extent as La Malibran.

Critics of the time give us little help — indeed, can the written word ever really evoke all the characteristics of a singer whom one has never heard? Serious music criticism was then in its infancy; Berlioz and Schumann were only just beginning to create it, and neither has left us a description of La Malibran's performances. Other good critics of the epoch — Fétis, Chorley, Vitet — do bring us a little nearer to understanding La Malibran's gifts and defects — mainly her talents as a dramatic artist rather than a singer; but the average contemporary newspaper critic usually wrote banal and often largely meaningless phrases. For example: 'Malibran exerted herself to the utmost, and displayed a genius which excited her audience to a furore of delight and admiration, that found expression in universal and prolonged plaudits.'[9] What does this *really* tell us about her performance? The following does tell us something about her voice, but not how she sang: 'Her voice is of a very peculiar character, of the mezzo-soprano kind, beautifully harmonious and full in the lower notes, extremely sweet and touching in the higher, which resemble a falsetto . . .'[10] The critic who wrote: 'She exuded some kind of enchantment, which raised her above all other artists into a sphere destined for her alone'[11] was probably right; but he still does not tell us how she sang.

Henry Chorley, critic of the *Athenaeum*, is more helpful; like many others, he noticed that

> her voice was not naturally of first-rate quality [. . .] weakest in the tones between F and F — a weakness audaciously and incomparably disguised by the forms of execution, modification and ornament which she selected. Her topmost notes and deepest notes were perpetually used in connected contrast, whatever the song might be — whether it was the *bravura* from 'Ines de Castro' or Haydn's 'With verdure clad'. On the stage her flights and sallies told with electric effect.

But Chorley recognised that he could not really transmit to his readers a true impression of her performances. 'I feel,' he wrote, 'that there was something feverish, meteoric, ever changing into a new surprise, both in her nature and in her art, which dazzled while it delighted, leaving the witness with small readiness available for balance and comparison of impressions.'[12]

The comments of composers whose music she sang, and of other professional musicians, should be more explicit than the vague statements of journalists, but rarely are. Until 1832 La Malibran sang Rossini's music more frequently than that of any other composer. Rossini's famous comment on the singers of his youth does not greatly enlighten us: 'The most remarkable,' he said, 'was Madame Pasta; Madame Colbran [his first wife] was the foremost; but Madame Malibran was unique.'[13] on another occasion Rossini said that, although there had been many great singers in his day, there had only been three real geniuses: Lablache, Rubini, and 'that spoiled child of nature, Maria Felicia Malibran.'[14] We are still no wiser as to the precise nature of her genius. After 1833 La Malibran became one of the most successful interpreters of Bellini's music. Bellini heard her sing only in a garbled version of *La sonnambula* in English.* It is clear from his correspondence that he had the highest opinion of her talents; yet he, too, merely referred vaguely to her 'prodigious talent'.[15]

The list of other composers and musicians who admired La Malibran is long; it includes: Zingarelli, Spontini, Meyerbeer, Auber, Halévy, Donizetti, Nicolai, Vaccai, Paer, Liszt, Chopin, Paganini, Ole Bull, Julius Benedict, Thalberg, Moscheles, and many more; but none of their comments — usually confined to the word 'genius' or adjectives in the superlative — tell us anything about the way she sang. The pianist Moscheles, for example, usually quite a stern critic, tells us: 'She always sings exquisitely, and with true inspiration; she is never the mere vocalist, but a musical genius. If obliged to repeat a cavatina, as is generally the case, she improvises new passages more beautiful than the first, unsurpassable as they seemed.' Then the sober Moscheles abandons his attempt at serious criticism, and tells us: 'Her very smile captivates the orchestra and conductor, and she kindles with a spark of her own spirit the most inanimate of orchestral players . . .'[16] As usual, we are left with the impression that it was charm, personality, vivacity, and the variety and originality of her performances that enabled La Malibran to excite audiences more than other great singers did. *How* she sang, we really do not know.

The comments of Fétis and Verdi, however, are so strikingly similar, although written at widely different dates, that they may, perhaps, be taken as the closest we can now get to the truth concerning La Malibran's style of singing. Fétis, who sometimes criticised her for lack of taste, nevertheless after her death considered her to have been 'the most astonishing singer of her century' — the adjective was probably particularly appropriate — and defined her talent as 'great, sublime, bizarre, and sometimes unequal.'[17] Verdi, who only heard her when he was a very young man, and never worked with her, writing forty years after her death said much the same thing. He remembered her as 'very great, but not always equal! Sometimes sublime, and sometimes eccentric! Her style of singing was not very pure, her technique not always correct, her voice was

---

* See pp. 178–80.

strident in the upper register! But in spite of everything, a very great artist, marvellous. But Patti is more complete.'[18]

Rossini, whose music she so often sang, and who probably knew her better than any other composer did, realised his inability to describe her art: 'Ah! That marvellous creature! She surpassed all her imitators by her truly disconcerting musical genius, and all the women I have ever known by the superiority of her intelligence, the variety of her knowledge and her flashing temperament, of which it is impossible to give any idea.'[19]

If we could hear and see La Malibran today, would we rave about her as her contemporaries did? Probably not. Improvisation and florid ornamentation have gone out of fashion; her exaggerated and idiosyncratic performances would probably not be acceptable to modern audiences, and certainly not to modern directors, conductors, and other singers who might have to perform with her. In La Malibran's day the concept of a corporate production by a team working together was virtually unknown; the star did exactly what she felt like doing, and everyone else had to fit in with her. La Malibran's temperament was such that she would have found it very difficult to submit to the discipline of a modern director or conductor.

La Malibran's dramatic ability was easier to describe than her musical talent; it obviously contributed enormously to her success, and we shall discuss it more fully in later chapters. Writers — Musset, George Sand, Vitet, Legouvé, Lamartine — were more explicit than music critics were about her singing. If the nature of her vocal performances must always remain obscure to us, what is clear is that La Malibran possessed a fascinating and unusual personality, and that she perfectly expressed the mood of the moment; her frenetic, often bizarre and exaggerated performances inflamed the Romantic imagination, and sometimes excited audiences to a hysterical pitch. Ten years earlier or ten years later, she would probably have had far less success; but she was the spirit of 1830 incarnate, and this was the real secret of her extraordinary popularity.

Sontag, already well known in Paris, received far less attention than La Malibran after Galli's benefit; but she had her band of admirers, who supported her ardently and vociferously. The rivalry between the two singers in private was far more intense than that of their supporters. They refused to speak to each other; and although they often appeared at the same private concerts, they would not sing together. Several attempts were made to reconcile them, notably by Rossini who, on one occasion, put his arms round both girls at the same time and drew them together; but then each turned on her heel and stalked away. 'This rivalry was pushed so far between the imperious Juno and the blonde Venus,' wrote a contemporary, 'that they could not remain together in the same room. Upon the stage, when they sang in the same opera [. . .] their stupendous jealousy manifested itself by malicious cadenzas and rockets of sound which inflamed their hearers . . .'[20]

A reconciliation did eventually take place at Countess Merlin's house, where the two singers were finally persuaded to sing a duet. But although they fell in each other's arms and embraced when it was over, it is to be doubted that either suffered a real change of heart.

After La Malibran's outstanding success at Galli's benefit the Paris theatres, as well as theatres abroad, were all doing their utmost to engage the new star. Wild rumours circulated about her exorbitant demands: some said she was asking 35,000 francs for the season, others said 50,000 francs or even 75,000 francs. Although later in her career La Malibran was to earn such fees, in 1828 the larger sums mentioned in the press were a gross exaggeration; they merely reflected the star status which she had already attained, and the public's estimation of her worth.*

The Opéra let it be known discreetly that the person who could persuade her to join the theatre could have 2,000 francs for his pains; but it was to no avail. Even Rossini could not persuade her to join the Opéra, although she said that he was 'never out of her house'.[21]

Maria realised that the Opéra — more French, more conventional, and more official than the Théâtre Italien — was not the right place for her. 'I'll never join it, under any pretext, no matter what it might be,' she told her husband. 'First and foremost no sum of money would make me change my mind. It's a different career to follow, and once you join it you only get out of it twenty years later.'[22]

---

* She had asked the directors of the Opéra for 30,000 francs per year 'in order to get rid of them', for she knew that they would not agree to such a sum (letter to E. Malibran, 7th Feb., 1828, Teneo, p. 460). Six months later she obtained 35,000 francs for a six months' season at the Théâtre Italien in Paris, and 40,000 francs for a three months' season in London (letter to E. Malibran, 2nd August, 1828, Teneo, p. 469).

On 3rd March she was able to tell her husband that she had achieved her ambition: she had been engaged to appear at the Théâtre Italien; for the next four years she was to be its brightest star.

2

It is not difficult to see why La Malibran wished to join the Théâtre Italien; as one of her contemporaries said: 'The Opéra is a fashion and a taste; the Théâtre Italien is a NEED and a PASSION.'[1] Therefore, to be the greatest star of the Théâtre Italien was to be something much more than to be the greatest opera singer in Paris. In the late 1820s and the 1830s the Théâtre Italien was not just a theatre, it was a way of life. By engaging the finest singers in Europe, at a time when Italian opera was enjoying an unprecedented success in France with a wide public, the directors of the Théâtre Italien had made it first fashionable, then a cultural centre for the Romantics, and finally the temple of a cult.

Music had never before played such an important part in French life, and perhaps never has since; the popularity of opera, in particular, was at its zenith. To the Romantics there were no frontiers between the arts, and music was the bond which united people, breaking down barriers of class, nationality and profession, as it did again in the western world in the 1960s. Each art — music, literature, the graphic arts — was fed by the others. Poets, such as Vigny, Musset and Nerval, were inspired by music, and were very knowledgeable about it. Musicians, such as Berlioz and Liszt, were inspired by literature. Novelists, such as Stendhal, Balzac and George Sand, also wrote about music. Among painters, Ingres's love of music has become proverbial, and Delacroix's diaries and letters are a rich source of information about the music and literature of his day. Gautier, who began life as a painter, became a poet and dramatic critic; Victor Hugo's paintings are, we now see, almost as worthy of interest as his poetry. A real brotherhood of the arts existed.

The Théâtre Italien was the centre and meeting-place of a mainly young, cosmopolitan, enthusiastic and talented audience, 'whose first rule was never to miss a single performance'.[2] People went there first and foremost to hear the music — principally Rossini's music — and to witness the drama. They went there so frequently that they knew most of the operas by heart, and could detect the smallest nuances between different performances. Legouvé, for example, went to hear Rossini's *Otello* 60 times.[3] People went to hear the finest Italian singers of the day, and were extremely critical of performances, and dedicated in their support of their favourite singers.

But they did not only go to the Théâtre Italien for the music. They went to see, and to be seen; they went to meet their friends, to carry on intrigues or business, to learn the news, and to create it. Some, like Balzac, went to digest their dinners in comfort, while listening to the music and observing the human comedy. Others, like Stendhal, went to kill their *ennui* with the aid of the music they adored. Delacroix found that the music often 'inspired him with great thoughts'; but he was also 'deliciously affected' by the women in the theatre.[4] Philothée O'Neddy, one of the minor Romantics, revelled in the voluptuousness of the atmosphere, and envisaged the Théâtre Italien as the ideal setting for a sublime suicide.[5] All went to bask in the heady atmosphere, compounded of music and drama, powerful emotions, talented men and women, lavish décors, jewels, scent, intrigue, wit, conversation, gossip, scandal — a wealth of sensual and intellectual stimuli, all to be found in one place at the same time, three times a week.

It was to this audience that Maria Malibran made her début in Rossini's *Semiramide*,* on 8th April, 1828. The dilettanti and the many professional musicians who crowded the theatre that night in order to assess the new prima donna saw before them a frail-looking girl, who was excessively nervous.

She was not tall and was, by the standards of the time, too thin. Her hair was very dark, her complexion ivory. Her features were irregular, but very mobile. She had a fairly large mouth, beautiful teeth, and a shortish nose. The purity of line of her neck and shoulders, and 'a refinement in the form of her head'[6] were particularly noticed. Her most striking feature was her large, dark eyes, '. . . eyes which *had an atmosphere*. Virgil has said: *Natantia lumina somno*, eyes swimming in sleep; well, Maria Malibran had, like Talma, eyes swimming in I don't know what electric fluid, from which her glances flashed, both luminous and at the same time veiled, like a sunbeam passing through a cloud. Her glances seemed all charged with melancholy, with reverie, with passion . . .'[7] 'She

---

* In the part of Semiramide (soprano); she was later often to appear as Arsace, a mezzo-soprano breeches part in the same opera.

may not have been beautiful,' wrote H. F. Chorley, who saw her in 1830, 'but she was better than beautiful.'[8]

She began to sing. At first, her extreme nervousness inhibited her; but eventually she was able to bring it under control, and could then give full play to her amazing vocal and dramatic powers. By the end of the evening, her success was complete. It was not the greatest performance of her career, but it was the most important one; to have failed at the Théâtre Italien would have been to fail in all Europe. Fétis (and other, less critical reviewers), predicted a brilliant future for her: 'Nature has given her everything which goes to make great artists,' he wrote. 'Experience will do the rest.'[9] The delirious audience fully agreed with him.

La Malibran's début inaugurated a celebrated era in the annals of the Théâtre Italien. For the next four years she was to be the principal attraction there, and those who were lucky enough to witness her performances remembered them with nostalgia for the rest of their lives.

A week later she wrote to her husband: 'I've appeared in *Semiramide*, which was a mad success, then *Otello* which goes crescendo terribly, *Il barbiere idem*, and this very evening I performed *La cenerentola* for the second time. What enthusiasm, I won't tell you if it's deserved or not, but I can tell you that I hold my audience, and that it likes everything I do.'[10]

She certainly held her audience; and since that audience was largely made up of creative artists, she not only held it, but was soon to begin to influence it. It was Ludovic Vitet, the historian and future Inspector of Historical Monuments, who, writing in *Le Globe* about her first appearance as Ninetta in Rossini's *La gazza ladra*, was the first in Europe to refer in print to 'the truly *romantic* manner in which Madame Malibran envisages her art';[11] but he was surely not the first to notice it. From her very first appearances it was obvious to the Romantics that they were seeing the personification of their ideals, and watching their own dreams and fantasies being played out on the stage.

Everything about La Malibran was romantic: her exotic Spanish (or gypsy) origins; her originality; her unpredictability; her lack of Classical restraint and her love of excess; her passionate acting; her ability to mix tragedy with comedy; the freedom with which she squandered her physical and emotional powers; and, to crown it all, the cloud of melancholy — of tragedy, even — which never left her, even in her brightest moments.

Melancholy was then all the fashion; Alexandre Dumas, not much given to melancholy himself, explained his contemporaries' taste for it at that time:

> There are moments like that in society; everything is calm, except people's imaginations. Bodies are in no risk of danger, so minds want imaginary perils; human pity must fix on something. Twelve years of calm made everyone want emotions; ten years of smiles made everyone call for tears.[12]

La Malibran was protean; each member of the audience could find in her performance his own ideal, and could identify with the emotions which she portrayed on the stage. She was all things to all people. To Stendhal, a passionate addict of Italian opera, she was above all an amazing singer; he foretold that she would become 'the greatest singer in the world'.[13] To Etienne Delécluse, theatre-goer, connoisseur of acting, and student of Shakespeare, she was merely an agreeable singer, but 'above all an excellent actress'.[14] The young Liszt, three years La Malibran's junior, told her she had 'more than genius', and that she had 'made such an impression on him that he needed to see her'.[15] The poet, Alfred de Vigny, was moved by her nobility, her performances 'which come from her heart';[16] another poet, Gautier, said simply, 'she was music, as Taglioni was the dance.'[17] Alexandre Dumas thought her 'dazzling, melodious, melancholy'.[18] She made George Sand 'weep, shudder, suffer'.[19] Lamartine thought her supernatural.[20] To Ernest Legouvé she was 'the purest and most moving interpreter of poetry, of love, and of sorrow'.[21]

'The character one finds in all the débuts of that epoch,' wrote Gautier, 'is an overflowing of lyricism and the quest for passion'; and La Malibran's début was no exception. She herself fully subscribed to the ideals of the young Romantics: 'To develop freely all the caprices of thought, even if they shock taste, conventions and rules; to hate and, as much as possible, to reject what Horace called *profanum vulgus* [the ignorant masses], and what the bewhiskered, long-haired students call grocers, philistines or the bourgeoisie: to extol love with such ardour that it burns the paper, to set it up as the sole aim and sole means of happiness; to sanctify and deify Art, considered as the second creator.'[22]

The Romantics deified art and love, and saw La Malibran as the high priestess of their new religion, which was soon to be reflected in the literature of the day. The Théâtre Italien was 'the temple of music'.[23] The thirteen-year-old Charles Gounod, hearing La Malibran there on his first visit to the theatre, sensed this, as everyone did: 'I felt that I was in a temple,' he wrote, 'and that something divine was about to be revealed to me.'[24] The theatre was 'the court of heaven',[25] attended by 'the faithful, its congregation';[26] there was 'a religious silence'[27] there; hostile criticism was 'blasphemous';[28] the singers were 'sacred nightingales';[29] and the supreme mystery was to be revealed by La Malibran 'in ecstasy, singing the Willow-Song.'[30]

3

La Malibran's interpretation of the *Willow Song* became the quintessential Romantic set-piece, an unforgettable experience of which her contemporaries never tired. The Romantics identified her with Rossini's Desdemona; she herself had anyway always identified with the part since her earliest performances in America, but for rather different reasons.

Most writers and painters depicted La Malibran as Desdemona in Rossini's *Otello*, accompanying herself in the *Willow Song* on the harp. It was probably her greatest part, at least until she began to interpret Bellini's operas, and *Otello* is the most Romantic of Rossini's operas.* The libretto† is lamentable; but the French Romantics admired the theme and Rossini's music so much that, as Stendhal said, 'we invent our own libretto to match.'[1]‡

'One cannot praise Rossini's *Otello* too highly,' said Alfred de Musset. 'I don't know if it will go out of fashion [. . .] but for us, who are of our own time, it is a masterpiece.'[2] A century and a half later, it has gone out of fashion; but in the early nineteenth century the combination of Shakespeare, albeit very garbled, of Rossini and of La Malibran proved irresistible. In particular, the *Willow Song* in Act III had, at that period, a greater significance for the French than any other operatic aria.[3] 'The *Willow Song*,' said Musset, 'is poetry itself. It is the highest inspiration of one of the greatest

---

* Except, perhaps, *La donna del lago*, based on Walter Scott. This is not to say that Rossini's operas *are* Romantic, although Delacroix (*Journal*, p. 326) considered that they were.

† By Marchese Francesco Beria di Salsa after — a long way after — Shakespeare. The opera was first produced at the Teatro del Fondo, Naples, on 4th December, 1816, with Isabella Colbran, Rossini's first wife, as Desdemona.

‡ Stendhal's attitude to *Otello* was ambiguous: he sometimes praised it extravagantly, but also damned it as 'Germanic'. (See his *Life of Rossini*, trans. Richard Coe, 2nd ed., London, 1970, p. 221).

masters who ever existed.'[4] Musset alluded to it in no less than four different poems;[5] it is frequently mentioned by other French writers of the period.[6]

The *Willow Song* occurs in the last act of *Otello*. Desdemona, full of foreboding, is left alone in her room. Through an open window she hears a gondolier singing Dante's famous lines:

> *Nessun maggior dolore*
> *che ricordarsi del tempo felice*
> *Nella miseria.**

She takes up her harp, and begins to sing a melancholy song; at one moment, overwhelmed with grief, she breaks off, unable to continue; then she begins her song again. When it is over, she falls asleep. Otello enters with a lantern and a dagger. After a brief, final exchange, he kills her.

The harp accompaniment to the *Willow Song*, which Rossini makes very prominent, had great significance at that time; the fact that La Malibran could actually play it herself, rather than have someone play it for her in the orchestra, greatly heightened the excitement of her performances. It was the Romantic instrument *par excellence*,[7] and was extremely fashionable as a solo instrument until the mass-production of pianos made it redundant. It was often used to accompany *romances* in private houses; the *Willow Song*, called in French *La Romance du saule*, was, to all intents and purposes, a *romance* interpolated in an opera. The harp was usually played by young girls; it showed off the beauty of their arms and shoulders, and the instrument is itself beautiful.

The harp also had a mythical and poetic significance; it was the instrument of angels, of Ossian, and of beautiful women, 'the harp which makes the woman who plays it adored [. . .] the joy of David and of God',[8] 'an instrument which transports one from earth to heaven.'[9] It was, therefore, entirely fitting that the priestess of Romanticism should play it.

'Rossini's *Otello*,' said Musset, to whom it meant so much, 'is not Shakespeare's. In the English tragedy — a magisterial tragedy,

---

* Dante, *Inferno*, Canto V.

> There is no greater sorrow
> than to remember the time of happiness
> during misfortune.

if ever there was one — human passion is the entire mainspring.
Othello, courageous, frank, generous, is the play-thing of a traitor
who is his subordinate, who poisons him slowly. Desdemona's
angelic purity struggles by means of gentleness alone against all
Iago's efforts. Othello listens, suffers, hesitates, ill-treats his wife,
then bursts into tears; finally, he succumbs, says farewell both to
glory and to happiness, and strikes. In the opera a terrible, inexorable
fatality dominates. From the beginning to the end of the action the
victim is predestined [...] Shakespeare's Othello is the living
portrait of jealousy, a terrifying dissection of a man's heart; Rossini's
is only the sad story of a young girl who is slandered, and dies
innocent.'[10]

Shakespeare's play is about Othello; Rossini's opera is about
Desdemona, the predestined victim, which is how La Malibran came
to see herself — the victim of her father, of her husband and,
eventually, of the public.

4

Sudden fame changes people's lives, and sometimes alters their character. In the case of Maria Malibran fame came anyway at a time of transition in her life — from adolescence to maturity — and, although it did not change her character, it swiftly developed it. She had arrived in France alone from a distant, pioneer country; she had scarcely ever been on her own before, but always under the tutelage of her parents or her husband. She came to Paris immature, inexperienced, provincial, unsure of herself both as a woman and as an artist, lacking friends and even funds. Within six weeks she had become a celebrity, and thereafter everything changed: she was invited, courted, adulated; everyone, both in Society and in the intellectual world, wanted to know her. Always very quick to learn, she had rapidly assimilated Parisian ways and manners, and her provincialism was disappearing as fast as her self-confidence was increasing. Money was no longer a problem. She had grown used to being on her own, to taking her own decisions, to thinking for herself. Her basic character — frank, impetuous, generous, original — was never to alter; but, after her arrival in Paris, her attitudes did change, and they changed fast — most fundamentally in her attitude to her husband.

When she had left New York it had been agreed that he was to join her in France when he had paid off his creditors, when she had made enough money to help him. She had parted from him on very friendly terms. She told him in her first letter, written on board ship, that the parting from him had been 'cruel', that she missed him dreadfully. 'Remember me to your brother,' she wrote, 'make him really feel what it cost me to leave you, tell him how hard it is to be separated from people *one loves*, from you.'[1]

Eugène Malibran was, apparently, jealous; his wife frequently had to reassure him on that count. 'Once again, my dear little husband, get it well into your head that I only want *what is proper*.'[2] This appears to have been true. Maria was obsessed with keeping an unsullied reputation, with behaving in such a way that no one could

criticise her on that score. She refused to go anywhere in Paris
without a chaperone, and settled in her sister-in-law's house so as
to be beyond reproach. If, as a young married woman, she had lived
alone, she would have been considered too emancipated; at that
time, it was extremely important for actresses and singers to be
considered irreproachable if they were to be tolerated by Society,
since Society was only just beginning to be more flexible in its
attitude to them.

Soon after arriving in Paris, Maria wrote to tell her husband about
her successes and her plans. She told him that she was delighted
with his family; and she asked him to let her know precisely when
he intended to join her, because she was thinking of signing a
contract to sing in London, and would insist on a special clause in
it, stipulating that she would only go to London when her husband
had joined her.[3]

But, a fortnight later, the very day after her sensational début at
Galli's benefit, when she wrote to tell her husband about it, her
letter was quite different. It was much shorter than her preceding
letters; its tone was terse, and it concluded thus:

'Remember, Eugène, when you arrive in this Country, *to be well,
remember that I was ill as a result of your <u>imprudence</u>.*

'I haven't much faith in you and although you have a great deal
of experience, you make *mistakes*, and <u>*very great mistakes*</u>. My
health is much better *than when I was in New York*.'[4]

After two months' separation from her husband Maria was no
longer recalling his good qualities. As the date of his arrival in
France seemed to be approaching, she began to remember the unsatisfactory side of their relationship much more vividly; and certain
aspects had, it seems, been very unsatisfactory.

'You tell me to love you,' she wrote to him on 7th February. 'I
love you as I did at the beginning, not love, for I've never know it,
but friendship, that's all I can promise you if you deserve it, and if
your conduct towards me is the same as you say it will be in your
letters. In order to set your mind at rest I can tell you that all the
men I see, handsome or ugly, are like statues to me, like logs, no
more effect than that — I never feel the slightest desire, and even if
people talk about anything connected with what you appear to like
so much, I feel such disgust! . . . Ah! I don't even want to think
about it . . .'[5]

Although one letter,[6] written soon after her marriage, contains
some mild and friendly sexual banter, it seems clear that Maria's

sexual relations with her husband had not been happy, and that she was not anxious to resume them. Her references to health in the letter quoted above may imply that her husband had given her a venereal infection.

While Maria was still not sure of herself or her position, she was happy to live with her sister-in-law's family; but as soon as she had made her name and was able to earn well, her in-laws began at first to irk her, and very soon to infuriate her. Pages of complaints about them were dispatched across the Atlantic.

'As you know very well, my friend,' she told her husband, naming his two sisters and various members of their family, 'they are not agreeable people because of their company or good education.'[7] And indeed, Maria's catalogue of complaints against them does make them sound singularly unattractive. Narrow-minded, avaricious, limited in their interests and social connections, they were clearly at a loss how to deal with the super-star who had suddenly landed in their midst; but they were quite astute enough to exploit her financially, taking advantage of her inexperience and sudden affluence.

The atmosphere in the house grew tense. Maria, who needed someone to chaperone her, and who found her in-laws more and more hampering and socially inadequate in the grand circles in which she was already moving, began to look round for someone to replace them. Her choice fell on Madame Naldi, the widow of a singer who had worked with Garcia. Garcia had, in fact, been the involuntary cause of her husband's death; he had invited Naldi to see a novelty which he wanted to demonstrate — what appears to have been an early version of the pressure-cooker. The pressure-cooker exploded, and Naldi was killed instantly. The families remained friendly all the same; Madame Naldi had a daughter a little older than Maria, who had been a singer, too, but she had achieved the ambition of most singers, had made a grand marriage, and had become Comtesse de Sparre.

Madame Naldi was a rather severe lady and no longer young; but she came from the same theatrical background as Maria, who felt much more at home with her than she did with her husband's family. She spent more and more time with Madame Naldi, and finally left her in-laws and moved into Madame Naldi's house. Her husband's relations took this badly, and no doubt wrote to her husband implying the worst. Maria wrote a long letter of justification to her sister-in-law, in which the following significant passage occurs:

Don't bother to worry what my husband may think; for, if he were here, and were to lock me up in a tower, that wouldn't prevent me from being the very worst of wives (if I felt like being that) as I've often told you. So leave me in peace to earn money *for my husband*, and for myself, without disturbing his mind, or mine. Remember that *he has no one but me*. Remember too that *I shall do everything* so that he may lead an agreeable life, so long as he remembers to behave towards me as I believe I deserve (that is to say as a wife who *in and for everything* can only do him honour) and so, instead of blackening the motive for my actions, be disposed to believe that I shall do only what will be perfectly seemly.[8]

She wrote to her husband to explain why she had moved to Madame Naldi's house; and, in a postscript to the same letter, she referred to another question about which she felt very strongly:

I have received a letter from Maman, and she says that she will be able to embrace us when the sum which they are owed has been paid. If you cannot fulfil your obligations to them, I beg you not to give them false hopes. Don't ever let them think that *I will pay what I don't in any way owe*, do you understand me?[9]

Eugène Malibran owed Garcia money — perhaps, the $50,000 which he is said to have promised as his part of the marriage settlement.[10] Garcia badly needed money; on his way back from Mexico he had been attacked by bandits, and robbed of all he possessed. Maria was willing to work to pay off her husband's other debts, but not this debt to her father.

Her sense of duty towards her husband remained, but his financial affairs caused her increasing concern. She heard from his family that he was proposing to join her soon, but had not settled anything with his creditors. Maria was horrified; how could he contemplate leaving New York without first repaying his debts? '*I don't imagine that you will come back to me with a dishonoured name?*' she wrote cuttingly. 'As to the remarks you make about fearing to be a burden to me — I'll tell you, when I married and thought that I wouldn't have to do anything any more, I didn't think I'd be a burden to you, now that the situation is reversed I don't think of doing anything but my duty.'[11]

On receipt of these disconcerting letters from his wife, Malibran had apparently written to defend himself, and had said that he thought he had done his best to please her. Her reply was crushing:

> You know, when people get married each one has an aim in view. Mine was to be happy and peaceful, you know that I have a loving nature, and it was entirely up to you that it should continue to be so, but do you remember ... one can forgive, but never forget. That was my aim. I don't want to know what yours was.[12]

The deterioration in Maria's relations with her husband was not caused by love-affairs, but by the fact that she had had time to think over the two years she had spent with him, to compare her marriage to other marriages, and to realise that she had not been happy. In Paris she suddenly became aware that she could have whatever she wanted: fame, money, admiration, love. She was surrounded by men, most of them younger, more attractive, more distinguished and more amusing than her elderly husband. She did not yet particularly want any of them; but she now knew that she did not want Eugène Malibran. At last, for the first time in her life, she was happy: with Madame Naldi, with all her new friends. If her husband were to join her, her new-found happiness would be in peril. She resolved to do everything possible to defend it.

She chose to do so first by writing a letter to her American friend, Mrs Wainwright; she sent the letter to her husband, unsealed, in order that he might forward it. She knew that he would read it.

'Ma chère Madame Wainwright,' she began, but continued in her own brand of English:

> I hope that this letter will find you in good state of ealthe as well as your Dear family. I am as much loved hear as I was in New York by the generosity of the poeple. I can say with truth that I am not as foolish as I was and I have taken a good dose of quietness which I wanted so much. You know that I have been for two months in my husband's family, well, they are not a society suitable for me — they have not the least Idea of education, and besides that, I have been cheeted of money (in some manner) by them, they have left me at last alone in the house, and if I had not found a dear old friend of my family (wich we know from nine ears) at this time perhaps poeple would say many things seeing me alone in a house.
> I am happy and fat, and want nothing but my dear friends

— they tell me my husband grows fat, God bless him and kip him so for a long time, and make *him remain ther* — I don't want him hear.[13]

Malibran did read this letter, but did not send it on to Mrs Wainwright; he kept it with Maria's other letters to him, and wrote in what must have been reproachful terms to his wife. Here is her reply:

I couldn't understand what you were trying to say to me when you spoke of an unsealed letter which I sent to you and which you did not send on to the person to whom it was addressed. If the letter contains something which concerns you and which displeases you, I can assure you that what I say can only be true, especially as you know that I've never liked deceiving anyone and you must have been the first to realise this, on account of my too great frankness. What's more, I declare that whatever the contents [of the letter] may be, I repent of nothing I may have said, and if there is something which you don't understand, I'll explain it to you even if it is to your disadvantage.[14]

Someone more sensitive than Malibran would have realised by this time that he was not wanted; but he failed to take the hint. Later she would again try to get her message across to him. In the meantime, she went on writing to him about her successes, and the news of the day. But when she heard from New York that her husband now had money, but was still not paying his debts, her resentment of the past flared up again, and she told him brutally that she had never doubted that his bankruptcy had been both 'dishonourable and premeditated'. 'You have lost your right to my esteem,' she added. 'Well, I must try to forget the past. For I am *ashamed* to talk about your affairs with anyone . . .'[15]

Finally, on 11th October, she told him bluntly what was in her mind:

There's an idea which has occurred to me often and which I've been putting off telling you, but as you know I'm frank you will take it in good part and you'll do what I'm going to tell you. I think a theatrical life demands a great deal of calm and the life of a virgin which is what suits me perfectly *I am very happy as I am now.*

I'm telling you this so that you don't hurry to come here at all — for, my friend, listen: You are fine, you're putting on weight — I am too and I'm peacefully earning, so it's better if we only meet again when *my fortune is made*. Then, I shall have only one duty to fulfil. Several things [at once] are not good for me, so it would be better for your happiness and mine if that's how it will be. Don't show my letter to anyone; this idea must be only between ourselves. So, take my advice — stay there — and let me follow my career *honourably* as I have done until now, and when it's all over, we'll meet again in peace.[16]

It was the beginning of the end, but still Malibran did not seem to realise it; nor, strangely enough, did Maria fully realise it herself. Malibran did not abandon his plans for joining his wife, but he seemed to be in no hurry to do so. At that time Maria desired nothing more; so long as her husband remained in New York she was prepared to be his wife, to be faithful to him, to help him financially, and to write to him from time to time. She may even have really believed that one day, when she had 'made her fortune', they would 'meet again in peace'.

5

Elevated by public opinion to the status of High Priestess of the new religion of Art, La Malibran fulfilled her duties admirably. Her exceptional musical and dramatic talents set her apart from her colleagues in a class of her own, and marked her as different from, and superior to, ordinary people. She was not quite a Vestal Virgin; but her husband was far away and soon forgotten by everyone including, increasingly, La Malibran herself. Had she not told him that a theatrical career demanded 'the life of a virgin'? That was the life she led; she was dedicated only to her vocation. She had no lovers, and chose her male friends amongst elderly, and therefore relatively safe, men, such as Bouilly and Lafayette, or middle-aged men, such as Lamartine. Young men, such as Ludovic Vitet, who fell in love with her, were gently but firmly rebuffed unless, like Legouvé, they were able to transform their love into pure friendship. Such was her virtue that it was even rumoured that she was not a completely formed woman physically;[1] her boyish figure and habit of wearing men's clothes when riding or in the country[2] added to the androgenous effect which she sometimes produced, and to the belief that she was different from ordinary mortals.

As befits a priestess, a sense of mystery surrounded her; she was known to have 'secrets', and unhappy ones; and many people felt that she was consumed by a sacred fire. Her doctor had noticed this in New York, when she was still a girl: 'She may be said to be consumed by the fire of her own genius.'[3] Castil-Blaze saw her as 'devoured, consumed by the fire which burned in her breast';[4] Madame Merlin remembered 'the divine fire which fermented within her.'[5] Lamartine wrote of her 'beauty, which shone through her frail tissue like light through alabaster. One felt,' he said, 'that one was in the presence of a being whose fabric had been eaten away by the sacred fire of art.'[6]

Thus, virginal, dressed in the vestments of her calling, consumed by the sacred fire, she nightly performed a mystery in the theatre. She conjured up visions; she revealed people to themselves. To become, or be possessed by, an alien character, convincingly to express alien emotions, is a mysterious gift; and however much the audience knows that it is witnessing an illusion, it still feels that there is something unnerving, supernatural, about the actor's ability to transform himself so completely.

In the case of La Malibran, her dramatic genius, coupled with her versatility, made her performances particularly disturbing.* It was relatively uncommon at that time for an actress to play both comedy and tragedy, and some purists even considered it improper to do so. La Malibran would play Desdemona or Romeo one night, and Rosina or Fidalma (the old aunt in *Il matrimonio segreto*) the next. She would even play several parts in one evening; on one occasion she performed two acts of *Figaro* (as Susanna), the last act of *Otello* and the last act of *Giulietta e Romeo*.[7] To the audience, she *was* Susanna, she *was* Desdemona, she *was* Romeo; she was not only possessed by one alien character, but by two or three, sometimes of different sexes, within the space of a few hours. This was very potent magic indeed.

Despite her mythical status, La Malibran was, in fact, all too human, and her performances varied according to her mood, her health, the audience, and many other factors. Not all were perfect; not all reached that stage of 'ecstasy' when she appeared to be completely carried away by her part and the audience really was carried away by her performance. But her less-inspired performances only reinforced the illusion of some religious mystery. The gods do not always answer when they are invoked; only occasionally, and after much preparation, much supplication, when all the congregation is in a state of heightened tension, does the miracle, the revelation, occur. This is the '. . . *mens divinior*, which sometimes makes a great artist become a sibyl, invaded by her god.'[8] When

---

* Countess Merlin thought that La Malibran's performances were sometimes 'unseemly' — '*pas convenable*' (Merlin II, p. 207 and p. 232). Hogarth also considered that the realism with which La Malibran played peasant parts was rather shocking (see Part II, Ch. 6, Note 5). It is very difficult to tell exactly what was considered 'seemly' or 'unseemly' at that time; but a Society lady such as Countess Merlin was probably more prudish than most people. However, it may be that La Malibran's performances were sometimes sexually provocative — although no one could or did say so — and that this was one of the elements which helped to explain her success.

such a rare moment occurred to Sarah Bernhardt she, too, expressed it by saying: '*Le dieu est venu.*'[9]

Such transports, which only some actors and actresses experience, become, according to one's beliefs, either a quasi-religious experience, a form of ecstasy, or a form of hysteria; they reinforce the link between the theatre and religion. Both are, or can be, a true vocation; both have their mystics and their saints and martyrs. François Mauriac considered the actor's art to be: 'A magnificent and dangerous profession, which consists in losing oneself, and then finding oneself again.' And he believed that between those two states, some actors experience another, perhaps without realising it themselves, when they may approach a 'redoubtable threshold,' which only the mystics have crossed.[10]

Did such moments occur to La Malibran? Perhaps; but rarely — certainly much more rarely than her audiences imagined. Legouvé said that she was 'sometimes so violently gripped by the dramatic situation that she was as if possessed.'[11] Others saw her as a 'sibyl',[12] or spoke of her as being 'in ecstasy'.[13] It is difficult to decide whether she was one of those actresses who was herself possessed by the character she was playing, or whether, on the contrary, she it was who took over the part and possessed it. What is certain is that 'it was impossible not to identify with her, because she herself identified with her part [. . .] and communicated to others the feelings which she felt and expressed so well.'[14]

But there were many routine performances, when La Malibran was not 'possessed', but was simply professional. The violinist Ole Bull, standing in the wings one night, was moved to tears by the pathos of her performance as Desdemona. Suddenly she caught his eye and, turning her face from the stage, made a ridiculous grimace at him. Ole Bull was shattered. 'The discovery of her entire self-control while she moved others to the utmost was a disappointment which he could not afterwards disguise, but she laughingly excused it by saying: "It would not do for both of us to blubber." '[15]

On another occasion La Malibran 'proved' to a friend to what an extent she analysed her parts, and 'laughed at those who so much praised her so-called *improvisations* in singing and acting, which, in actual fact, had been prepared long beforehand, and partly noted in her *baule*.'[16]*

---

* The notebook in which singers noted fiorituri, ornaments, variations, facial expressions, details of their parts, was called '*une baule*'.

This would have pleased Diderot who, in a famous and still controversial pamphlet: *Paradoxe sur le comédien*,[17] asserted that too much sensibility or emotion makes for bad acting; a great actor, he believed, should be coldly detached — it is not his heart, but his head which should control his performance. The Romantics, however, believed exactly the opposite: heart, sensibility, emotion, feeling, were to them what produced great art, and they deplored cold detachment. Only a few close friends knew that La Malibran could often play a part and remain completely detached, and she did not enlighten the public on that score. They would not have believed it, anyway; La Malibran was the personification of Romanticism, and therefore, *ipso facto*, spontaneous, deeply emotional, abandoned in all she did.

Critics and admirers were so convinced of her genuine emotion that it is difficult now to separate truth from fiction in accounts of her performances, in which the words 'spontaneity', 'genius', 'inspiration', 'improvisation' abound, sometimes all in the same sentence: 'Everything in her genius was spontaneity, inspiration, effervescence,' said Legouvé.[18] The American, Nathaniel Willis, saw her as 'a soul rapt and possessed beyond control with the melody';[19] but it seems unlikely that she could often have been 'possessed beyond control' and, at the same time, act and, above all, sing as she did. The whole art of singing is a matter of control, and genuine, as opposed to feigned, emotions make it almost impossible for singers to control their voices.

However, great artists are sometimes possessed by their parts, and yet still able to give musically coherent performances. Tito Gobbi has described how, when playing *Wozzeck*, he felt himself being 'slowly but surely pervaded by the character until I lived inside his tragic, miserable life and came to identify with Wozzeck both musically and dramatically.' Gobbi explains this situation with great clarity: 'As an artist who loves his work and resolves his task of interpretation with great conscientiousness, I sometimes find myself carried away into *being* my characters. Normally I can separate myself from them and represent them with the detachment and objectivity which long theatrical experience permits. With Wozzeck that has not been, and never would be, possible. His torments

penetrate one's flesh like witchcraft . . .' Gobbi's '*dédoublement*'*
was so complete that when he wrote a letter to his wife at the end
of a performance of *Wozzeck* he signed it 'W'.[20]

Thus, the Romantic critics were probably not entirely wrong. La
Malibran may well sometimes have experienced '*le dédoublement*';
she was often spontaneous, and did improvise a good deal. 'Catch
me where you can in the last scene,' she would say to her partner
in *Otello*, 'for at that point I can't answer for my movements.'[21]
Only Bordogni, middle-aged and lazy, refused to alter his habits
when acting with her. 'Look here, Maria my girl,' he told her, 'just
don't you imagine that I'm full of fire and energy like you, and that
I want to tire myself out and fling myself about like you do. If you
want me to kill you, you come over here.'[22]

On at least one occasion La Malibran's improvisation had unfortunate results. When playing the scene in *Otello* when Desdemona
questions the knights about the outcome of the fight between Otello
and Rodrigo, she seized a member of the chorus and dragged him
to the front of the stage in order to address him. The poor man had
no idea what was going on, and was quite unable to rise to the
occasion; the more Desdemona questioned him, the more vacantly
he gaped at her. The whole scene nearly misfired, and there were
stifled titters in the audience.[23]

Long after La Malibran's death her brother Manuel Patricio and
Eugène Delacroix had a discussion about Diderot's *Paradoxe sur le
comédien*. Delacroix supported Diderot's thesis that the actor must
be completely self-controlled, although he thought that Diderot, in
saying that the actor must be devoid of sensibility or feeling, did
not make sufficient allowance for the part imagination plays in an
actor's performance. Manuel Garcia defended the necessity for sensibility and true passion. The conversation turned on La Malibran.

Manuel Garcia maintained that his sister had never known how
she would play a part, performing the same rôle differently every
time. Delacroix, so Romantic in his own art, disliked the excesses
of Romanticism in others; he had not admired La Malibran's style

---

* *Le dédoublement* — literally: 'splitting in two', or 'dual personality' —
is the French term used to describe the state which actors and actresses
sometimes experience when they become one with, or are taken over by,
their part. There is no satisfactory English word for it. (For some interesting
examples, see André Villiers, *La Psychologie du comédien*, p. 192 *et seq.*)

of acting, which he considered 'exaggerated and misplaced', and, in his opinion, this was one of the reasons why she had never achieved true greatness or nobility.[24]

Today, we would probably agree with Delacroix. By modern standards, it does seem that La Malibran overacted to an unacceptable degree. 'She walked precipitately, she ran, she laughed, she cried, she smote her forehead, undid her hair . . .' But, Musset added, 'at least she was genuine in her disorder. Those tears, those laughs, that loosened hair belonged to her, and it was not in order to imitate some actress or other that she threw herself on the ground in *Otello*.'[25] In *Maria Stuarda* she would tear her handkerchief and gloves to shreds; as Romeo she would do a sensational fall; in general she would fling herself about the stage with too much movement and too little discipline. Taxed with this, she replied: 'You're right, it isn't beautiful, but once I'm in my part I no longer think about what effect I make. At that moment I am really afraid, and I behave as I would if I were pursued by a murderer.'[26]

La Malibran's acting was frenetic; but so was the epoch she represented, and she gave her audiences what they wanted. It is noteworthy that, of her contemporaries, only Delacroix failed to be moved by her — and she could hardly have made much impression on a man who, in the theatre, admired above all the Classical restraint of Racine and Corneille. Even Mendelssohn, who did not share the Romantic frenzy and sometimes found La Malibran's performances 'disagreeable', succumbed in the end.[27] It is also noteworthy that other singers and actors — Talma,[28] Kean, Macready, Nourrit, Duprez, Marie Dorval — admired her acting; and composers, such as Rossini, Bellini, Pacini, Meyerbeer[29] and Balfe — saw her as their ideal interpreter.

On stage, La Malibran portrayed the spirit of her times. As Gautier, the chronicler of Romanticism, foresaw, it is impossible for later generations who did not live through that era fully to understand the Romantic fever:

> Present generations [Gautier was writing in the 1850s] must find it difficult to imagine the effervescence in people's minds at that time; a movement similar to the Renaissance was taking place. The sap of new life was germinating, everything was budding, everything was bursting out at the same time. The flowers gave out heady scents, the air made one intoxicated, people were mad with lyricism and art.'[30]

6

In London, where La Malibran was engaged to sing in the summer of 1829, scents were not quite as heady and people's minds not quite as effervescent. The English Romantic movement, which had fired the whole of Europe, was subsiding. Lord Byron, Keats and Shelley were dead; Sir Walter Scott was old; the French Revolution had been a sobering example of what too much effervescence in people's minds can do; the Napoleonic wars had left Britain victorious, but exhausted. When La Malibran had left Paris in the spring, the atmosphere there had been febrile; political, social and artistic ferment was steadily mounting, and everyone felt that some kind of violent upheaval was imminent. But in London, the aristocracy and the wealthy middle-class were calmly preparing for the annual and unchanging ritual of the social season, which revolved around the court of the ageing George IV. Lavish parties, balls and receptions were held almost every evening, and music played a great part in them. Concerts, usually in the morning, and the opera in the evening, were the principal entertainments, together with Ascot, the Derby and other sporting events.

La Malibran had left London in 1825 as a seventeen-year-old *débutante* of great promise; she returned to England in 1829 as a celebrity and a much-travelled married woman of twenty-one. Her reputation as a singer had preceded her across the Channel; but the semi-divine status which she had already been accorded in France meant little to the English. La Malibran was not the personification of English Romanticism, but merely a very talented, very accomplished prima donna, and it was as such that the English prepared to judge her.

From her first appearance — in *Otello* on 21st April, 1829 — it was clear to English critics that she had made enormous progress in the years she had been away, that she had amazing musical and dramatic powers, and had become at least the equal of the greatest artists of the day. She was compared favourably to Pasta,[1] who had recently appeared in London; and although, during the 1829 season, she was competing against Sontag, who was very popular in England, by the end of the season even Sontag's supporters had to admit that La Malibran was superior.[2]

Since, in England, La Malibran was an ordinary mortal, she was not above criticism. The *Times* critic, reporting her first performance in *Otello*, thought that she overacted disgracefully, 'abandoning herself to all the excesses of ungovernable grief.'[3] Mendelssohn, who was present at that performance, agreed.[4] This was the style of Kean; unlike the French, the English were used to it and, in London, it was already a little old-fashioned. Others criticised the realism with which La Malibran played peasant parts: Zerlina and Ninetta (in *La gazza ladra*), making them 'coarse country girls, with awkward demeanour and hoydenish manners.'[5] But the general consensus of opinion was that she was an outstanding vocal and dramatic artist; and from that first season until her death La Malibran was in constant demand in England.

English criticism of her performances, more objective and analytical than French accounts, and expressed in more sober language, nevertheless confirms that she was probably the greatest dramatic singer of her epoch, and shows that Delacroix was unfair when he spoke of the 'exaggerated panegyrics'[6] of her French contemporaries. English critics wrote of '. . . the versatility, nay, universality of her histrionic genius';[7] of her 'independence and versatility, which are almost the same as the creative faculty';[8] of her 'devotional pathos' (in Mozart's *Agnus Dei*) which, 'in the opinion of eminent judges', was 'never surpassed'.[9] 'Our admiration is excited not merely by the delivery of so much beautiful music,' wrote another English critic, 'but by the mind which imparts to it an additional charm . . .'[10] One can only conclude from such comments by sober English critics that the French, for all their Romantic fervour, did not exaggerate La Malibran's greatness.

Although La Malibran found English audiences cold compared to the French,[11] she realised that she was much appreciated and was happy to return every year, especially as the fees she earned in England were high. Her knowledge of English was an enormous asset; it helped her to make friends, and she was able to sing in English, which few other first-class international stars of that period could do. As a result, she reached a far wider public in England than she did in France, since she sang frequently in concerts and oratorio at English provincial festivals; she became a familiar figure in Norwich, Gloucester, Chester and other provincial cities, whereas in France she could only be heard in Paris.

La Malibran was not received by English Society, although she frequently sang in aristocratic houses, for no singer was received by high Society at that time. But she had many friends in England, and not only amongst musicians and actors. Her charm, her vivacity and lack of pretention made her popular, and the fact that she was a superb horsewoman was an added advantage. Lord William Lennox lent her mounts, and Lord Burghersh and Sir George Warrender escorted her to the Derby. Disraeli met her at Miss Mitford's; he thought her 'a very interesting person', and there and then decided to write an opera for her, although nothing seems to have come of it.[12] But Disraeli was the exception; La Malibran did not inspire writers and poets in England as she did in France; and although she spent a great deal of time in this country, made her début in London and died in Manchester, there is little trace of her in English literature.*

* She is mentioned fleetingly in the *Ingoldsby Legends: The Execution: A Sporting Anecdote.*

7

So far La Malibran had represented only one of the twin aims of Romanticism as defined by Gautier: the deification of Art. But what about the other aim: 'to extol love with such ardour that it burns the paper, to set it up as the sole aim and sole means of happiness'?[1] A bourgeois marriage to a businessman twice her age and the other side of the Atlantic hardly fitted that bill, and La Malibran seems to have realised that her admirers expected something more Romantic of her.

One day, when her friends were teasing her about the passion she aroused in one of her admirers, she said: 'Yes, I think he does love me, but what's to be done? I don't love him. I don't want to appear as a heroine of virtue. I know that, young as I am, independent, married to a man who could be my grandfather and who is two thousand leagues away, surrounded as I am by dangers, I shall end by falling in love one day; but then I won't play the coquette, I shall quite simply tell the man who appeals to me, and then it will be for life.'[2]

She rejected the cold, pedantic and erudite Ludovic Vitet, who wrote articles about her in *Le Globe*. He was a historian by training, and later went on to make a brilliant career as Inspector of Historical Monuments, then Deputy, and he had reached the haven of the French Academy by the time he was forty-three. Intelligent and, according to Stendhal, unutterably boring,[3] Vitet was normally 'an icicle';[4] it was his misfortune, at the age of twenty-six, to fall hopelessly in love with Maria Malibran.

Vitet was introduced to her soon after her arrival in Paris. He reviewed her first appearance at Galli's benefit in guardedly enthusiastic tones, and devoted a good deal of his article to demolishing Sontag, whom he could not abide. His next articles about La Malibran were laudatory, but full of paternal advice; with all the experience of his twenty-six years, he told her in print and, no doubt, in conversation, exactly how she should play each part, interpret each aria. La Malibran was probably thinking of Vitet when she told her husband that she had made the critics acclaim her by *pretending* to take their advice.[5]

By the time Vitet came to write his review of La Malibran as Desdemona (*Le Globe*, 23rd April, 1828) he was completely conquered; from then on this scrupulously objective historian could write nothing but panegyrics about the object of his love. A month later he was comparing La Malibran to Mozart. Some of his friends, notably Mérimée, thought that his enthusiasm went too far.[6]

There is, so far, no evidence to suggest that La Malibran felt anything more for Vitet than friendship and, above all, gratitude for his championship of her in the press. Probably she led him on, gave him to expect more than she was actually willing to give. The intensity of Vitet's grief when she drew back from what might have become a serious love affair makes it clear that Vitet, at least, was deeply committed.[7]

La Malibran must have rejected many other suitors besides Vitet; most of the men who surrounded her were at least half in love with her.[8] But probably both her father and her husband had given her a distaste for sex, and she did not fall in love easily. However, no true Romantic could reject love for ever, and the public expected a Romantic muse to have a Romantic passion. La Malibran's choice finally fell on the Belgian violinist Charles de Bériot.

They first became close friends during the 1829 London season. They had met before, in Paris; but Bériot had then been courting Henriette Sontag, and had not paid much attention to her Spanish rival. By 1829, however, it was clear that Bériot was not going to win Sontag; she was already living with Count Rossi, had had a child by him, and he intended to marry her. Sontag's friends believed that Bériot was at least as interested in her income, which was considerable, as he was in her beauty and personality; but when she rejected him he gave himself Byronic airs and let it be known that he was broken-hearted. This, of course, made him interesting and, since he was also good-looking, aroused much feminine sympathy. La Malibran was not immune to such feelings, and on one occasion in Paris Bériot's playing had reduced her to tears.

In London Bériot and La Malibran both took part in a concert at the Argyll Rooms, at which Mendelssohn also played. At that concert she sang 'some beautiful and highly difficult' variations which Bériot had composed.[9] Three days later she appeared with Bériot again, when he gave a concert of his own. Fétis tells how Bériot approached him and asked him to use his influence to persuade La Malibran to take part in the concert. At first she was not very eager to do so; Bériot's well-known admiration for her rival, Henriette Sontag, both as a singer and a woman, did not predispose her to help him. 'Why doesn't he ask the singer who charms him so?' La Malibran replied to Fétis. 'Their two talents are very pure, really made for each other. My talent is too untamed.'[10] It was a prophetic remark; Bériot was always to find La Malibran 'too untamed'.

Finally, she reluctantly agreed to take part in the concert; and from that moment her fate was decided. At that concert, says Fétis, a bond of affection was established between La Malibran and Charles de Bériot, which soon developed into love.* Sontag's friends alleged that Bériot had suddenly realised that La Malibran's earning capacity was quite as great as Sontag's.

Charles Auguste de Bériot was born on 20th February, 1802, in Louvain. He was very remotely of Spanish origin; an ancestor, Don Christavas di Barrio y Barrio, a native of Castille, had served in the Spanish armies in the Low Countries, and had died when Governor

---

* Countess Merlin's account, hallowed by repetition, of how La Malibran suddenly declared her love to Bériot in public at the Château de Chimay in Belgium, is probably pure romantic fiction. The countess was not there; and Fétis implies that the relationship had begun earlier. In any case, for a married woman who valued her reputation for respectability, as La Malibran did, it would have been extremely indiscreet to declare her love for another man in public. However, in Countess Merlin's account, La Malibran, rather than Bériot, took the initiative; from what we know of their characters, this is very likely correct. This is Countess Merlin's version:

> One evening [. . .] Bériot had just finished playing one of his own concertos. As everyone applauded, Maria went up to him; pale, her eyes moist, she took his hands in her own trembling hands and, with an indefinable expression, said to him: 'I'm very happy at your success.' 'Thank you, thank you,' Bériot said to her, while listening to several people all congratulating him at the same time, 'and I am very flattered by your support.' 'Oh no, it's not that, my God!!! Don't you see that I love you?'
>
> Moved, charmed by a feeling so sincere and so naïvely expressed, Bériot did not know if he were dreaming, or if Maria, carried away by the enthusiasm of the moment, had not uttered rash words.
>
> From that moment, an intimate bond of feeling was established between the two artists.
>
> Merlin, I, 99–100.

of Lierre, in 1678. This Spaniard's descendants prospered, the Spanish name Barrio eventually became Frenchified as Bériot; the Bériots married well, and had some pretensions to nobility. But Charles de Bériot's parents had lost all their wealth, owing to 'the revolution [presumably the French Revolution] and unfortunate speculations.'[11] When Charles was ten and his sister Constance thirteen, both their parents died. Constance was then brought up by her mother's family, and Charles was handed over to his god-father, François Tiby, an excellent musician and a kind and enlightened man, who was Professor at the College of Louvain.

François Tiby realised that Charles was exceptionally gifted as a violinist, and did everything to educate him and to further his career; he was also advised by his friend, André Robberechts. In 1821 Bériot went to Paris, where he was praised by Kreutzer, had some lessons from Bailliot, and perhaps also from Viotti, the two most distinguished violinists of the French school. By 1823 he was already established as a soloist. He divided his time between Belgium and Paris, and after his first visit to England in 1826 was frequently in London. In 1826 he was appointed '*premier violon de la Chambre de sa Majesté le Roi de France*', and the following year he received a similar appointment from William I, King of the Netherlands.

Bériot was an excellent violinist. His technique and intonation were impeccable and, after Paganini, he was the first to make use of a wide range of technically brilliant effects: harmonics, arpeggios, pizzicato, and so on. His playing was elegant and refined; but his style was too sweet for some people, and he was often criticised for playing inferior music — showy variations and drawing-room pieces, often of his own composition. He was the founder of the distinguished Belgian school of violin-playing; Henri Vieuxtemps was his most famous pupil.

Bériot's character appears to have been a little colourless. As a violinist he was very well known and went everywhere with La Malibran, yet few of his contemporaries bothered to record anything about him, and when they did it was not always flattering. Karoline Bauer called him 'cold and calculating',[12] Moscheles also thought him 'cold',[13] and Liszt described him as 'a rather contemptible fellow'.[14] His family had a fairly prominent social position in Belgium, with strong middle-class prejudices, and he considered himself both morally and socially superior to the ordinary run of musicians. As a young man he was deeply religious, an ardent Roman Catholic; in his early youth he was influenced by Lamennais, who had not yet become a controversial figure in the eyes of the Church, but this influence did not last. Controversy did not appeal to Bériot, and he was something of a prig. At the age of nineteen he wrote to a friend:

> How true it is that if men were only to read good books they would never stray from virtue, but the depraved minds of our time never make reflections about that, and they are afraid of reading religious or moral books, because they find themselves condemned in them.[15]

Whatever Bériot's moral characteristics may have been, there was little disagreement about his physical appearance; he was, like his playing, elegant, and very good-looking.

It was natural that La Malibran and Bériot should become friends: they often appeared at concerts together, knew the same people, were both young and strangers to London. At precisely what date their relationship became more intimate, it is impossible to say; in all probability it was in the summer of 1829, at the end of the London season.

In August, La Malibran visited Belgium, at Bériot's invitation. The proprieties were observed, since she was chaperoned by his sister. During the previous months, however, her correspondence with her husband, already greatly diminished before she left France, had become even more spasmodic; only three letters to him from this period have been preserved. In them she told him that she had no time to write — 'In half an hour I have to dress in order to go to four concerts' — and she replied evasively to her husband's questions about her financial affairs.[16] She had become 'a golden prima donna',[17] and from then on was never to be sure if she was valued as a person, or for her money.

She had other problems, too. In 1829 her parents and small sister had returned to Paris from Mexico. When she first heard of their plans, she wrote to tell her husband that she was 'very frightened' that she might have to live with them again. She offered Garcia money, but he took offence and said that the 4,000 francs a year which she had offered him was a 'wretched pittance'.[18]

La Malibran did not see her parents when they first arrived, for she was still in London. In the autumn of 1829, however, when she was probably already Bériot's mistress, she returned to Paris and met her parents again after three years. The situation was delicate; Madame Naldi had lost no time in telling the Garcias about Bériot.

Garcia had always hated Eugène Malibran, but that did not make him approve of Bériot. His jealousy of his daughter's admirers — perhaps sexual jealousy — had not abated, and he did not approve an extra-marital love affair. A bigamist himself, like most men of his time Garcia believed in one law of morality for men and another for women, particularly for his own daughter.

An uneasy truce between father and daughter was established. Garcia managed to secure an engagement at the Théâtre Italien where he appeared in some of his old parts with Sontag, and also with La Malibran.* His first appearance with her, in *Don Giovanni*,[19] was a great theatrical event and was acclaimed by the critics. But La Malibran was unable to conceal what a great strain it was for her, as Zerlina, to be seduced on stage by her father, and the press noticed this. The *Journal des débats* commented: '. . . in the theatre, and above all if it is a question of singing, one portrays agitation rather badly if one is oneself agitated.' *Le Globe* (probably Vitet) was more perspicacious: 'Madame Malibran suffers too much for her own good.'[20]

But most journalists, unaware of the sordid details of La Malibran's childhood, greeted the appearance of father and daughter on the stage as a happy event. La Malibran knew what was expected of her, and played up to the audience. For example, during a performance of *Don Giovanni*, when, as Zerlina, she had finished her part, she left the stage to witness the final scene from a box. As her father, the Don, was being dragged down to hell by devils, she called out to them to be careful, and 'to treat her father with as much gentleness and consideration as the situation allowed.'[21]

This pleased the audience but did not represent a real change of heart on either side. In public, with her vast success, La Malibran could afford to be magnanimous to 'the old lion', whose voice and dramatic powers had pitiably declined, and who could no longer hold his audience. In private, it was different; she had neither forgotten nor forgiven her unhappy youth, and fiercely resented any interference by her parents in her new-found happiness.

Garcia had come back from Mexico old and embittered. He soldiered on at the Théâtre Italien for a few more performances with ever-diminishing success, and finally retired from the stage for ever in January, 1830.

* See also p. 124.

8

At first La Malibran's love-affair with Charles de Bériot did not displease the public; they made a handsome couple and, to begin with, they were extremely discreet. Although they were probably living together from the summer of 1829, they did not at first set up house together, and if the general public noticed their relationship at all, it was probably seen as a Romantic friendship.

There can be no doubt that La Malibran was in love with Bériot, and he was probably the only man whom she ever loved. Bériot's attitude to her is less clear. She entered into the love-affair in true Romantic fashion, without counting the cost, and saw love as 'the sole means of happiness'. (See p. 79.) However, the theories of Romanticism did not always translate well into practice, and the first few months of their liaison were not happy.

Bériot was insensitive to La Malibran's position — as a married woman and an actress — and suggested that they should make a concert tour together. La Malibran was deeply hurt by this proposal which, if accepted, would compromise her, but not him, and would classify her as just another actress of easy virtue. There were probably other disagreements as well.[1]

That winter, and in the spring of 1830, the lovers were frequently separated. Bériot made his concert tours alone, and in the spring La Malibran went to London, where she was to sing during the summer season. Their relationship was at a low ebb; Constance de Bériot, Charles's sister, whom La Malibran had already met in Belgium, became the intermediary between them.

Three years older than her brother, Constance was probably the most important woman in his life. Brother and sister had been left orphans so young that Constance had, to a great extent, taken over the role of mother, and the two had a very close relationship.*

* After Constance's death her son-in-law, Lieut-General H. E. Wauwermans (see p. 109), found 'an important correspondence' between her and her brother which, Wauwermans considered, was too intimate to be published. (Wauwermans, p. 13). Its whereabouts is not known.

Constance was obviously the stronger character, and in moments of crisis it was she who took the lead. When La Malibran first met her, Constance was unmarried; the following year she was married to her cousin, Joseph de Francquen de Boquet, a cavalry officer.

It was fortunate for La Malibran that she made friends quickly with Constance, who was ten years her senior and came from a completely different social background. Had she not done so, her relationship with Charles would have been far more difficult than it was. She probably realised this; at any rate, when her love-affair with Charles appeared to be virtually at an end, she appealed to Constance for help.

'Does Charles love me?' she asked. 'As for me, I love him for life. What's to be done?'[2]

What indeed? La Malibran was probably already pregnant by Bériot, and the question of a divorce from Eugène Malibran became paramount in her mind:

> In my despair I had already written to Viardot, who did all he could to console me. I was so unhappy that I told Lady Flint, my good friend, what my misfortune was. She spoke about it to one of her friends, an excellent man, who told me that, in a similar case, he had himself been helped out of a difficulty by consulting one of his friends, a very elderly Lord (he is seventy) who, so it appears, knows the law inside out. This morning at 12, Sir George Warrender, who is the *old friend* of the older man, is coming to talk to me about it. Since I risk nothing, I shall tell him as much as is necessary (not more) so he can give me a useful opinion which will slightly assuage my heavy heart.[3]

On 1st May Constance had written to La Malibran enclosing a letter from her brother. The contents of his letter are not known; but when La Malibran read it she 'cried bitterly, like a child, and sent a bitter reply to it.'[4]

At about the same time she received news — false, as it turned out — that her brother had been killed in Algiers. These two blows had a grave effect on her health.

On 21st May she won her usual acclaim in a performance of *Semiramide*; but the audience which applauded her had no knowledge of the events, far more dramatic than Rossini's opera, which had preceded her appearance.

The previous day, La Malibran had suffered one of her 'fainting fits'; but this 'fit', the only one to be recorded by a doctor,[5]* was probably more serious than usual. She froze into a kind of trance, neither hearing nor seeing anything for several hours and, while in this state, fell down a stone staircase, cutting herself badly. She remained in a trance for most of the night. Next day, she insisted on going to the theatre; she 'was lifted into her carriage, not being able to stand — was taken out in the same manner — was dressed, while sitting, for her part in the *Semiramide*; and when the moment came that she was to appear, to the unutterable astonishment of her friends she rushed on the stage, and drew down thunders of applause by her unrivalled acting and singing.'[5] As soon as the performance was over, she relapsed into a trance again.

There now began those frequent 'indispositions' which were to be such a feature of La Malibran's career, and which were eventually to alienate her from the public and from many theatre directors. They were usually caused by emotional stress, or pregnancy, or both. She was soon taken ill again, in Bath, where she had gone on a lightning trip to give some concerts; and by 2nd June she had forfeited fees to the tune of 300 guineas.

At this point Bériot arrived in England, and Constance decided to intervene in the love-affair on La Malibran's behalf. A reconciliation between the lovers took place, and Constance set about trying to solve their problems.

These appeared to be insoluble. La Malibran wanted to be, not Bériot's mistress, but his wife; she was, however, already married to Eugène Malibran. If she lived with Bériot openly and bore his children, she would lose her good name and her precarious footing in Society, and Eugène Malibran would be entitled to some form of redress — at least of a financial nature. Bériot's family, too, considered marriage the lesser of two evils. The family was middle-class and Catholic; a marriage to an actress was, therefore, highly undesirable, but it was perhaps better than a liaison which would

---

* Dr Belinaye, who attended La Malibran on this and other occasions, (until, in April, 1833, he was succeeded by her homœopathic physician, Dr Belluomini), considered that '... the pursuit of her vocation, accompanied by great private sorrows, over-excited her nervous system' and made her 'subject to fits of hysteria, akin to epilepsy, and to attacks of catalepsy, such as I have never seen elsewhere, and hope never to see again.'

(*Morning Post*, 24th October, 1836).

inevitably be much publicised, and illegitimate children which the family might not be able legally to control. The family also took La Malibran's earning capacity into consideration.

Since Constance de Bériot now acted with some precipitancy and La Malibran was 'in despair', she probably was pregnant. Constance would hardly have behaved as she did had this not been so; but in her old age, when she told the story to her son-in-law,* she said nothing about a pregnancy — it was no longer necessary to do so — maintaining that she had merely wanted to smooth the course of true love.[6]

In order to do so she 'summoned a council', composed of 'the elders' of the family, in order to find a solution acceptable both to Bériot and his family, and to La Malibran. It was agreed that a marriage was desirable; apart from any other considerations, 'since Charles and Maria practised the same art, they complemented each other, and together could acquire a fortune and lasting glory.'[7] This rather mercenary consideration was undoubtedly uppermost in everyone's mind, except La Malibran's; Charles de Bériot had no money, and even as a successful solo violinist earned only a small fraction of the fees she commanded.

The family council — which included Bériot's uncle Blargnies, a

---

* Lieutenant–Général Henri Emmanuel Wauwermans (1825–1902) married Bériot's niece, Angélique-Antoinette de Francquen, in 1860. After a very distinguished career in the army, he retired, and published a large number of scholarly papers, mainly on archaeology, military history, and geography. At the time of his marriage, Constance de Francquen was still alive; she often used to talk to him about La Malibran. Like so many people (Pougin, for example) he succumbed to La Malibran's posthumous charm. When his mother-in-law died, he inherited the family papers; he left some papers concerning La Malibran, together with various objects which had belonged to her, to the Brussels Conservatoire. Wauwermans wrote a biography of La Malibran, not for publication, but for the family; the typescript is dated 1902, the year of his death. In it he used some of the letters and documents which are now in the Brussels Conservatoire, and some other letters which are not there. Although much of Wauwermans' biography is based on well-known sources, such as Countess Merlin, and some of it is incorrect, it contains some material which is available nowhere else; and although both Constance de Francquen and her son-in-law were at pains to show La Malibran, Bériot and his family in the best possible light, and were therefore biased, Wauwermans' typescript remains an important source.

distinguished lawyer, who later helped to draft the Belgian consti-
tution — decided, firstly, that the civil marriage between Maria
Garcia and Eugène Malibran in New York was invalid as the French
consul had not been competent to marry the couple and that, therefore, Maria's marriage should be terminated by an annulment rather
than by divorce.[8] Eventually, in 1836, this is what happened, but
only after six years of extremely complicated legal wrangles. In 1830
no one could have foreseen that result; Constance, talking to her
son-in-law years later, was being wise after the event.

The family council next decided that 'there had been no religious
ceremony, as it had not been possible to find a Catholic priest' as
Catholic priests were 'very rare in the United States at that time.'[9]
This, of course, was quite untrue; Maria had either concealed her
church marriage from Bériot's family, or lied to them about it. It
was not a lie which could be easily maintained for long: her husband,
her family, the Catholic clergy, and most citizens of New York knew
about it. But at that time New York was very far away, and she
may have hoped that no one from there would turn up in Europe
and disclose the fact that she had had a church marriage. Her
parents, however, were already in Europe.

The family council assumed — wrongly — that Maria was, 'from
the canonical point of view, just as free as Charles to contract a new
marriage;'[10] but it recognised that this would not be possible in
France or Belgium where, by law, priests could not marry couples
without a civil marriage certificate.

At this juncture:

> one of the members of the council, inspired by the idea of
> the secret marriage between Count Rossi and La Sontag, and
> probably also by the episode in the novel, *I promessi sposi* by
> Manzoni, which was published in 1827 and which at that time
> everyone was reading (the marriage of Lorenzo and Lucia),
> suggested that the difficulties could be overcome by an
> immediate *church* marriage, invoking an ancient canonical law
> which considered the union of two strolling players valid if they
> went to the priest of the parish without confirmation or prior
> notice, and declared before witnesses that they would take each
> other as husband and wife.[11]

This idea was based on a slight distortion of the facts.* There

* See pp. 125–7.

was no ancient canonical law which enabled a priest to *marry* strolling players, but priests could often be found who would give the union of two actors a blessing, and in some liberal dioceses they might even perform a marriage ceremony, providing neither party was already married. As La Malibran was, no priest could marry her.

That the idea of a secret marriage was, in part, inspired by Manzoni's novel is yet one more example of the Romantic desire to turn literature into life, and *vice versa*.

The family council decided that, if such a 'marriage' were to take place, absolute secrecy would be necessary, so as not to prejudice divorce proceedings against Eugène Malibran, and also 'to protect the priest who would perform the ceremony.'[12]

They also decided that if divorce proceedings against Malibran were eventually unsuccessful, the couple might, 'by changing their nationality, for example by becoming Roman citizens,' regularise their civil status.[13]

Constance told her son-in-law that this solution — a secret marriage by a priest who would marry them as strolling players — was immediately accepted by Bériot, but met with 'serious objections'[14] from La Malibran. This is hardly surprising, since she knew that in the eyes of the law and the Church she was already married. But the 'serious objections' attributed to her by family legend were that she did not wish the marriage to be kept secret. It does seem that La Malibran, in a panic about her pregnancy, wanted the world to believe that she was Bériot's wife and about to be the mother of a legitimate child. Her grasp of reality had anyway always been tenuous; she was inclined to believe fiction true and reality false. Her church marriage to Malibran was inconvenient, therefore she seems to have come to believe that it had never taken place, just as she came to believe that she had been forced to marry Malibran against her will. She insisted to Bériot's family that a *secret* marriage 'would take away from her all semblance of legality';[15] she appears not to have realised that an open marriage would be even more damaging.

According to Constance, the summer was spent arguing about this, and Maria consulted some of her friends, including Lamartine. She received 'very varied' replies.[16] Her friends, some of whom probably knew the truth about her church marriage to Eugène Malibran, must have been at a loss as to how to advise her.

In any case, again according to Constance, the idea of a secret marriage won the day. During the summer of 1830, probably in Paris, the couple appeared with two witnesses before a priest who, at first, 'could not understand anything'. The situation was explained to him and absolute secrecy was promised. He was not asked for any written declaration. Some sort of ceremony — a benediction? — was performed.[17] From then on Maria, Charles and his family considered them to be married, and Charles referred to her as his 'wife'. It is, perhaps, ironical that La Malibran's greatest success that season was in Cimarosa's *Il matrimonio segreto*.

What are we to make of this fantastic story, which even a librettist might find a bit far-fetched? It is almost impossible to believe that La Malibran, whose salient characteristic was frankness, could have concealed her church marriage from Bériot; but she did, later, conceal important information from him, through fear,* and may have been able to conceal her church marriage from him for a time. The story of a secret marriage was probably not invented by the family after her death; both Maria and Charles repeated it to several of their friends.[18] When Maria lay dying in Manchester in 1836, she told the landlady of her hotel 'that she had known De Bériot nine years, and had been seven years of that time married to him, but that she had not been able to make their marriage known till within the last two years.'[19] Either a secret (and bigamous) marriage did take place, or Charles and Maria came to believe that they were married.

In August that year La Malibran returned to Bath. While she was there she was so ill that she almost died.[20] She probably had a miscarriage or a child which did not survive for long. After that 'illness', whatever it may have been, her mood changed; she was no longer 'in despair', but was again the all-successful prima donna. For the time being, the problems which had threatened her private life had receded; she turned her attention to her public life again and began to negotiate a new contract with the Théâtre Italien.

Her demands were outrageous, but the directors of the theatre were eventually forced to submit to them. 'We absolutely must have her,' Robert told his colleague Severini, 'and whatever the cost, for after all she can take three different kinds of part, soprano serio and buffo and contralto . . .' They had to 'drink the hemlock', and give in to the 'rapacious blood-sucker'.[21] La Malibran obtained the extra-

* See p. 212.

ordinary fee of 1,075 francs per performance, and the exclusive right to play all the principal roles. But, as Robert reminded his colleague, so far as talent went, she was 'unique in the world'.[21]

9

The goddess of Romanticism could not be indifferent to the artistic ferment of her epoch. On stage, she portrayed the Romantic spirit; off stage, she lived the life of the Romantic generation. She threw herself into the artistic life of Paris and, like the other Romantics, saw no barriers between the different arts.

Her own talents were multifarious. She drew well, and usually carried a paint-box and sketch book in her bag. She made portraits of her friends, sometimes designed her own stage costumes, and sketched views while travelling. She had a gift for caricature — sometimes of herself — and she would entertain her friends with imitations of ridiculous people whom she had met in Society. She was fond of writing rhymes, of puns, riddles and party games. She was a good linguist, and an excellent sportswoman — she fenced, rode and went shooting; but she was a clumsy dancer. 'Above all,' said Rossini, 'she wrote. Her letters are masterpieces of subtle intelligence, of verve, of good humour, and they display unparalleled originality.'[1] She often illustrated them with little drawings.

She was also a voracious reader. She read that great Romantic precursor, Madame de Staël — she was herself later to be compared to that writer's Corinne — and Xavier de Maistre.[2] She could, like all her generation, expatiate on Byron; we are told that she read Dante and Goethe.[3] She admired the poetry of Hugo, Lamartine and Musset; read the novels of Balzac and, later, of George Sand; and considered Dumas to be 'the regenerator of the French theatre'.[4] Dumas was flattered to see her at the first performance of his *Henri III et sa cour*, leaning out in excitement from her third tier seat — the only one she had been able to obtain — and clutching on to a pillar to prevent herself from falling.[5]

At the ill-starred dress rehearsal of Berlioz's *La Mort de Sardan-apole* at the Institute, La Malibran could only find a place in the orchestra pit, sandwiched between two double basses; but she was there. She was so overwhelmed with emotion when she first heard a performance of Beethoven's 5th Symphony that she had an attack of convulsions, and had to be carried out of the hall.[6]

She went to see and applaud Marie Dorval, the leading Romantic actress. She visited her in her dressing-room after the performance and found her own portrait hanging on the wall. The two great Romantic artists fell in each other's arms and, when La Malibran left, Marie Dorval dissolved into tears.[7] La Malibran also visited the dirty little Théâtre des Funambules, to see the great mime, Deburau. Throughout the performance she kept on exclaiming: 'What an artist he is! What a lesson for me!'[8] She was friendly with Harriet Smithson, the Irish actress who had just revealed Shakespeare to the French, and who was to become Berlioz's first wife.[9] She appeared on the stage with Marie Taglioni,[10] the initiator and personification of the Romantic ballet.

If La Malibran went to see other performers, everyone went to see her; newcomers to Paris made a point of seeing her as Desdemona at the earliest possible opportunity. Paganini, the only person in Europe who was as great a star as La Malibran, went to see her in *Otello* as soon as he arrived in Paris, and he met her at a party the next day, when he improvised on an aria which she had just sung.[11] With Bériot she attended Paganini's first concert in Paris; while she recognised Paganini as her peer, Bériot realised that, from then on, his chances of being the leading solo violinist in Europe were at an end. He had already had to take second place to La Malibran, whose reputation had long ago dwarfed his own.

In 1831 Chopin, newly arrived in Paris, made the obligatory visit to the Théâtre Italien to see La Malibran in *Otello*, and was not, at first, much impressed. It was unfortunately the night when, copying Pasta, she had chosen to play Otello to Madame Devrient's Desdemona. Chopin thought the sight of La Malibran, small and frail, grappling with her huge German Desdemona, was ridiculous.[12] But later he changed his mind, and thought her 'fabulous', the 'leading European prima donna'.[13] Aurore Dudevant, not yet George Sand, who had also arrived in Paris that year, also went to see La Malibran in *Otello*; she went one further, and called her 'the foremost genius of Europe'.[14]

La Malibran's political ideas were probably not highly developed, but she sympathised with the liberal causes of the day, and greeted the July Revolution with enthusiasm.[15] She considered music to have an educative role, and advocated art for the people. 'Like religion,' she used to say, 'harmony should have temples where there would be no privileged people, where everyone should be equal.'[16] She shared the idealism and dedication of her friend and colleague, Adolphe Nourrit,* and was influenced by the ideas of another friend and mentor, Louis Viardot.

By now La Malibran had become the greatest singer in Paris, perhaps the greatest singer in the world. Sontag had retired; Pasta's voice was deteriorating, and she excelled only in tragedy; Wilhelmine Schröder-Devrient was, perhaps, as great an actress as La Malibran, but she was not as great a singer. It had taken La Malibran just two years to achieve her unique position. She was still very young — twenty-two — and already a star of such magnitude that she seemed beyond criticism. She had found independence, and love; she had found herself. A new period, when the possibilities seemed unlimited, was opening for her. Courted, adulated, she had become a great public figure, a trend-setter, the idol of her generation, and other great public figures were proud to be her friends. She could indulge all her whims; money was no longer a problem; she could dictate her terms in the theatre, sing whichever parts she chose. There was nothing she could not have, except official marriage to Bériot; it was the only thing she wanted.

She lived at a pace which left ordinary mortals gasping, and which seemed strangely at variance with her fragile physique. After a performance at the theatre — and performances were very long in those days — she thought nothing of singing at several private parties, or dancing at a ball until the small hours. Even then, when she got home she would do gymnastics, jump over the furniture

---

* Adolphe Nourrit, six years older than La Malibran, studied with her father, and became the most distinguished French tenor of his epoch. Nourrit was an intellectual and an idealist; he treated his work as a true vocation, and was much influenced by Saint-Simonism. He was the first to introduce Schubert's songs to Paris; he wrote the scenario for *La Sylphide*, the archetypal Romantic ballet; and was the friend and inspiration of many French writers and musicians. Nourrit was eventually supplanted at the Opéra by Gilbert Duprez; Nourrit then left for Italy. Although he was well received there, he became more and more depressed, and felt that he was harassed by the public and his colleagues. In 1839 he committed suicide by throwing himself from a window in Naples. Nourrit and La Malibran had much in common — a fact often remarked on by their contemporaries, and which they themselves realised. She dedicated one of her last songs to Nourrit, 'the companion of my stormy childhood and my musical misfortunes'.

until she was too tired to move. When Bériot or her friends remonstrated with her, she replied: 'No, you're mistaken, you don't know my nature; I can't plan rest in my head; it must become indispensable for me because of tiredness.'[17]

Riding and horses played a great part in her life. After going to bed very late, she would get up early, and insist on her somnolent friends getting dressed in order to accompany her on long and daring rides. She was an intrepid horsewoman, quite without fear, and tackled jumps with the same courage and obstinacy with which her father had taught her to tackle musical difficulties. 'She did not merely have contempt for danger,' said one of her riding companions, 'but a passion for it.'[18] Others said: 'Donna Maria sings like an angel and rides like a devil.'[19] The pianist Kalkbrenner, who used to ride with her, called her his 'dear little centaur';[20] another friend said: 'For want of a hippogryphe, she had a horse.'[21] Since she was already becoming a mythical person, people associated her with mythical steeds.

La Malibran made long, and sometimes unnecessary, journeys all over Europe at high speed, on bad roads. She often drove the horses herself, or sat with the coachman. She suffered from what the French call '*la bougeotte*', an inability to keep still; her friends noticed her 'feverish need to scour the country, without respite or rest.'[22] Such frenetic activity — 'a singularly violent hurry to play and to live'[23] — was a symptom of the times, and as usual La Malibran expressed it. Philarète Chasles saw his contemporaries as 'a crowd of chariots with burning wheels, which don't take long to burst into flame as they go, burning up their drivers.' He saw Death, 'that terrible mistress', as urging his generation on. It was, he thought, as if the end of the world were approaching; 'the universal order of the day is this: "Let us use up life, let us hurry to exist." '[24] That is how La Malibran lived.

In spite of her vast success, she remained unpretentious. In her small house in Paris she would talk to her friends and admirers while doing her hair in her little drawing-room. She chatted to everyone unselfconsciously, holding her own with the distinguished men who formed her circle, never playing the flirt. Her conversation was, according to Marie d'Agoult, 'original, like her art.'[25] Although amusing, she was not malicious; and, unlike some actresses — Mademoiselle Mars, Marie Dorval — her conversation never went beyond the bounds of propriety. 'Her remarkable shrewdness and insight were mixed with charming good nature, which hid no *arrière pensée*.

Her conversation — simple, natural, without pretension, enlivened by pleasant and exuberant gaiety, sometimes contained magnificent outbursts, and rose to the highest eloquence when she tackled matters of art . . .'[26]

The men who surrounded her, says Ernest Legouvé, who was one of them, were all more or less in love with her; but they were not jealous of each other, since it was obvious, and she made it clear, that the only man who deeply mattered to her was Charles de Bériot.

Those who frequented her *salon* were mostly much more interesting than Bériot; but, with one or two exceptions, they were a good deal older than he was. The pianist Kalkbrenner was fifty-two. Lamartine, a close friend, in 1830 was forty, and the most famous and popular poet in France. If, in 1830, his popularity was about to be challenged by the young Victor Hugo, Lamartine's position as the father-figure of the young Romantics was still unquestioned. The mystical lyricism of his *Harmonies poétiques*, published that year, powerfully evoked one of the moods of the moment. Lamartine was rather an incongruous figure in La Malibran's *salon*, with his elegance, 'half-military and half-aristocratic, which smacked of the Life Guards and the gentlemen of the Court'[27] (he had been a member of the Royal Guard). But the informality with which La Malibran received her friends, and her own spontaneous high spirits, made even Lamartine unbend and relax in her house. When she was abroad, she corresponded with him. 'The pleasure of talking to someone who understands one is infinite,' she told him. 'This affinity of ideas delights the soul.'[28] And one evening, 'intoxicated with poetry, music, inspiration', she sang for Lamartine alone until three o'clock in the morning.[29]

Her friendship with Jean-Nicholas Bouilly dated back to her childhood; in 1830 he was almost seventy. Bouilly had once intervened when Garcia was ill-treating his daughter; she never forgot it and, when she grew up, repaid the debt by trying to fill the place of Bouilly's beloved daughter, who had died. Bouilly was an old Jacobin, a friend of Mirabeau, a poet and well-known librettist; his *Les Deux Journées*, for Cherubini, was considered a model, and his *Léonore*, written for Pierre Gaveaux, is the source of Beethoven's *Fidelio*. La Malibran was later to give a celebrated and controversial interpretation of the part of Leonore. Bouilly, known for his mawkishness, corresponded with La Malibran and his letters do not belie that reputation; but he sincerely loved her. 'The affection which I have dedicated to you,' he told her, 'is based on so many sources in my mind and heart, that it can only end with my life . . .'[30] But, old though he was, he was to outlive La Malibran.

Louis Viardot, left-wing intellectual, writer, journalist and trans-lator, was younger — thirty in 1830 — but he was an old young man. He, too, had known La Malibran as a child. As a student of nineteen in Paris he had gone without food in order to buy tickets to hear her father in *Don Giovanni*. He had subsequently become acquainted with the Garcia family, had learned Spanish, visited Spain, and was to become a famous translator of Cervantes. When La Malibran returned to Paris as a married woman and celebrity, they met again. Viardot, an intelligent but reserved man, who always kept in the background from choice, won La Malibran's friendship by refusing to flatter her, and by always telling her the truth, as few people did. He came to occupy a special position in her life, as confidant, adviser, and sometimes business manager. After her death he was to marry her younger sister, Pauline.

Although La Malibran knew many men of her own age or younger — Dumas, Liszt, Mendelssohn, Gautier — her friendship with them was never as close as it was with her elders — Bouilly, Lamartine, Viardot and, later, Lafayette. The only exception was Ernest Legouvé, who was a year older than she was.

Legouvé was one of La Malibran's closest friends and, eventually, her biographer. He came from a literary family, and made a precocious début in the world of literature, winning an important prize when he was twenty-two. He spent the rest of his life as a literary man, became a member of the French Academy, and died at the age of ninety-six. He was successful in his day, writing many plays, poems and novels, but he is only remembered today as the co-author (with Scribe) of *Adrienne Lecouvreur* (1849), and for his delightful but not totally reliable *Soixante ans de souvenirs*, in which his biography of La Malibran appears.

Legouvé first met La Malibran soon after she arrived in Paris, in 1828. He was more than a little in love with her and, although there is no evidence that she reciprocated his feelings, she did confide in him, and wrote him some very intimate letters. Unlike other admirers, whom she rebuffed, Legouvé was able to turn their relationship into one of friendship.

When Legouvé first heard La Malibran sing, music was, to him, 'just an agreeable art', and nothing more. Her singing was a revel-ation to him; she was, he said, a 'wonderful genius who feels every-thing and makes everything felt, who floods the heart with emotions . . .'[31] After a performance of Zingarelli's *Giulietta e Romeo* he was so overwhelmed by the experience that he went straight home and wrote a letter to La Malibran to tell her of the emotions her performance had aroused in him:

'It is on one's knees, Madame, it is on one's knees that one must speak of you; I've just come from Romeo, I need say no more . . .' Needless to say, he did say a great deal more — several pages, in fact.

But Legouvé was as much intrigued by La Malibran's personality as he was inspired by her art:

When I was introduced into your house, and heard you talking, I admired the shrewdness of your instinct and the soundness of your arguments. I listened to you talking, and your conversation astonished me; I was surprised that, in the midst of so many compliments, there was room in your life for reflexion; a few words which you let slip, some profound ideas, proved to me that you have thought a great deal and suffered a great deal . . .[32]

Legouvé was not the only one to notice that some tragic mystery hung over her. Lamartine also recalled that

a mystery, which she one day half-revealed to us personally, hovered over her life like a cloud over the source of a river. This cloud darkened her beauty. It diffused over her features, which were dazzling with youth and inspiration, a tinge of sadness. This melancholy would sometimes clear, but it never lifted entirely. She had suffered too much for her smile not to retain a certain languor and a certain unconscious bitterness . . .'[33]

Lamartine, recalling the day when she 'half-revealed' her mystery to her friends, may have been thinking of the same occasion to which Legouvé referred in a letter to La Malibran:

I have only learned to know you since last Friday; delicious and dreadful evening! Ah! Madame, how moving they were, those tears which you shed in your old friend's arms, and how they would melt the hardest heart! You — unhappy! . . . I cannot tell you how bitter and painful such an idea is to me . . . [. . .] I'll tell you that you have torn my heart and that, in doing so, you have filled it with esteem and affection for you.

Manuel Garcia as Otello. Lithograph by G. Engelmann. *Copyright Royal College of Music, London*

(*Above and below*) Water-colour sketches by La Malibran; signed by M. F. Garcia, so probably made before her marriage in 1826. *Le Cesne Collection, Paris*

La Malibran in *La cenerentola*, artist unknown.

Mme Malibran-Garcia, by Henri
Grévedon, 1829. *Crown
Copyright Victoria and Albert
Museum* (*Theatre Museum*)

Henriette Sontag. Engraving by
A.C. after Carloni. *Copyright
Royal College of Music, London*

Charles de Bériot by Paul Gauci
after Corneille Kruseman.
*Copyright Bibliothèque royale
Albert Ier, Brussels* (*Cabinet
des Estampes*)

Sketches of La Malibran as
Ninetta in Rossini's *La gazza
ladra*, 1829. *Crown Copyright
Victoria and Albert Museum
(Theatre Museum)*

La Malibran as Desdemona,
1830. Engraving by Chs.
Turner, after the portrait by
Henri Decaisne (which is in the
Musée Carnavalet, Paris).
*Crown Copyright Victoria and
Albert Museum (Theatre
Museum)*

[. . .] You voluntarily poured out some of your noble secrets
in our presence, and yet I almost reproach myself for knowing
them, as if I had stolen them . . . [34]

Whatever La Malibran's secrets may have been, they certainly
affected her deeply. 'Do you know what?' she wrote to Legouvé,
'My happiness is Juliet! It is dead, like her, and I am Romeo, and
weep for it.'[35]

Although Legouvé promised La Malibran that 'no secret will ever
be better kept. I will preserve it as a perfume of you, and I will not
even remember it in your presence,'[36] he probably did later reveal
her secret, not in his biography of her, but in a novel, *Max*.

10

In 1832 Legouvé visited Italy for the first time, and saw a good deal of La Malibran and Bériot who were then in Rome. He published *Max* in Paris in 1833. The novel contains many Italian scenes, prompted by Legouvé's first impressions of Italy, and much of it was clearly inspired by La Malibran. The conversations which he had with her in Rome — significantly, just after the death of her father — may have given him further insights into her 'tragedy', which she may have already partly confided to him in Paris.

The novel tells the story of two young men, Max and Williams, and their relationship with a prima donna, Giuditta Darini. Although La Darini has Pasta's Christian name and is, unlike La Malibran, blonde and Italian, in most other respects she is obviously modelled on La Malibran. Many of La Darini's sayings are to be found, word for word, in the letters from La Malibran which Legouvé later published in his biography of her.[1] Some anecdotes about La Darini are to be found in other sources with reference to La Malibran:[2] like her, La Darini suffered from 'fainting fits';[3] like her, she had had an unhappy childhood;[4] like her, she was full of contradictions — one moment gay, impulsive, delighted with some pun she had made, the next moment, with no transition, talking of death and eternity.[5] Like La Malibran, La Darini held court in her sitting-room, while doing her hair and talking to her admirers.[6] The journalist in the novel, Delon, is probably a portrait of Vitet, while the sensitive and high-minded Williams seems to be a self-portrait of Legouvé.

Like La Malibran, La Darini has an aura of melancholy, and Max, echoing Lamartine's words about La Malibran, speaks of the 'mystery of misfortune' which surrounds her.[7] Max resolves to find out what that mystery was. He eventually does so: La Darini is leading a double life. In public, she has sensational successes, is admired and fêted; in private she is living out a sordid tragedy, a hideous nightmare: her father has an incestuous passion for her, and is trying to seduce her; eventually he kills her.

In Rossini's *Otello* Desdemona sings: 'If my father abandons me, from whom can I hope for compassion?' Garcia did, indeed, reject La Malibran when she was expecting Bériot's child; but perhaps La Darini's paraphrase of the words in *Otello*: 'If my father *dishonours* me, who then will respect me?'[8] also applied to La Malibran who considered that, like Esmeralda in Hugo's *Notre Dame de Paris*, she was 'not innocent, but pure'.[9]

Does *Max* reveal the true nature of La Malibran's relationship with her father? It is, of course, impossible to accept a novel as firm evidence, and the truth will probably never be known for certain. But the gutter press of the day, no doubt reflecting contemporary gossip, did allege that Garcia had an incestuous passion for his daughter,[10] and other, more reliable sources, such as the anonymous English friend writing in the *Manchester Guardian*, hinted at the same thing after her death:

> Those who knew La Malibran's secrets knew those things which they never would have expected, and which explained most honourably all the actions of her life. Those persons likewise knew that no woman on earth suffered greater agony of mental torture than she did from the age of fifteen until her marriage.

The period specified exonerates both Malibran and Bériot, but incriminates her father, the only person (apart from her mother) with whom she had close contact during that period. The same English friend goes on to link La Malibran's adolescent sufferings to her 'fainting fits' — probably correctly, since they began when she started to study with her father, and almost always occurred in connection with him: 'The effect those sufferings produced can never be forgotten by those who saw them. She would remain sometimes for hours in a state of unmovable "exstasis", gazing on vacancy.'[11]

If the incest in *Max* is based on La Malibran's life, did Legouvé, by writing the novel, betray her confidence? He did take certain precautions so that the connections between La Darini and La Malibran would not be too obvious; he changed many of the details. For example, in *Max* La Darini's father is not a singer, and does not appear with her on the stage; some of the action of the novel takes place in Venice, which La Malibran had not then visited; and so on. Legouvé waited until La Malibran had left Paris for good before publishing his novel there in 1833. His precautions appear to have been effective; no one, it seems, made the connection between La Malibran and La Darini then, or, indeed, until now.

Legouvé is careful to point out, in his preface to *Max*, his aim in writing it: 'In this book,' he wrote, 'I protest strongly against over-indulgence in the false sentiment of poetry'; and he went on to complain that, at the time when he was writing, at the height of the Romantic fever, if someone committed a crime, murder for example, everyone would say: 'There's something poetic about it.'[12] Alfred de Musset, in his ironical analysis of Romanticism in his *Lettres de Dupuis et Cotonet*, said the same thing: '. . . four incests and a couple of parricides, in period dress, is great literature.'[13] Although, in his youth, Legouvé was a Romantic, he knew La Malibran too well to romanticise her sufferings; he knew that incest is not usually poetic; but he also knew that his contemporaries might think it so.

Legouvé's biography of La Malibran (1880) is charmingly written, and contains no breath of scandal. In it he was at pains to show her as the delightful woman he remembered, rather than the mythical creature she had by then become. The biography contains a few errors of fact; Legouvé was writing almost half a century after the events, and his memory sometimes failed him. For example, he tells the story — and he is the only one to tell it — of a touching reconciliation between La Malibran and her father on stage at the end of a performance of *Otello* in Paris, after Garcia's return from Mexico in 1829.[14] According to Legouvé, when the curtain was coming down at the end of the performance, he could see La Malibran moving across the stage towards her father; when the curtain was raised again, her face was black — she had embraced Othello, and his make-up had come off in the process. Garcia and La Malibran gave only three performances of *Otello* in 1832, all very widely reported in the press, but there is no mention of this incident. However, in an interview which Garcia gave to the press at that time[15] he told the same story, but said that it had taken place in Mexico with a Mexican prima donna. It seems that Legouvé vaguely remembered the story, and either came to believe years later that he had witnessed it, or simply improved it for literary effect. This is a good example of how legends grow; many other examples of the same sort could be found.

11

In the theatre, La Malibran reigned supreme, and she knew it; but in the wider world, her social position was extremely precarious, and she knew that, too. The thought of what lay outside made her choose to see the theatre as reality, and she lived in a 'magic palace [. . .] where she savoured her triumphs in a dream.'[1] Within the theatre world and her circle of close friends, she was a goddess, and sure of her divinity.

In Society she was merely a woman and an actress, a doubly-disadvantaged person. As a woman, she had no rights; but her husband could, at any time, claim his conjugal rights, and her money. Nor was she on an even footing with Bériot; pregnancies interfered with her career, and any child born of her liaison with Bériot would be illegitimate, and would have a difficult life as a result. Her own position, if she were to have an illegitimate child, would not be enviable; she would be condemned as an adulteress, and would forfeit the small social concessions she had won as a result of her modest behaviour; she would lose all her women friends, except those whose own morality was doubtful. Bériot, on the other hand, would still be *persona grata* with everyone. She did become pregnant; but, at first, she was able to conceal or terminate her pregnancies. The fear haunted her, that she would not always be able to do so.

Even if La Malibran had not been living with Bériot, and had been entirely virtuous, her position in Society was very equivocal. In France theatrical performers had been socially ostracised for so long that, even though opera singers were not officially condemned by Church and state, as other stage people were, the public and some priests and officials treated them in exactly the same way.

The prejudice against actors and, particularly, actresses goes back so far in antiquity in almost all civilisations that it is difficult to establish its origins with any certainty. The link, often official, between the stage and prostitution is also very ancient, not only in Europe but in China, Japan and India. Although the prejudice is perhaps based on irrational fear, it is often rationalised by the idea that the actor or actress, like the prostitute, sells him- or herself to provide pleasure, and that the instrument used is his or her body.[2]

In France the Gallican Church, invoking the Councils of Arles (in the years 314 and 452), which had validity only in France, considered all those on the stage to be excommunicate, despite the fact that 'no general condemnation against theatrical people was ever pronounced by the popes or by a single oecumenical council.'[3] Actors and actresses in France were therefore denied all the sacraments: they were denied the right to take Communion, to marriage, absolution, and Christian burial, unless they renounced the stage; the story of Molière's funeral is well known. This state of affairs remained unchanged until 1849, when the Council of Soissons gave theatrical people in France their religious rights after more than 1,500 years.[4]

During that time the attitude of the clergy to people on the stage varied enormously; sometimes excommunication was strictly adhered to; and sometimes bishops and priests ignored it, and actors and actresses received the sacraments and were in no way disadvantaged. But when they were refused marriage by the Church, at a time when only church marriage existed, they were obliged 'to live in sin', and their children were illegitimate. Some liberal priests in some dioceses would bless the union of actors, although they could not officially marry them. As musicians were not excommunicated, actors would sometimes pass themselves off as musicians in order to get married.[5]

The attitude of the state in France was not consistent, but from the middle of the seventeenth century until the French Revolution it hardened. Actors had no civil rights; they could not be witnesses in court, and could hold no public, municipal or military office. The state put them in the same category as heretics, prostitutes and public executioners.[6]

In 1789 the National Assembly gave theatrical people civil rights; civil marriage and death certificates were issued, and the administration of cemeteries was taken away from the clergy, so that they could no longer control who was buried in consecrated ground. But actors and actresses still could not have a church marriage or Christian burial unless they renounced their 'criminal'[7] profession for ever; many, when they thought they were dying, did so; but many, like Talma, refused.

The Revolution had given actors their civil rights; but the Restoration gave power back to the Church, and a decree of 1816, under Louis XVIII, took actors' civil rights away again.[8] They were finally granted the same rights as other citizens in 1829[9] — although they still remained excommunicate — a year after La Malibran reached Paris.

Women on the stage were inevitably particularly disadvantaged.[10] Classed as prostitutes by the state, and denied Christian marriage by the Church, there was little they could do to retain their respectability in the eyes of the world, although many of them led eminently moral lives and retained their self-respect and the respect of their colleagues. But men unconnected with the theatre considered actresses easy game, and were only too ready to take advantage of them.

Attractive actresses — including La Malibran[11] — were deluged with propositions from men who wanted to buy their favours; inevitably, many succumbed. They had little to lose, except their self-respect. They all came from poor backgrounds and had little money apart from what they earned — and very few earned the colossal sums paid to La Malibran or Sontag. Most actresses dreamed of retiring from the stage, of being kept by a rich protector or, if they were lucky enough, of marrying a rich man and gaining respectability, as Sontag eventually did. The theatre was a hard profession, and the working life, particularly of singers and dancers, was short. Most actresses were haunted by the thought of a destitute old age, or by the possibility of having to go on earning their living, in order to feed themselves, in fourth-rate provincial theatres, their voices, their looks, and their ability to hold an audience gone. Many sold themselves in order to avoid this fate. Thus, in the public mind, the idea, fostered by Church and state, that actresses were prostitutes or of easy virtue, was confirmed by well-known examples. This is why, in 1828, when Sontag had an illegitimate child, La Malibran considered that she had let down 'the honour of the team.'[12]* If

---

* At the end of the summer season in London in 1828 it became known that Henriette Sontag was pregnant. With a certain amount of glee, La Malibran informed her husband of this news (letter of 8th September, 1828, Teneo, p. 470), saying that 'people think her voice has greatly declined and that she *no longer has such a pretty waist* . . .' Sontag is alleged to have accounted for her disabilities by saying that she had slipped on a cherry stone. Count Rossi was the father of the child; he was a man of honour and subsequently married Sontag, but his diplomatic career would

public opinion was to change, actresses' behaviour had to change also.

In a pathetic desire to ingratiate themselves with Church and Society, and to atone for their 'criminal' profession, stage people went out of their way to be generous to the poor, and to give alms to the Church which, with the utmost cynicism, often asked them for money. At one period the state taxed actors, and they had to give a sixth of their income to the poor.[13] This habit or tradition continued long after they had been given their civil rights. La Malibran was a case in point; there are innumerable anecdotes about her generosity to the poor.* Although she probably was a genuinely compassionate and generous woman, these anecdotes, true and false, must be seen in the context of this ancient theatrical tradition of trying to buy the Church and the public's favours through charity.

---

have been at an end, because he had married a singer, had not the King of Prussia intervened, and given Sontag a patent of nobility. The marriage was a success; as Countess Rossi, Henriette was received by everyone, and was very popular in aristocratic circles. She was particularly in demand at charity concerts. However, some years later (1849) Sontag went back to the professional stage, ostensibly because she needed the money, but perhaps also because she missed her profession. As a result, her husband had to resign from the diplomatic service, and she found that her aristocratic friends would no longer receive her. Sontag's second career was successful; she went to the United States in 1852, and was very well received there. She died of cholera in Mexico in 1854.

* The anecdotes about La Malibran's generosity are very numerous — too numerous to be quoted, and not all of them are verifiable. However, some are: there is the autograph ms. of a letter from La Malibran to an un-named correspondent (29th November, 1829) in the Bibliothèque de l'Opéra, in which she promises to give the addressee the 5,000 francs which she had offered, but insists that it should remain a secret. In the same library there is a newspaper cutting (unfortunately unidentified and undated) in which Louis Viardot tells how, in 1829, a young English girl in the chorus of the Théâtre Italien did not have enough money to return home. La Malibran sang at the Duc d'Orléans' concert, and gave the fee which she had received to the English girl. This story is repeated, with variations, by other sources; but Viardot says that he was present when it happened. La Malibran's kindness to young musicians at the beginning of their careers — Ole Bull, Benedict, John Orlando Parry — is well documented, as is her generosity to the theatre director Gallo in Venice, (see Pougin, pp. 181–5); and see also Quicherat, Hogarth, Wauwermans and, of course, Merlin for many other anecdotes.

It might be thought that the public, which applauded nightly in the theatre, would have had some sympathy for the plight of their heroes; but opinion was 'manifestly hostile'.[14] Napoleon contemplated giving Talma the *Légion d'honneur*; but even he dared not do so, although Talma was France's greatest actor at the time, and very popular.[15] Public opinion in France remained hostile to stage people long after they had been granted their civil and religious rights and certainly well into the twentieth century. Although liberal and enlightened individuals always condemned this attitude and defended actors' rights, the prejudice was so ingrained amongst the general public that vestiges of it can probably be found to this day.

It is difficult to estimate what psychological effect such attitudes had on successive generations of theatrical performers. To be applauded in the theatre and treated with contempt outside it, must have been deeply damaging, and increased the problem of identity which is anyway inherent in the actors' art. Who were they? Gods, or outcasts?

The ambivalence seriously affected La Malibran, and she was acutely conscious of it from an early age. One of her reasons for marrying Malibran had been to escape the theatre; and later, despite her vast success, she often dreamed of leaving the stage, for reasons which she explained to a woman friend:

> Then I shall no longer feel that the name of actress, said with contempt, nose wrinkled, will come to undo the calm of my existence or to make you, my friend, blush. Don't think that I *despise* my art; but it is so distressing to be associated pell-mell with those who are the cause of the word *actress* only being understood in the most unfavourable and the most revolting sense of the word. I don't know why I come back over and over again to a subject which is so painful to me; in spite of myself, my pen traces this familiar thought of mine. After all, it's my profession, and I must practise it. I wish everyone who does so had the same way of thinking as I have, and then it would be fine . . .[16]

Apart from the deep-rooted prejudice in France against actors and actresses, there was also, all over Europe, a social prejudice against musicians and other performing artists. Musicians were not condemned by Church and state in France, but there, as elsewhere, they were not considered acceptable in high Society. This was a class prejudice, which was just beginning to change at the beginning of the nineteenth century, and which had almost disappeared by the end of it. The free-lance musician, not the hired servant of some aristocratic or royal patron, was a relatively new phenomenon. Haydn's menial position at Esterház and Mozart's at Salzburg are well known, as are Mozart's financial difficulties when he left Salzburg and held no official court position. The rise of the virtuoso instrumentalist — Paganini, Thalberg, Liszt and many others — made musicians socially more prominent; but they had to fight to be accepted in Society. 'Good' families did not wish their daughters to marry musicians; Chopin was a victim of this prejudice.

In the 1830s social snobbery concerning musicians began to relax a little. Some hostesses were beginning to treat musicians not yet as friends and equals, but as something a little better than servants. Countess Merlin, La Malibran's patroness, had a notable musical *salon*, and was very friendly with her protegée; but she was an exception. Born in Havana, she was not influenced by the Gallican Church, and she was a good amateur musician herself, a pupil of Garcia.

La Malibran was often snubbed socially. Mendelssohn 'was quite indignant at the way paid artists were isolated from the guests [in London], nor could he forget having seen Malibran sit in a remote corner of the drawing-room, shut out and looking miserable'; but Mendelssohn's father, from a solid bourgeois background, was worried by the 'ardent interest' which his son took in the singer.[17] The situation was little different in Paris; Marie d'Agoult, very well-born and snobbish, who in 1833 was herself to abandon her good name, her husband and her child in order to elope with Liszt, has left a description of how musical *soirées* were organised at that time:

> Enthusiasm [for singers such as La Malibran] was universal. Yet composers and singers still kept to a place apart; they appeared in drawing-rooms only in a subordinate way, in spite of the eagerness people had to have them there [. . .] They all arrived together at the appointed time, by a side door; they all sat together near the piano, they all left together, after having received compliments from the master of the house and from a few professional *dilettanti*. The next day, Rossini [who usually organised the musical side of such *soirées*] was sent his fee, and the host and hostess considered that their obligations to him were at an end. In some more modest houses, in families where music was cultivated from preference, relations between artists

and members of Society were established with more affability. Madame Malibran, after having sung the *Willow Song*, or the cavatina from *La gazza ladra*, charmed us with the lively grace of her wit. When the concert was over, she gladly stayed on after the other artists, and grew animated while talking. Her conversation, like her talent, was original. She did not allow any pretension to show, and I believe she had none. Mademoiselle Sontag was quite different. Spoiled by adulation in Germany, obsessed with aristocracy and fine manners, avid for praise, even more avid for money, and with very little wit, she tried to play the great lady, and she set about it badly.[18]

La Malibran knew that the small concessions she had won by her modest behaviour — that Society ladies sometimes treated her as an ordinary human being — would be instantly forfeited if the slightest breath of scandal were ever to be connected with her name. She was keen to be accepted by Society — mixed Society, for men without their wives always could and did accept her — not from snobbish reasons, but because she was tormented by the thought that, because of her profession, she was not considered to be a respectable person, and that people valued her only for her talents. She would often come home after having sung at some aristocratic house and collapse in tears, saying: 'Nothing but an artist! That's all they see! . . . the slave they pay to give them pleasure!'[19] La Malibran's friend, Adolphe Nourrit, expressed the same thought just before he committed suicide: 'You know very well, I'm the plaything of the public.'[20]

It is understandable that La Malibran was interested in the early movements which advocated women's rights, and which campaigned for granting artists — actors, musicians and so on — an honourable position in Society. We are assured by one of her biographers that she was too sensible and well-behaved 'to lend the support of her name and influence to the cause of the free woman and other eccentricities of the same type'; but the same source tells us that she was interested for a time in Saint-Simonism,[21] which advocated complete equality of the sexes, and divorce, and considered artists to be superior beings, who should have an honourable and honoured place in Society. It was the artist's mission, the Saint-Simonites believed, to raise the rest of humanity to a higher level. The sect also had a quasi-religious side, which eventually became predominant. After the July Revolution, it gained many new members, and set out to recruit artists, particularly musicians, who could propagate its ideas. Liszt, Berlioz and Nourrit, La Malibran's friends, were interested in the sect for a time, and she attended some of its meetings (although she was later to deny it,*) in the hope of finding some way out of her many problems.

Issues which affected her — the emancipation of women, the emancipation of actors and actresses, and the artist's place in Society — were later to be taken up and campaigned for by her friends Legouvé† and Liszt,‡ and by George Sand,§ who did not know her personally, but greatly admired her. All three were, in part, influenced by her case; but, although they campaigned valiantly, and ultimately with some success, for these causes, their efforts came too late to help La Malibran.

* See p. 155.

† Legouvé. For his defence of women see, for example, *La Femme en France au dix-neuvième siècle* (*Conférences de la Salle Barthélemy*, 2ème série, Paris, 1864) and various other publications. For his defence of actors, see *La Croix d'honneur et les comédiens* (Paris, 1863). These themes can be found in many of Legouvé's other writings.

‡ Liszt. See, for example, *De la situation des artistes et de leur condition dans la société*, originally published in *La Revue et gazette musicale*, republished in *Pages romantiques* (Paris, 1912). In this article (p. 79) Liszt quotes La Malibran's friendship with Lafayette as one of the first to break through the class barrier. All his life, Liszt was interested in, and campaigned for, the artist's proper place in Society, and references to this subject can be found in his writings and letters. Because of his superior intelligence, personal charm, and vast success, he probably achieved more for this cause than anyone else in the nineteenth century. Despite his love affairs and some other indiscretions, and despite the indiscretions of his daughter Cosima, Liszt himself was received by the aristocracy all over Europe in his old age.

§ See Chapter 12.

12

In January, 1831, Aurore Dudevant, née Dupin, shortly to become George Sand, arrived in Paris. After nine years of unsatisfactory marriage, she had decided to separate from her boorish husband and to lead her own life; she would spend six months of the year in Paris, and six months at Nohant, her country house, with her two children. She was twenty-eight years old. In order to live in Paris she had to earn her living; like many women in the nineteenth century and later, she decided that she was best qualified to do so by writing. She and her lover, Jules Sandeau, were given some journalistic work by the editor of *Le Figaro*; they also dreamed of writing novels. At first, they collaborated, each contributing something to articles and stories which were then signed, at Aurore's request, by Jules Sandeau or by 'Jules Sand'.

They were both fresh from the provinces, and avid to taste all the artistic experiences which Paris had to offer. 'When one wants to write,' Aurore told a friend, 'one must see everything, know everything, laugh at everything. Oh, my goodness, long live the artist's life! Our motto is freedom!'[1]

High on their list of priorities was the Théâtre Italien; Aurore was passionately fond of music, and had received a good musical education from her grandmother — she was particularly affected by the human voice, as many references in her later works testify. Very soon after her arrival she went, like everyone else, to hear La Malibran as Desdemona. The experience was shattering. 'She made me weep, shudder, in a word, suffer as if I had witnessed a scene of real life. This woman is the foremost genius of Europe, as beautiful as one of Raphael's virgins, simple, powerful, naïve, she's the foremost singer and the foremost tragic actress. I am in raptures about her.'[2]

This enthusiasm directly inspired ideas, themes and whole passages in some early works in which Aurore Dudevant and Jules Sandeau probably collaborated: *La Prima Donna*,[3] *La Fille d'Albano*,[4] *La Marquise*,[5] *Rose et Blanche*;[6] and *Pauline*,[7] which is entirely the work of George Sand. Sandeau's later work makes it clear that most of the ideas in these works were Aurore's, but he, too, was interested in La Malibran, and referred to her in later works.[8]

The principal themes in these first, very immature works were to be reiterated and gradually refined throughout George Sand's life; they were to find their most complete and mature expression in *Consuelo* (1842–3), which was directly inspired by La Malibran's younger sister. The main theme in the early stories is the artist: his or her place in Society; the choice — especially for women — between art and love; art as a vocation and dedication; true and false artists — those who aspire to a noble and disinterested art, and those who only want to win fame and popularity, and strive after effect alone. A secondary theme, also to be partially developed later, is women's liberation. In all the five works mentioned above, the hero or heroine is some kind of artist (two prima donnas, one painter, and an actor and an actress), and four out of the five are women.

Although these stories all owe something to La Malibran, they contain some misunderstandings and misinterpretations of her true situation, attitudes and personality. As George Sand did not know La Malibran personally, she romanticised her. She tended to romanticise performing artists all her life, both those whom she knew personally, and those whom she described in her novels; but when she later got to know Liszt, Nourrit, Marie Dorval, Chopin, Pauline Viardot and others, her portraits became more refined and authentic, and her ideas on the subject matured.

The theme of *La Prima Donna* and of *La Fille d'Albano* is that the artist cannot be, must not be, made to conform to the restrictions and conventions of ordinary society, but must be free to follow his or her vocation. In both these stories the artist is a woman, and the restrictions and conventions applied particularly to women. In *La Prima Donna* the heroine, Gina, a prima donna, having married into a 'good' family, naturally has to leave the stage. But 'from the first day she felt constricted' in her new life of affluence and leisure. 'Farewell to the artistic life, so full and fiery; farewell to the excitements of the theatre, the intoxications of glory!'[9] Gina pines away, finding her new world 'so cold and dry, like a rich man's heart.'[10] Fearing for her survival, the doctors suggest that, in order to save her, she be allowed to appear once more in the theatre. When she does, she is so overwhelmed with happiness that she dies on stage, in the last act of Zingarelli's *Giulietta e Romeo*.*

There are many reminiscences of La Malibran in this short story, written just after Aurore had seen her as Desdemona. There is a long description of Gina singing the *Willow Song*, 'melancholy like the night, which seemed to groan with her, foretelling her terrible destiny . . .'[11] This description, too long to quote in full, tallies with other accounts of La Malibran's performance in the part.[12] There are other similarities. Gina is 'pale, her hair divided into two shining, black braids';[13] she, too, has suffered; and, like La Malibran's voice, hers lingers in the listener's memory long after the event.[14]

La Prima Donna is a very immature work. What Gina misses most is excitement, fame, glory. This is not what George Sand's artists want in later novels; they are above such things, they are dedicated to Art. But there is little doubt that La Malibran would probably have felt the same as Gina.

In *La Fille d'Albano* the heroine is a painter and, like La Malibran, Spanish. She is saved in the nick of time from a 'good' marriage by her elder brother, also an artist, who persuades her to escape with him back to the *vie de bohème* of artists. The story is rather weak; it consists mainly of a long monologue by the brother, extolling the joys of a free life, and describing the horrors of conventional marriage. It clearly reflects Aurore's thoughts as a result of her own long and unsatisfactory years as a wife. La Malibran is not directly portrayed, but one of the themes touched on directly concerned her. In *La Fille d'Albano* vestigial ideas of feminism make their appearance; the author or authors advocate liberation for women, but only for women of talent:

> Genius has no sex. The woman born to perpetuate her kind, and the artist who lives the life of a whole world are quite different. The artist does not belong to herself, the details of ordinary life do not fit her. Soon disgust and boredom, agonizing boredom, torture, the terrible end of an active soul, will come to tarnish for her the false brilliance which normal life in vain offers. Ah! You had so promised yourself never to be anything but an artist! You were so proud of your freedom . . .
> [. . .] They will say: She was famous, she has become obscure;

---

* Gina plays Juliet; La Malibran almost always played Romeo.

she had a great destiny, and she has stifled it in her domesticity . . .[15]

Aurore did not, at first, understand the problem of the artist's position in Society. Having just succeeded in escaping from a boring conventional marriage in a Philistine society, she could exult in the freedom of the liberated woman, leading an artist's life, unhampered by social conventions. La Malibran, as a theatrical person, had been born and bred outside Society. She had the opposite desire: to belong, to be respectable and respected. As a woman on the stage, La Malibran's position was particularly humiliating; but other artists — Liszt and Chopin, for example — although men and not on the stage, also wished to be respected and accepted by Society. It was the aristocratic or middle-class young — Marie d'Agoult, Musset, George Sand herself — who could afford the luxury of flouting social *mores* and living a bohemian life. They could reject Society, because they had been born into it.

In *La Marquise*, written almost eighteen months later than *La Prima Donna* and *La Fille d'Albano*, Aurore's literary talents and ideas about artists had already considerably developed. A Society lady falls in love with an actor whom she has seen on the stage, and whose acting is noble, simple, grandiose. When she first sees him off the stage, in everyday clothes, she realises that he is insignificant, ordinary, vulgar. But she agrees to meet him again, for by now he is in love with her. When he arrives for their second meeting, he is dressed in his theatrical costume; thus clad, he is able to express his love and the noble sentiments which he has learned from the great authors whose plays he performs. But, although the Marquise and the actor love each other, they part; they realise that a social barrier exists between them, which neither can cross.

The future George Sand already understands actors much better. The social problem is seen to be more complex; and the problem of an actor's identity — whether he is himself, or the characters whom he portrays — is touched upon.

Rose et Blanche is not a story, but a long novel about a nun — Blanche — and an actress — Rose. Rose becomes a great singer who eventually rejects one vocation — the stage — for another — God. The complicated plot need not concern us here; but the portrait of Rose, who appears on the stage as La Coronari, is already much more subtle psychologically, and prefigures George Sand's mature portraits of artists. La Coronari finds inspiration in La Pasta's performances, but many of her own characteristics are modelled on La Malibran. Like La Malibran, she is vivacious, daring, an intrepid horsewoman. Like her — and unlike La Pasta — she can play tragic and comic roles with equal ease. But Rose's mentality does not greatly resemble that of La Malibran; and indeed, how could it, since Sandeau and Aurore did not know her.

It has been suggested[16] that in *Pauline*, completed after Aurore Dudevant became George Sand (which she did with the publication of *Indiana* in 1832) not only La Malibran is portrayed, but her mother and sister as well.* By the time *Pauline* was published (1839) La Malibran was dead, and George knew her sister and mother personally; the portrait of La Malibran, if such it is, would therefore be based on their memories of her, which were probably very subjective. It is possible that Laurence, the actress heroine of the novel, owes more to Pauline Garcia than to her sister.

La Malibran was the first prototype for George's early portraits of artists, which are often naïve and incomplete, but which foreshadow her later, more complex creations. La Malibran's performances provided the initial impetus for George's thoughts on the subject, which other artists were to enlarge, and which La Malibran's sister was to complete. When George Sand later met Liszt and Nourrit, came into contact with the Saint-Simonites and, through Liszt, with Lamennais, she, like them, began to see the artist as a being set apart from the ordinary run of people, dedicated to raise Society to a higher level.

Afterwards, she came to know other artists — Marie Dorval, Chopin, Meyerbeer — who did not really share her philosophical ideas about their calling, but who nevertheless gave her first-hand knowledge of many aspects of the artist's life. But only one artist fulfilled all George's ideals, and was prepared to put her ideas into practice. This was La Malibran's sister, Pauline Garcia, seventeen years younger than George, who was to complete what her sister had begun. She was young enough, and willing, to be moulded by George.

Pauline[17] was probably just as talented as her sister — their voices were comparable, and they sang many of the same rôles. Pauline was an excellent actress, a first-class pianist and organist, and quite a talented composer. But she was very different from her sister.

---

* Although she bears the same Christian name, Pauline in the novel certainly bears no resemblance to Pauline Garcia.

Calm, plain, intelligent and well-balanced, she had had a happy childhood and had never been ill-treated by her father. She was in no way a Romantic; indeed, her début, in 1839, coincided with the decline of Romanticism, with the début of Rachel, and the revival of the Classical drama. Although she did play Romantic parts, her greatest triumphs were in the operas of Meyerbeer and in Gluck's *Orphée*.

The difference in the sisters' temperaments was very apparent in their interpretation of the part of Desdemona in Rossini's *Otello*. Musset, who had seen and admired them both, remembered that 'La Malibran played Desdemona as a Venetian and a heroine; love, anger, terror, everything about her, was exuberant; even her melancholy was emphatic, and the *Willow Song* burst from her lips like a prolonged sob.' Pauline's interpretation of the part was one of overwhelming gentleness and resignation. Musset thought that she played Desdemona '. . . not as a beautiful Amazon, but as a girl who loves naïvely, who wishes people to pardon her love, who weeps in the arms of her father at the very moment when he is about to curse her, and who is brave only at the moment of death.'[18]

George was as enthusiastic about Pauline Garcia as she had been about her sister. She thought her 'the foremost, the only, the great, the true singer,'[19] and valued her just as much as a woman. They became close friends, and remained so for the rest of their lives.

As soon as they met, George realised that Pauline could became the ideal artist of whom she had so long dreamed, and she set about ensuring that this would happen, with Pauline's willing co-operation. George arranged Pauline's marriage to Louis Viardot, twenty-one years her senior, whom Pauline liked, but did not love. George believed that Pauline's vocation as an artist could best develop within the safety of such a marriage, which would give her tranquillity and security, and protect her from stronger passions which might interfere with her career. And, in this case, George was right; the marriage was a success. Pauline sacrificed passion to art, and became all that her mentor desired: a great and dedicated artist who was, it seems, fulfilled by her vocation.

Pauline's marriage to Viardot solved the problem of the artist's place in Society. They were an entirely respectable couple, and even Turgenev's long attachment to her could not be described as a scandal, since he was very friendly with her husband, and the laws of Society were never openly transgressed. In addition, the climate of opinion was changing fast; in Pauline's day stage people were no longer considered outcasts, and Pauline herself, by her intelligence and discreet behaviour, did much to make them acceptable. The Viardots were received by the aristocracy and even by royalty, and they and their children were honoured and respected members of Society. It is small wonder that Pauline and her husband were at pains to conceal some details of the Garcia family's past.

In 1842–3 George Sand published *Consuelo*, perhaps her greatest novel about an artist.* The heroine is composed partly of what Pauline Viardot already was, and partly of what George wanted her to become. Pauline entirely approved of her portrait, and dutifully strove to copy it. She told a friend to read *Consuelo* if he wanted to understand her.

La Malibran would not have been so malleable. A true Romantic, unlike her sister, she wanted art, and love, and passion, and personal happiness, and fame, all at the same time, and was not prepared to sacrifice any one for another. Nor was she prepared to sacrifice the present for the future; she rightly suspected that her future would be short.

One more work by George Sand was inspired by La Malibran. This was her '*histoire lyrique*' *Le Contrebandier*,[20] written in Switzerland in 1836, and inspired by Liszt's *Rondeau fantastique*[21] on Manuel Garcia's *polo*, *El contrabandista*.

El contrabandista, the song of a smuggler, an outlaw, occurs in Garcia's *El poeta calculista*.[22] The song was an immediate hit in Spain and, when Garcia performed it with his usual verve in Paris in 1808, it created a furore. Some authorities consider that 'it launched the Spanish popular [musical] idiom on its way round the world.'[23] Garcia himself thought the song was a summing-up of an artist's life. The idea of the smuggler, living outside society, appealed greatly to the Romantic imagination; Mérimée's *Carmen* is the most celebrated example. Victor Hugo used the words of Garcia's song in his first novel, *Bug Jargal*; Berlioz 'often sang' the song and taught it to Alfred de Vigny, who taught it to Augusta Holmès when she was a child.[24] More recently, it figures in F. Garcia Lorca's *Mariana Pineda*.

La Malibran often sang *El contrabandista*, and it was her performances of it which inspired Liszt and George Sand. Like everything

---

* *Les Maîtres sonneurs* (1853), which deals with popular music and musicians, may be considered the pendant to *Consuelo*, which deals with courtly music.

to do with her father, this song always affected her deeply, and on one occasion, at least, she fainted after singing it. George Sand attributed La Malibran's emotions to 'memories of her native land' (which she had never visited), and to 'childhood memories'.[25] She was probably right about the childhood memories.

Liszt and George Sand wrote their respective works in Switzerland towards the end of September, 1836. La Malibran died on 23rd September, but the news can scarcely have reached Geneva before they were completed; by the time *Le Contrebandier* was published, in January, 1837, it had become a kind of elegy. It is not a work of great literary distinction, but reiterates the theme of the free artist, living outside Society, so dear to George Sand's heart.

13

While La Malibran was in England in the summer of 1830, political tension had been mounting in France. A series of decrees published at the end of July — they included the abolition of the freedom of the press, the dissolution of the chambers, and the repeal of the electoral laws — brought things to a head. On 26th July a rehearsal of *Guillaume Tell* took place at the Opéra; when in Act II Guillaume Tell pronounced the words '*Ou l'indépendance ou la mort!*' people watching the rehearsall— singers, stage-hands, carpenters — took up the cry with such vehemence that it was impossible to proceed. Many of the men seized any weapon they could find, and ran out into the street. Two days later, revolution broke out. As a result of the 'July Days', 28th, 29th and 30th July, '*les trois glorieuses*', Charles X abdicated, and the Duc d'Orléans, as Louis-Philippe, was proclaimed king of France. Liberalism had, it seemed, triumphed; and a new and better age appeared to be dawning. Victor Hugo's Romantic slogan, 'freedom in Art, freedom in Society!', was on everyone's lips.

Writing to his wife from Paris a month later, Mendelssohn's father told her: 'In all classes and trades here young people's brains are in a state of ferment; they smell regeneration, liberty, novelty, and want to have their share of it [. . .] The young ones want to rule, and the old ones do not like it . . .'[1]

La Malibran wrote to Legouvé from Norwich bitterly regretting that she had not been in Paris to witness, or even to take part in, the great events.

> Do you think that armed soldiers would have been able to prevent me from shouting long live freedom? They tell me that things still aren't quiet in France, write and tell me; I shall go there! I want to share the lot of my brothers. They say that well-ordered charity begins at home, with oneself! Well, others are *my myself*. Long live France![2]

Whether Bériot greeted the revolution with as much enthusiasm has not been recorded; as a result of it, he lost one of his main sources of income, his appointment as principal violinist to Charles X.

He was soon to lose his other source: his appointment to the King of the Netherlands. On 25th August, a performance of Auber's *La Muette de Portici* was being given at the Théâtre de la Monnaie in Brussels. In 1830 the story of Auber's opera, which concerns events in Naples in 1647 when the fishermen rose against their Spanish oppressors, was sensitive material. The Belgians had long been dissatisfied with their status as what they considered to be an oppressed minority under the King of the Netherlands, and recent events in Paris had set them an example. As the opera proceeded, with frequent appeals to liberty on the stage, the audience became frenzied with excitement, and people rushed out into the street, shouting: 'Let us copy the Parisians!' A mob formed, and began to destroy public buildings and the homes of unpopular officials; the revolt soon spread to the provinces. The Bériot family, French-speaking and Catholic, supported the Belgian cause.

In spite of the fact that Charles and Maria were having a kind of honeymoon in England, his first thought was for his sister; he left England immediately for Brussels. Maria continued to fulfil her engagements in the English provinces alone. They did not meet again for almost three months.

Charles remained in Belgium, consoling and supporting his sister, whose fiancé, Lieutenant Joseph de Francquen, was taking a more active part in events than Charles, fighting with his regiment against the Dutch. For his part, Charles composed some patriotic songs, for which he was given the Iron Cross. At the beginning of November, he was about to leave Brussels to rejoin Maria when he heard some worrying news about the fighting round Anvers, where his future brother-in-law was. He at once wrote to Maria:

'This bad news put my poor Constance in such despair that I couldn't dream of leaving her [. . .] Constance assures me that you would be cross with me if I were to abandon her in her present uncertainty. So, till tomorrow [i.e. in another letter], my good little wife.'[3] Not every 'good little wife' would have been as tolerant of Bériot's order of priorities — his sister always first, Maria second — but Maria seems to have realised that, if she wanted to keep Charles, she had to keep Constance, too.

La Malibran returned to Paris in the autumn of 1830, as the goddess of triumphant Romanticism. Freedom in Art, freedom in

Society was the order of the day, and she personified it. On stage, her performances contained all the revolutionary artistic excesses which her contemporaries craved; off stage she no longer hid her liaison with Bériot, but set up house with him. Her friends saw this as yet another Romantic gesture; and indeed, this was one of the first of the great Romantic liaisons. Others already existed, or were soon to follow: Alfred de Vigny with Marie Dorval; Victor Hugo with Juliette Drouet; Balzac with Madame Hanska; Liszt with Marie d'Agoult; Aurore Dudevant with a succession of lovers culminating, when she had already become George Sand, in her liaisons with Alfred de Musset and Chopin. These Romantic love affairs, seen then and by posterity as the ultimate Romantic gesture of artists who sacrificed everything for love, are in many cases better remembered today than the works those artists created.

At La Malibran's first appearance in the theatre that season she was acclaimed as 'the foremost lyric tragedienne' no longer of the world, but 'of the universe'.[4] Every time she appeared there were extravagant scenes in the theatre, and extravagant articles in the press.[5] Like the Romantic movement — euphoric, but soon to begin to diversify and disintegrate — La Malibran had reached her peak.

She was twenty-two years old, and living with the man she loved. In the theatre she had no rivals, and there seemed no limit to what she might achieve in her career. The public adored her. Her friends included the most celebrated and talented men of the day. Love, fame, wealth and happiness were hers. Only one thing could spoil her future, and this now occurred: her husband Eugène Malibran arrived in Paris.

No letters from La Malibran to her husband between July, 1829, and December, 1830 — in other words, after the beginning of her relationship with Bériot — have been preserved. Perhaps she did not write any, for even before that the correspondence had become very irregular. Eugène Malibran had probably been kept informed about events in Paris by his sister and other relations. Probably news of his wife's liaison with Bériot had eventually reached him in New York, and the vast sums of money which she was earning were mentioned in the papers. He decided to come to Europe to claim his rights.

Eugène Malibran had rights; but his wife had none. The threat to her happiness with Bériot terrified her. Moreover, if she had gone through some bigamous marriage ceremony with Bériot, Eugène Malibran could ruin her. She refused to see him. Instead, she sent him a note, in which her handwriting clearly betrays the emotion with which it was written:

> Since you have the intention of making me happy, *leave at once*, or if you stay, do so only in order to consent to a *divorce*, do you understand? It is the only way left to you to prove what you say. I beg you for this purpose to go to see Monsieur Labois, No. 42, rue Coquillière. *Say who you are*, he is informed of my intentions. Consent, and by this means you will be able still to find a little gratitude in the heart of
>
> Marie, née Garcia[6]

Eugène Malibran did not relinquish his rights immediately, or comply with her request. Desperate, La Malibran mobilised her friends to help her. Louis Viardot, always reserved and discreet, was involved in negotiations between husband and wife. But soon a much more powerful person than Viardot came to her assistance. Three days after writing the note to her husband, she received a letter from General Lafayette:

> You know, *chère Madame*, that we have to pay a visit today. Monsieur Rives, Minister of the United States, has sent me a reply which is very kind both to you and to me, offering all his advice and all his help.

As La Malibran had been married in New York, the help of Lafayette and of the American minister in obtaining a divorce was of great importance. However, Lafayette went on to say:

> I don't suggest that we should see the minister at mid-day, because I saw yesterday evening that you were not feeling well; I was even told the sad reason. [The 'sad reason' was, in all probability, another pregnancy.] You will not doubt the tender sympathy which I feel for your misfortunes. There was something instinctive about the first feelings of interest in you which I felt; but since I have got to know you, *chère Madame*, I cannot express to you all the attachment you inspire in me, or how much I would be happy to bring some consolation and some remedy to your sorrows. You have been good enough to choose me as your guardian; I beg you, my dear ward, to accept my fond affection,
>
> Lafayette[7]

The General, who had participated in the American Revolution

'After playing Fidalma in Cimarosa's opera Il Matrimonio Segreto Malibran went into a pit box to see the ballet, or rather to afford the Public a better opportunity of appreciating her powers of transformation.   July 31st, 1830.'

By A. E. Chalon, R.A., from his *Sketch Book*. *Crown Copyright Victoria and Albert Museum (Theatre Museum)*

Maria Malibran by Léon Viardot, brother of Louis. *Les Lettres et les arts, Vol XIV, p.94, 1889.*

Portrait in oils of La Malibran. Artist unknown; has sometimes been attributed to Delacroix. *Private collection*

La Malibran by François Bouchot (oils). According to Pauline
Viardot, this portrait, which is unfinished, is the only one which
truly resembled her sister. La Malibran is holding a horse, the
head of which can be dimly discerned behind her. *Collection of
Monsieur Robert Maupoil, Paris*

Giuditta Pasta.
*Collection of
Anthony Gasson, Lo*

Vincenzo Bellini.
*Collection of
Anthony Gasson, London*

— he had been made a Major-General of the United States by Congress in 1776, when he was twenty — who had played a prominent part in the French Revolution of 1789 — although not in its excesses — had once more, during the Revolution of 1830, played a leading rôle in events. He had taken command of the National Guard, and was the great popular hero of the day.* Now seventy-four years old, he was immensely distinguished, immensely influential, and immensely respected. That he could spare time out of his extremely busy official life to help La Malibran over her divorce was a compliment indeed.

In his old age, Lafayette still had an eye for pretty girls. Stendhal alleged that he spent his time pinching girls' bottoms, and that at the age of seventy-five he had a passion for a Portuguese girl of eighteen. 'His glory all over Europe, the innate elegance of his talk, [. . .] his eyes which light up as soon as they are a foot away from a pretty bosom — everything combines to make him pass his last years cheerfully . . .'[8]

Perhaps, when Lafayette told La Malibran that there had been at first 'something instinctive' about the interest he had taken in her, he was merely being frank. But he was also being sincere when he told her that, when he got to know her, his feelings changed into something deeper and more paternal. There was gossip about her relationship with him. Cuvillier-Fleury noted in his diary:

> *La Quotidienne* alleges that he [Lafayette] is in love with her and wants to marry her. It's a good joke, which greatly amuses people in society, where there is no respect for anything. It's certain that that crazy woman [La Malibran] is enamoured of the general, and that she is trying to get a divorce from her husband through his influence.[9]

In fact, Lafayette's letters to La Malibran are not at all amorous, but deeply affectionate; and there is something rather touching about this immensely distinguished old man's solicitude for his young ward.

At a performance of *Tancredi* that season, La Malibran showed her gratitude to him. As Lafayette made his way to his box, he

---

* Lafayette was so popular that the actress Marie Dorval, bored by all the fuss about him, said: 'Let him be awarded a tricolour wig, and don't let anyone mention him to me again!' (Marcel Bouteron, *Muses romantiques*, Paris, 1934, p. 143.)

received an ovation from the audience as the hero of the day — and of so many other days. The opera began; Tancredi (La Malibran) made his entrance, dressed as a warrior, with helmet and sword. La Malibran went towards the footlights and, fixing her gaze on Lafayette, presented arms to the old soldier. 'One can well imagine how, at that epoch of general excitement, when all hearts were so easily overcome by emotion, a thunder of applause greeted this gesture, which was as felicitous as it was unexpected.'[10]

No heart was more touched by this gesture than that of Lafayette himself. He referred to it in a letter to La Malibran written over three years later[11] when he had fallen from favour with Louis-Philippe and she was in Italy. He remembered the incident as having taken place not in *Tancredi*, but in *Semiramide* — Arsace in *Semiramide*, a part often taken by La Malibran, is also a warrior.

As Eugène Malibran did not at first agree to a divorce, Lafayette made what was probably a half-hearted attempt to persuade Maria to agree to a reconciliation. He wrote to Eugène Malibran on 2nd January, 1831, to tell him what had happened:

> You are familiar with the character of my new ward, and in spite of her friendliness and respect to me, you know that her thoughts are sharp, and her whims strong. Her first reaction on arriving at my house was fear that she might meet you there, and then, after having listened to everything I could tell her about your desire for a reconciliation, her refusal was so peremptory that there remains no possibility of my using my influence . . .

Lafayette went on to try to persuade Eugène Malibran that, since a reconciliation was impossible, it would be more dignified for him to grant his wife a divorce, rather than to try to enforce his rights with the aid of the law. Lafayette pointed out that public opinion would be against Malibran, since his wife was adored by the public. He also pointed out, with tact, that his refusal to grant a divorce might lead to some strain on La Malibran's 'virtue, unspotted until now, and on your name, which she has not yet ceased to make respectable.'[12] Here the General was treading on thin ice, for he knew about La Malibran's liaison with Bériot, and that she was probably pregnant by him.

Lafayette's advice, together, it is said, with large sums of money from La Malibran,[13] had some effect on Eugène Malibran. He did not pursue his rights; but the fear that he might do so, and perhaps also the fear that he might denounce her as a bigamist, never left her. The question of divorce became an obsession with her, and was to haunt her continually for the next four years. It became the most important thing in her life — more important than her career, more important, perhaps, than her love for Bériot, for without peace of mind there could be no happiness.* She spent vast sums of money, mobilised lawyers all over Europe; but, although the lawyers grew rich, the law was infinitely slow. Since the Saint-Simonites believed in divorce, La Malibran supported them.

Although his wife and, consequently, all her friends, vilified Eugène Malibran and made him out to be a monster, in fact he seems to have behaved in as dignified and gentlemanly a way as was possible under the circumstances. La Malibran was his wife, and he, it seems, loved her. He was perhaps naïve enough to imagine that, in the two years during which they had been separated, she had not changed, and had remained the same immature and affectionate person he had known. Until he arrived in Paris he can have had little idea, despite her letters, of the extraordinary and unique position she held there. He made some attempts to win her back, and when he saw that his cause was hopeless, resigned himself to his position. It was not an enviable one. The elderly, cuckolded husband of a super-star is, at best, a figure of fun, and at worst a villain. La Malibran, who saw life as opera, chose to cast him as a villain; for the rest of her life she gave, to anyone who would listen, a completely false account of her marriage and of her relationship with her husband. But there is no evidence that Malibran, after his initial attempt to win back his wife had failed, ever tried to harm her by word or deed. He remained a passive and forgotten spectator of her meteoric career, lonely and ageing, far removed from the brilliant circles in which she moved. No one bothered to defend him in his lifetime, and history has accepted his wife's version of their story.

As the year 1830 drew to a close, La Malibran and Bériot were happy, despite their problems. It had been a momentous year for France, for Belgium, and for them personally. They were now setting up house together in Paris. Charles wrote to his sister — his 'dear

---

* From a letter to one of her lawyers it is clear that, at one point, La Malibran hoped to sue her husband, 'the bear Malibran', but she had to abandon this plan. In the same letter she refers to 'this lawsuit, this devil, which makes my life a torment'. (Ms. letter to Labois, n.d., Brussels Conservatoire).

heart' — to ask her to send him his furniture, his piano, his violins and his music. He wished her 'for the year 1831 the happiness which I am enjoying at the end of 1830'. Maria added a postscript to the letter, in which she told Constance to look in her mirror, where she would see a resemblance to Charles. 'Do it often, and think of my happiness . . . with all my heart I wish you as much happiness as I have.'[14]

14

By the beginning of 1831 the mood of optimistic euphoria, which had overwhelmed the youth of France in 1830, was beginning to dissolve, and disillusion was already setting in. The Romantic movement had lost some of its momentum, and the high hopes which had been set on the July monarchy were beginning to fade. The political situation was anything but calm; there were frequent riots, and the government was obliged to employ more and more repressive measures.

Artistic life was as intense as ever, but it took place in an uneasy atmosphere. Cuvillier-Fleury who, as tutor to Louis-Philippe's son, lived with the royal family in the Palais Royal, noted in his diary:

> At a quarter to seven I was going to dress for the concert in the evening, when I heard a great clamour in the square; it was a riot; twelve hundred wretches were shouting: Long live the king! and wanted to break down the doors of the palace, they were asking for bread, and were staggering from drink. Twenty-five soldiers charged them with rifle-butts and dispersed the groups, after having taken about thirty prisoners, all riff-raff [. . .] Two hours later, a brilliant concert in the salons of the palace had drawn a numerous and select audience; the voices of Madame Malibran, of Bordogni and Nourrit had succeeded the bandits' howls; patrols were circulating round the palace, which seemed a besieged place, to which the sentries only admitted men in evening-dress and women loaded with diamonds and flowers.[1]

Although many great Romantic triumphs in the arts were still to come, the excitement and spirit of unity which had been engendered by *Hernani* had proved a peak which was never quite recaptured again. The young Romantics who had supported Hugo were now beginning to follow their own independent paths. Despite a magnificent performance by Marie Dorval, Hugo's *Marion Delorme* (11th August, 1831) was only a semi-success; the battalion of young

Romantics, mobilised as a *claque* for *Hernani,* no longer rallied to their leader in quite the same way. Political and personal disagreements were beginning to make the group split up. They were all still Romantics, but each one followed his own individual bent; some moved towards aestheticism, others towards committed art, others towards religion or the supernatural.

With the decline of the idealism of 1830, commercial interests were beginning to cash in on Romantic ideas. Originally the inspiration of a small dedicated group of creative artists, they were now beginning to be taken over, in a distorted and cheapened form, by the wide public. What had begun as an artistic movement was fast degenerating into a fashion. The public was getting used to Romanticism and to the Romantics; both had lost some of their power to shock; long hair and odd clothes no longer attracted much attention in the streets.

In the world of opera, three astute men had already noticed this trend and were preparing to take advantage of it. Dr Véron, director of the Opéra, saw great possibilities in Eugène Scribe's libretto, *Robert le diable,* and in Meyerbeer's score for it; he decided to put the opera into production. He set about it slowly and carefully, and no effort or expense was spared.

Véron, Scribe and Meyerbeer were made for each other. Véron supplied the business acumen, organising ability, cynicism and flair for publicity. 'He sensed,' wrote Philarète Chasles, 'that literature was going to become industrial,' and he became 'the Mercury of intellectual materialism.'[2] Scribe supplied his skill as a librettist, and his excellent sense and knowledge of the theatre. Meyerbeer's contribution was his thorough German musical technique, tempered by much experience in Italy; his adaptability; and his flair for sensing what the public wanted. He was very skilled in the use of publicity, and had a network of spies and what we would now call PROs throughout Europe. Véron, Scribe and Meyerbeer were the first great artistic publicists of the new, bourgeois era; they realised that commercial success in the theatre in future depended on attracting the middle classes.

The result was that throughout the summer and autumn of 1831, people in Paris talked of nothing but the new opera which was being prepared at the Opéra, and awaited its production with the greatest excitement. Anything else which was performed in this waiting period aroused little interest. At the Théâtre Italien, for so long the leading operatic theatre in Paris, the great Pasta, now past her prime, failed to draw the public, and Bellini's *La sonnambula*, his first opera to be heard in Paris, received tepid reviews.

La Malibran returned to Paris at the beginning of November. The directors of the Théâtre Italien hoped that she would draw the public back to their theatre, as she always had done in the past. She made her first appearance in *La gazza ladra* on 8th November, and was given a tremendous welcome by her admirers. But, almost immediately, things began to go wrong. She was not in good health, and there were again frequent cancellations of performances; her voice seemed to have deteriorated. Her benefit performance, on 20th November, was singularly ill-timed, for it was on the evening before the long-awaited first night of *Robert le diable* at the Opéra; as a result, the Théâtre Italien was half-empty.

On the following night, *Robert le diable* was first performed at the Opéra. There was an all-star cast: Mademoiselle Dorus-Gras, Madame Cinti-Damoreau, Nourrit, Levasseur, and Marie Taglioni in the important ballet. The décor was extremely lavish and striking. The performance was an unparalleled success. People talked of nothing else for months; Véron made a great deal of money; the Opéra became the most fashionable theatre in Paris; and Rossini's supremacy in Paris was broken. A new era had opened — the era of Meyerbeer and French grand opera, which was to last for more than a generation.

Robert le diable provided everything which the new middle-class public wanted: a magnificent spectacle, star performers, value for money, and current artistic trends watered down for popular consumption. It was like a sumptuous Hollywood musical. Although it contained all the visible and external ingredients of Romanticism, it was not Romanticism, but an artificial brew concocted by three clever men for commercial reasons. The public loved it — the spectacle, the music, the supernatural element, the simplified Faustian theme, and the midnight orgy of ghostly nuns led by Taglioni. And it must be admitted, in fairness to Meyerbeer and Scribe, that many discerning people admired it, too.

On the night of the première a young poet, Antoine Fontaney, went to the Théâtre Italien. He noted in his diary: '. . . *Tancredi* was performed. Rubini sings deliciously; and Madame Malibran, how beautiful, graceful, ravishing she is in *Tancredi*! God! what charm music has! I was almost crying! What an inconceivable thing!'[3] But the theatre was half-empty; everyone had gone to *Robert le diable*.

A half-empty theatre, the knowledge that she was no longer the principal attraction in Paris, and indifferent or even hostile reviews, were a shock to La Malibran who had never encountered anything like that before in her whole career. But she had another, much more serious problem; she was again pregnant, and this time everyone knew it, it was the talk of the town, just as Sontag's pregnancy had been in 1828. And the town was even less indulgent to La Malibran than it had been to Sontag, for La Malibran was married, and not living with her husband. In 1828 Maria had herself been none too charitable to Sontag, and had noted that her reputation had collapsed 'like a soufflé'.[4] Now it was happening to her. She was fast ceasing to be a goddess, and was becoming just an actress, an outcast, classed with prostitutes, rejected by Society.

The first person to reject her was her father. 'My daughter's conduct offends and dishonours the whole family,' he said. 'A bohemian life is one thing, but it is a totally different matter that Mariquita is now expecting a child, when it is well-known to everyone that she has been separated from her husband for years . . .'[5] The fact that most, if not all, of Garcia's own children were illegitimate or born of a bigamous marriage did nothing to soften his rage, and his rages had not diminished with the years. He refused to see his daughter; as in the past, her mother surreptitiously kept in touch with her.

La Malibran was now enacting in real life a scene which she had played innumerable times on the stage. In Act II of Rossini's *Otello*, Desdemona sings:

> *L'error d'un infelice*
> *ah Padre, mi perdona.*
> *Si il padre m'abbandona,*
> *da chi sperar pietà?*

To which Elmiro (Desdemona's father) replies that she does not merit any pity, and the chorus sings:

> *Se metre nel suo petto*
> *un impudice affetto*
> *giusta è la crudeltà.*

'If my father abandons me, from whom can I hope for compassion?' Garcia's reply was as implacable as Elmiro's: 'If you take on a shameless love, cruelty is justified.' Art was being transformed into life. Despite her father's faults, his approval had always been more important to Maria than that of any audience; in this moment of crisis, he rejected her.

The next person to do so was Madame Naldi's daughter, the Comtesse de Sparre. She refused to receive La Malibran; as the daughter of a singer who had succeeded in marrying into the aristocracy, she had to be particularly careful. This second rejection cut Maria to the quick; she and the Comtesse de Sparre were old friends, and were roughly the same age. 'Not even a glance, not even a nod!' she said. 'Why, it's as if she had never known me! What disdain!'[6]

Other houses where La Malibran had been received in the past became closed to her; people who had once seemed to be very friendly greeted her coldly, or not at all. She felt that everyone was talking about her, unkindly, behind her back. Someone suggested that she could solve her problem by going back to live with her husband, in which case she would be received by everyone, as in the past.

'What!' she replied. 'Repudiate all I love and commit the most base, the most vile act in order to escape what your prejudices call dishonour! No, I'd rather suffer.'[7]

And suffer she did. This pregnancy was particularly ill-timed; she knew that it would become visible before the end of the season, that she might not be able to fulfil her obligations in the theatre. She knew that people would talk about it; and they did. Mérimée discussed it — in terms which were exceptionally crude, even for him — in a letter to Stendhal written on 1st December, 1831.[8] He said that she was then five months pregnant; he was probably right.

In addition to the real rebuffs which La Malibran received from her father and her 'friends', there was the criticism and hostility which she imagined. In the theatre, she was scrutinised by everyone in the audience; as her condition became more and more visible, she believed that everyone could see it, and was commenting on it. There was hostility to her from audiences at that time, but the real cause of it was probably the fact that so many of her performances were cancelled. With a touch of paranoia, La Malibran imagined that she was despised as a fallen woman; perhaps in some cases this was so.

She imagined, too, that her fellow artists had turned against her, and she wrote to the soprano, Madame Caradori-Allan, to accuse her of hostility. Madame Caradori-Allan, who had known Maria since childhood, had stood in for her that autumn during one of her indispositions, and there had been some disagreeable incident concerned with this, for which La Malibran appears to have been to blame. However, Madame Caradori-Allan, a good singer but not a great star, well known for her charm and good nature, sent La Malibran a friendly and tactful reply, denying that her attitude to her had changed.

> Doubtless you will say that I have allowed myself to be influenced by rumours which are circulating to your detriment. Well! To this I reply that I do not listen to them; I very well know that it suffices to be famous and admired to make anyone attack and slander one. [However, Madame Caradori-Allan did go on to say:] Your letter mentions things which I do not understand, and do not wish to understand; I cannot conceive how a *law** which is going to be passed can make you more or less estimable, but I desire with all my heart that it may increase your happiness.[9]

According to Madame Merlin, one evening during a performance La Malibran felt very unwell and depressed. She suddenly left the stage, went to her dressing-room, and locked herself in. Through the closed door she announced that she was too ill to go on with the performance. The theatre director tried in vain to persuade her to go back on the stage. The audience waited impatiently; there were hostile murmurs, and the stamping of feet. In despair, the director appealed to the Marquis de Marmier, a friend of La Malibran's, who was in the audience, and asked him to use his influence to persuade her. Marmier knocked at the door of her dressing-room, and announced who he was. After a moment, he was admitted. He found La Malibran half-lying on a sofa, almost completely undressed. Marmier saw at a glance the cause of her indispositions. La Malibran realised this and, in tears, said: 'I'm lost. You despise me already, and soon the public will despise me too.' Marmier, 'full of pity and, at the same time, embarrassed', tried to console her; he finally succeeded in persuading her to finish the performance. But the audience had been kept waiting too long, and was not inclined to be indulgent.[10]

There is little doubt that La Malibran did not want the child she was expecting. By this time she had had several pregnancies which had ended in miscarriages or abortions, and probably in at least one birth — when, and where, is not certain. At that time, illegitimate

---

* La Malibran had probably referred in her letter to the revision of the divorce laws, then being discussed in the Chambre des Députés.

children were concealed, farmed out to foster parents, never mentioned. There are no references to any of her children — including the son who survived her — in any of her letters which have so far come to light.

She had to defend herself on other fronts, too. The Saint-Simonite sect, which had started as a political and social movement, offering something genuinely new and an alternative life style, under *le père* Enfantin was fast degenerating into a farcical quasi-religious mumbo-jumbo with unsavoury sexual overtones. The sect recruited young people in an underhand way, cut them off from their families, and tried to get hold of their money. Mendelssohn told a friend:

> I attended a meeting last Sunday, where all the Fathers sat in a circle; then came the principal Father and demanded their reports, praising and blaming them, and addressing the assembly and issuing his commands; to me it was quite awful! A. has completely renounced his parents and lives with the Fathers, and his disciples, and is endeavouring to procure a loan for their benefit . . .[11]

Reputable people, who had originally been attracted by Saint-Simon's ideas, began to disassociate themselves from the sect, and the government was eventually forced to close it. La Malibran, who could ill afford another blow to her reputation, wrote to the editor of a newspaper:

> It is said by the public, and some newspapers have repeated it, that I belong to the Society of Saint-Simon, that I am one of its priestesses, that I have preached at the Salle Taitbout, and so on. I am anxious to contradict these rumours, which are completely false. I know the Society of Saint-Simon by name only. I have seen none of its members. I have never attended any of its meetings. [I am] exclusively occupied by the art which is my profession. It absorbs all my time and energy . . .[12]

Financial worries, caused by her pregnancy, were added to her other troubles. She and Charles had nothing but what they earned, and he was not earning very much at that time, due to Paganini's arrival in France and to the loss of his two royal appointments. La Malibran had not sung during the lucrative London season that year, due to an earlier 'indisposition'. Her popularity in France was waning, and directors now saw her as an unreliable star; moreover, as a result of the success of *Robert le diable* the Théâtre Italien, to which she was committed, was losing its position as the foremost operatic theatre.

She appeared infrequently in December; on 3rd January, 1832, she gave a performance of *L'italiana in Algeria* and *La prova d'un opera seria* with Lablache. On 8th January she appeared, visibly unwell, in a concert with Bériot, in which she sang only two arias. She was not merely six or seven months pregnant, but also had a very bad cold. The audience was moved partly by pity, and partly by admiration for the way she triumphed over her disabilities. Wrote the critic of *La Revue musicale*,

> It was one of those victories which only a great artist can carry off, but which are fatal to the victor. To be sure, so far as I am concerned, I am more than ever convinced that Madame Malibran is the foremost singer of our time, but Madame Malibran should not buy her glory at the price of ruining, perhaps sacrificing, her future.[13]

Her benefit performance, on 20th January, 1832, was as Desdemona in *Otello*, the Parisians' favourite opera. With a supreme effort, she seems to have regained some of her powers. But she was unable to finish the season, and had to break her contract.

The goddess of Romanticism fled incognito from the scene of her former triumphs. She went to Brussels, but Bériot and his family presumably feared the scandal of an illegitimate birth in Belgium, for Charles de Bériot, with La Malibran disguised in a blonde wig, returned secretly to Paris, where they had rented a house with a large garden. Hidden there, they awaited the birth of their child.[14]

Despite all their problems, a letter from Maria to Constance shows that it was a relatively happy period.

> I could never tell you enough what an angel dear Charles is to me. He's kind enough to say that he likes it here, that he's not bored, and would spend his whole life here with me! You know how much I take his heart into consideration; however, it could very well be that he's sincere in what he says for, for the last four or five days you've no idea what delicious things come into his head [...] We no longer say the slightest word about *composition*; the most perfect harmony reigns between us . . .[15]

One must assume from this letter that Charles was not always sincere, and that there had not always been perfect harmony between them in the past.

Their child* was probably born early in March, 1832. The event was hushed up, and the child did not, apparently, survive very long. By 25th March La Malibran and Bériot were back in Brussels, and appeared together in a concert there.

They had left Paris just in time. The year 1832 had not opened well for anyone; the mood was no longer one of hope, but of foreboding. On 22nd January the Saint-Simonites' headquarters was closed by the police; further repressive measures followed. One night, at the beginning of February, some people were walking home in fancy-dress after a party. One of them suddenly felt ill; he was taken to hospital, still dressed as Punch, but died on his way there.[16] It was the first case of a cholera epidemic, which was to kill thousands. The theatres were closed, even *Robert le diable* could not entice people out. 'Everyone, audiences and artists alike,' said Dr Véron, 'was trying only to save his own skin.'[17]

It is said that La Malibran vowed that she would never sing in Paris again until she was married to Bériot. In fact, she never again dared face a Parisian audience.†

---

* Although Fétis and other sources refer to this child as a daughter, Bernard Huys in *L'École belge de violon* (Brussels, 1978, p. 18) says it was a son, and names him: Franz. Huys says the child was born in February, 1832, which is probably roughly correct. However, Huys may have confused the name and sex of this child with Bériot's son by his second marriage, Franz-Charles, who was born in 1841. Fétis's statement that the child was born in November, 1832, is clearly wrong — by then La Malibran was already pregnant again (see p. 169) — but he also states that La Malibran 'already had a son'. Another source (Claude Cantal — *Vieux souvenirs*, n.d.) says their daughter died in Italy. There is no other evidence for this. The whole question of La Malibran's children remains obscure; the American edition of Countess Merlin's book merely says (I, p. 42) that she had 'several children' by Bériot, but gives no details.

† In 1832 Bériot and Viardot did try to negotiate another contract for La Malibran with the Théâtre Italien, but failed, perhaps because their terms were not acceptable, or because of the cholera, but most probably because the Théâtre Italien directors thought her too unreliable. (Letter from Bériot to Viardot, 24th February, 1832. Heron-Allen, p. 3.) In 1835 La Malibran turned down offers from Paris, saying that, as she had many other engagements, she would be tired, and did not wish to face a Parisian audience until she was on top form (letter to Baron Pérignon, 14th December, 1835, *cit.* Pougin, p. 192–3).

15

What had happened? How had a goddess, a priestess, become an outcast? Why had the greatest living prima donna suddenly been rejected by the Parisian audiences which had deified her? What had happened was that La Malibran, because of the grave problems of her private life — because she had not obtained a divorce, because of her illicit love affair and an illegitimate pregnancy — had shown that she was not divine, but all too human, and had sinned against the laws of Society. More seriously, by failing to comply with the public's wishes, by cancelling too many performances because she was depressed, out of sorts or pregnant, she had forgotten the law that stars are stars only so long as they do what the public wants.

The complicated and contradictory relationship that exists between a performing artist and his or her public must always be very delicately balanced, if the artist is to survive. The relationship can never be equal, for the public is always the master; and the artist's ability to remain at the top, in a dominant position, depends on his or her skill in 'conquering' the public, while in reality merely holding it at bay. The dividing line between love and hate in this relationship is thin indeed. For an artist to be faced by several hundred people is an exhilarating experience when they are friendly; when they are not, it can be a terrifying ordeal.

Until the end of 1830, when she was still only twenty-two, La Malibran's relationship with her public had been exceptionally long and unusually happy. Her first encounters with an audience, at the age of five or six, had been entirely successful even though, on one occasion, as we have already described, she had suddenly refused to go on performing. This early lapse had been forgiven, because she was a child.

At her first professional appearance in the theatre, at the age of seventeen, she was very favourably received, and from then on her career had had no significant setbacks. In America, where she had no competition, she was adulated; and her success when she first appeared in Paris was immediate and overwhelming.

La Malibran understood her public, and was a skilled professional. 'In that rare art, the power of exciting an audience,' said *The Times*, 'she is without a rival.'[1] She knew how to obtain applause, and rarely failed to receive it. 'Avid for popular successes, she neglected nothing to obtain them; she did not even disdain certain little tricks of charlatanism to achieve this end, although no one had less need of them.'[2] Mérimée noticed one of these tricks: how she would take a stance on the stage, 'as if saying to the audience: "Take a good look at me, sketch me, I'm posing." '[3] Accused of being too cold in the first scene of an opera, she said:

> You don't understand anything about it. The heads in the pit are, to me, a multitude of unlit candles, lined up in a basket; if one approaches them immediately with a mass of fire, the candles melt. If, on the contrary, you light them up gradually, you obtain a brilliant illumination. I *light up* my audience, little by little.[4]

Her performances in the theatre to a large audience were quite different from those she gave in private houses, where the audience was usually much more discriminating. 'My dear cross-patch,' she told Fétis, who had accused her of playing too much to the gallery, 'there are scarcely two or three connoisseurs in a large hall where I sing; it's not they who make a success, and it's successes I want. When I'll sing for you alone, I'll do it differently.'[5] And she did; accounts of her singing to real connoisseurs — Mendelssohn, the Novellos, Moscheles, Thalberg — show that, on such occasions, she abandoned 'her little tricks of charlatanism', and was capable of rising to great artistic heights.[6]

Despite her continual success, La Malibran was exceptionally sensitive to the public's reactions, for she was one of those artists who cannot perform well without strong encouragement. When applause was forbidden in a theatre because of protocol, she would go to great lengths to get the rules changed; in Naples, where the audience could not applaud until the king applauded, she personally asked the king to applaud as soon as she appeared on the stage.[7] Her whole mood depended on the audience's reaction; applause not only stimulated her, it was essential to her. She would have been unable to perform well, perhaps unable to perform at all, in a recording studio.

She looked on applause as her due, a recompense for her exertions. After singing an aria she would 'boldly throw up her little head [. . .] and look at the audience, as if she wanted to ask, "Well, have I done my part honestly? Then do yours as honestly, and applaud." And applause never failed to come.'[8]

Having 'conquered' the audience in the early scenes of an opera, and herself excited by the applause, she would then begin willingly to 'give herself' ever more to the audience, and a great performance, an act of love between artist and public, would take place. In such performances — and they were many — a perfect relationship between performer and audience was achieved. Each gave something to the other; and at the end of the performance artist and public would go their ways, excited, happy, fulfilled, satisfied, loving each other.

But the public, having made La Malibran into a great star — for, however great an artist's talent may be, only the public can make stars — considered that it owned her; without it, she was nothing, and it expected her to entertain it, to move it even, whenever it so demanded. If her private life was interesting, glamorous, *Romantic*, the public admired and applauded; but it did so only provided her private life did not prevent her from satisfying its wishes, and did not go counter to its rules.

Lulled by her amazing successes, and by her own Romantic love for Bériot, La Malibran forgot that the public owned her, and she began to treat it in an off-hand manner. Her 'indispositions' became too frequent; her performances were often cancelled. The public, at first disappointed, then annoyed at seeing her apparently perfectly well the next day, decided that her absences were due to caprice. They probably often were; but her frequent pregnancies seriously affected her health, her performances, and her mentality. She gave herself unwillingly, for money alone, and her performances were no longer an act of love, but more like prostitution.

The public, dissatisfied and jealous — for La Malibran had been unfaithful to it — took its revenge, and began calling her to order. She had ceased to be a goddess, and had become merely a recalcitrant singer. Audiences became cold, even hostile; having never experienced this before, La Malibran could neither understand it nor accept that it might be her fault, as a letter which she sent to Robert, director of the Théâtre Italien, shows:

Tuesday evening,
24th February, 1831

My Dear Robert,

For the first time in my life the public, in general so kind and indulgent towards me, has proved to be cold, glacial and almost malevolent to me! What have I done to displease it? Can the public have a grudge against me today because the opera was changed, when I, unwell, ill, scarcely in a fit state to sing the small part of Zerlina, consented, because Monsieur Sontini was indisposed, and above all so as not to oblige you to disappoint the public by closing the theatre, agreed to play a part which made me even more ill than I was and which obviously made me incur the public's disfavour, since it was very clear to everyone that the public attributed the change of opera to a caprice on my part — I am sorry, my dear Robert, to have to attribute to you the unpleasantness which I experienced this evening and I am hurt to the depths of my heart by it, since you did not inform the public of this fact. When I am fortunate enough to obtain some success I feel that I am amply rewarded for all the efforts I make to the detriment of my health. But when, having killed myself to please everyone, I get a cold reception which I certainly did not deserve, discouragement overwhelms me and I do not feel strong enough to dare reappear on the stage until I have fully recovered all my powers. I swear to you, my dear Robert, that I would not hesitate a moment to break my engagement and leave the theatre, were I able to do so without damaging your interests. To sum all this up, I beg of you to vindicate me instantly in the eyes of the public, either through the press, or by any other means before Saturday night — for to tell the truth I tremble at the thought of appearing again.[9]

The reception which La Malibran had had that night must indeed have been 'glacial' if she, Garcia's daughter, 'trembled at the thought of appearing again'.

From that time on, La Malibran realised that 'conquering' the public was an illusion; all she could do was to keep it at bay, or it would conquer her. She became afraid; the audience was no longer a lover to be wooed, but an angry mob to be placated. 'The public will kill you,' she warned a fellow-artist, 'either by their neglect or their exactions.'[10]

La Malibran could not satisfy the public's wishes because she was dedicated to the twin aims of Romanticism: Art and Love. But it is almost impossible to serve those two masters, as many Romantic artists were soon to discover. And for women, particularly in the nineteenth century, but perhaps also still today, a choice usually has to be made between private happiness and public fame. Unlike her sister,[11] La Malibran was never able to make that choice.

The general public, realising that La Malibran was not giving it her undivided attention and was not conforming to its rules, decided that she was just another actress, immoral like all the rest, and rightly censored by Church, state, and all right-minded people. Times had changed; Romanticism, it was felt, had been just a phase, and people were coming to their senses again. A few long-haired writers and artists might still go on talking about it, but life was getting back to normal, and a good thing, too.

The general public was wrong; many of the greatest manifestations of Romanticism were still to come: Taglioni in *La Sylphide*, Marie Dorval in Vigny's *Chatterton*, the music of Berlioz and Bellini, paintings of Delacroix, poems and plays by Hugo, Alfred de Musset, Gautier, Nerval, the novels of Balzac, George Sand and Stendhal, and many other works by lesser artists. These people — her friends — did not condemn La Malibran, or criticise her matrimonial affairs; on the contrary, they approved of her sacrificing everything for love, and saw her, more than ever, as the personification of Romanticism, their ideas made flesh. When she fled from Paris in 1832 she left behind her, amongst her peers, a memory which was never to be effaced; and her image was soon to be preserved in many Romantic works.

PART III

ITALY AND LONDON

1

By the spring of 1832 La Malibran and Bériot were in Belgium. She had, it seems, no child, and no engagement in the theatre. For the first time since her marriage to Eugène Malibran, six years earlier, she was free to lead the peaceful domestic life of which she had so often dreamed. But dreaming about peace and domesticity is one thing; enduring them is quite another.

Bériot was happy to be at home in Belgium, close to his sister. Plans for their new house at Ixelles went ahead; he hoped to make it a centre for the arts in Belgium, a base from which he and La Malibran could make concert tours throughout Europe. But Belgium was hardly an adequate setting for a star of La Malibran's magnitude, used to the great seasons of Paris and London, and able to shine brightest if supported by an operatic company in the theatre. She needed constant stimulus, movement, change and challenge; inactivity stultified her. Besides, she and Bériot badly needed money.

Therefore, when the bass singer Lablache, passing through Belgium on his way to Italy, suggested that La Malibran and Bériot should accompany him, she accepted with alacrity. Bériot accompanied her, as was his wont, passively but reluctantly. He disliked travelling, and was loath to leave his sister. '*Pauvre coeur*,' he told her. 'What a distance is going to separate us! But,' he added, 'one must make sacrifices for future happiness.'[1]

It is said that La Malibran was in extremely high spirits throughout the journey. It was an escape — an escape from boredom in Belgium, an escape from the humiliations which she had suffered in Paris, an escape from her husband, and an escape from her father — for Paris and its threats were too near Brussels for comfort. Italy represented her short, relatively happy childhood before her relationship with her father had begun to poison her life. Perhaps Italy would somehow restore her lost innocence; at any rate, in Rome she had hopes of obtaining a divorce or an annulment.

It would be a fresh start to her career. Italy was still the most important producer and consumer of opera in the world, although standards, particularly of orchestral playing, were low. La Malibran would not have much competition there, for there were no prima donnas of superlative quality in Italy at that time, except Pasta whom she admired but no longer feared. On the other hand, there were plenty of up and coming composers: Donizetti, then thirty-five years old, had already written many works, including *Anna Bolena* (1830); Bellini, then thirty-one, had already written most of his operas, including *Norma* and *La sonnambula*, both produced in 1831; Vaccai, forty-two, Mercadante, thirty-seven, and Pacini, thirty-six, although now forgotten, were then popular and successful; and Zingarelli, in whose *Giulietta e Romeo* La Malibran had often sung and who had known her as a child, was still very influential in Naples although then eighty years old. Verdi, nineteen years old in 1832, was still unknown; his first opera was to be staged four years later.

La Malibran needed new composers. She had sung Rossini's operas, and practically nothing else, ever since the start of her career. By early nineteenth century standards Rossini was already a little out of date, and no longer reflected the contemporary mood. La Malibran was trained in the Italian school, and French composers such as Auber and Halévy did not really suit her style. She was looking for, but had not yet found, her ideal composer, someone who would express the current mood, as she did, and who would compose an opera specially for her.

The travellers made their first prolonged stop in Rome. They had good letters of introduction, and were particularly kindly received by the painter, Horace Vernet, who was director of the Villa Medici where the French government housed winners of the Prix de Rome. La Malibran and Bériot became great friends with the Vernet family, and Horace Vernet later painted La Malibran's portrait.[2]

She had no difficulty in securing an engagement at the Teatro Valle, and preparations were going ahead for her first performance, in *Otello*, when La Malibran read in the newspaper, without any warning, of the death of her father.* She 'fainted' — or had one of her fits, which had, for a time, become less frequent.[3]

When she recovered she immediately wrote to Louis Viardot for confirmation of the news. '*Mon pauvre ami*!! What intense grief I am experiencing. It's the dagger of grief which pierces my heart a thousand times every instant.'[4]

* 9th June, 1832.

As she was then rehearsing *Otello*, so intimately connected with her father, the imagery of the dagger, although probably unconscious, can hardly have been fortuitous.

Was her grief sincere? Despite their relationship in the past, it seems that it was. Her father had been the most important influence in her life, perhaps the most important man in her life. He had made her what she was: the greatest singer of her epoch, and an unbalanced, unhappy woman. She had always feared him, often hated him and, at the same time, had been tied to him by some close bond of kinship or love. She had never been able to free herself from his poweful influence and personality. His death was both a liberation, and a grief.

They had not been reconciled before his death, although many friends had intervened. 'You know,' she told Viardot, 'that I did not want to reply to that letter which neither I nor you could conceive he could have written! Yet I had my pen in my hand a thousand times, I had such a need to write, to have news of them. [. . .] If only the cholera or the revolution could have carried off the *other one*!'5 The 'other one' was, of course, her husband.

Her instinct was to return to Paris, to her mother; but she was already engaged to appear in Rome within a few days; she went on rehearsing *Otello*.

Garcia had died at the age of fifty-seven, probably from a pulmonary infection, although it has sometimes been suggested that he was a victim of the cholera epidemic.6 Bad-tempered, violent, cruel, perhaps a pervert, he had all the same been a remarkable man who had left his mark on the musical scene in Europe and the New World, and had founded a great musical dynasty. The obituaries were numerous, and fulsome.

Garcia's younger daughter, Pauline, was eleven years old when her father died; he had not yet begun to train her voice, although he had already taught her a great deal about music and musicianship. Joaquina Garcia, after her husband's death, concentrated her not inconsiderable talents on making Pauline into a first-class singer, like her sister; in this she was helped by Maria and Bériot. Joaquina and Pauline went to live in Belgium in order to be near them, although they were hardly ever there.

With her journey to Italy and her father's death, a new epoch opened for La Malibran, the most successful of her life. The portrait of her by L. Pedrazzi (1834)* is very different from Henri Decaisne's portrait† of the distraught Desdemona painted four years earlier. Pedrazzi shows her as a beautiful, self-assured woman at the height of her powers; she is holding five flowers in her hand, the first letters of their names spelling out Bériot's name in Italian: Carlo.

After a brilliant début in Rome — although the tenor, Salvi, was no Garcia — La Malibran and Bériot went on to Naples where, despite the theatrical intrigues and cabals which were such a part of Neapolitan life, she established herself as the leading prima donna in Italy. At her last performance in Naples that season, she took twenty-five curtain calls during the performance, and six more at the end. From then on she could choose where she would sing in Italy, and name her price; the prices she named were very high.

For the rest of her life La Malibran was to divide her time between Italy and England.

* Now in the museum of La Scala, Milan.
† Now in the Musée Carnavalet, Paris.

2

La Malibran had been engaged for the 1833 pre-Lenten carnival season in Milan: forty performances, for a fee of 50,000 francs. 'That's good, even for Italy,' she told a friend. But, in the same letter, written on the day she heard of her father's death but, presumably, before she heard that news, since she did not mention it, she went on to say:

> There's only one worry, that is that I don't know if I'll have *time* to carry out this engagement in Milan . . . Sh! It's between ourselves — I hope to get out of this fix like *last time*. I'm not going to say anything about it this time, if I can transform myself . . . roughly into the shape of a broom-stick . . .[1]

But she was not able 'to get out of this fix like last time'; her son was born eight and a half months later. The contract she had with Milan had to be cancelled; this caused a lawsuit, which lasted for two years. Pregnancies cost La Malibran dear in every way.

La Malibran's son, Charles Wilfrid, was born in Brussels on 13th February, 1833. He was her only child to survive; although illegitimate, he was given his father's surname. Wilfrid, a rather uncommon Christian name in Francophone countries, happened to be one of Ernest Legouvé's Christian names.

The birth of her son did not change La Malibran's way of life. She had always lived at a fast pace; now the pace became very fast. For the next three years her life consisted almost entirely of journeys, performances and ovations. Her visits to Belgium, where her sister-in-law looked after her son, were brief and infrequent. Her little sister Pauline recalled in after years: 'I hardly knew my sister. She did not live with us, and was always away. She was mad, she could never keep still a minute, could never take up a book or some embroidery.'[2] When every theatre in Europe and some theatres in America[3] were clamouring for her services at almost any price, and the greatest composers of the day were convinced that she alone could guarantee the success of their works, La Malibran had little time, and less inclination, for embroidery.

The question of a divorce was now more urgent than ever. Her friends and numerous lawyers in different countries were mobilised to help her; but the whole business progressed very slowly. This does not appear to have been due to Eugène Malibran — on the contrary, after his initial attempt to win back his wife had failed, and having perhaps received some financial inducements from her, he seems to have given up any attempt to fight the case. The difficulties were legal: the fact that Maria Garcia, a Spanish subject born in France, had married a Frenchman who had become a naturalised American, and that the marriage had taken place in New York, gave the lawyers plenty of scope for argument and procrastination.

The question of her divorce was still a very sore point with both her and Charles; they spread rumours that it had, in fact, come through, and clung to the myth of a secret marriage. A friend reported: 'Married in very early years to a husband who had been forced on her, but liberated afterwards by special favour of the Pope, she had clung to De Bériot with true devotion, and now appeared in London as his wife.' Nothing in this statement was true, except that La Malibran had clung to Bériot with devotion. The writer went on to say that, in their 'marriage', 'hers was the unselfish, self-sacrificing part; for out of affection for her husband she not only sang in the opera, but, after the fatigues of performance at the theatre, appeared at private or public concerts.'[4] There is, indeed, much evidence to show that Maria did everything in her power to please Bériot, including earning a great deal of money, and that he accepted this calmly, as his due.

The pianist Moscheles was one of the many people who did not really like Bériot, or his playing. Like others, he found the contrast between the characters of Bériot and La Malibran disconcerting. 'Her sparkling genius, sunny cheerfulness, and never failing spirit and humour contrasted forcibly with his apathy, not to say coldness, more especially as the two artists were constantly seen and judged together.'[5] Audiences felt this, too; and Bériot was conscious of the fact that he was usually engaged only because, if people wanted to hear La Malibran, they had to hear him as well.

Bériot's powers as a violinist seem to have been already diminishing at this time. His talents were not much in demand in Naples, and he was galled by Ole Bull's immense success in that city. After the latter's concert Bériot sarcastically remarked: 'What sorcery must a violin possess to electrify the Neapolitans!'[6] La Malibran once told him that Ole Bull had a sweeter tone than he had, which did not greatly please him, either.[7] Moscheles suspected that La Malibran wrote, or at least contributed, to Bériot's compositions.[8] This is not impossible; she was quite a talented composer. But Bériot went on composing after her death, and there is no reason to suppose that he was incapable of writing the showy and vapid works that bear his name.

Not everyone disliked Bériot's style. In London, Mendelssohn's father heard him play in a string quartet by Haydn 'with sympathy, spirit and precision, in short very beautifully, although perhaps now and then adding some modern French effects.' Later on the same evening 'Madame Malibran sat down and gave us a Spanish song, then at Felix's request two others, then an English sea song, and finally a French tambour-ditty.' Abraham Mendelssohn, who had not previously admired La Malibran on the stage, was completely won over by this performance, and was at a loss to describe

with what flowing, glowing, and effervescing power and expression, what caprice and boldness, passion and *esprit*, with what assurance and consciousness of her means this woman, whom I now *do* appreciate, sang these ditties [. . .] one may truly say she sang songs without words [. . .] Felix, who justly, or at any rate wisely refused to perform after her, was fetched by her from the adjoining room and forced to the piano. He extemporised to everybody's delight and my satisfaction on the airs she had just sung.[9]

As their years together progressed, Bériot found many aspects of his relationship with La Malibran trying. His self-esteem was constantly wounded. She was an incomparably greater artist than he, and infinitely more popular; she earned colossal sums; he earned very little. She was a charming and attractive woman; he was cold and boring. He followed her all over Europe like a prince consort, always two paces behind. Everyone wanted to meet her, and merely tolerated him.

To be fair to Bériot, La Malibran cannot have been an easy person to live with. She was unbalanced, hysterical, prone to fits, hyperactive; she appears to have been a manic-depressive; and she was not interested in their child.

Her depressions were deep; she would remain silent for hours, overwhelmed with black thoughts. These periods were succeeded by phases of extremely high spirits, manic physical and mental activity, elaborate practical jokes, and exaggerated gestures, often involving some slight risk. She threw herself into deep water, although she could not swim, trusting that people would not let her drown. When someone inadvertently gave her the wrong medicine just before a performance, and huge blisters appeared all over her mouth, she seized a pair of scissors, cut the blisters, and went on stage to sing. On another occasion she swallowed a whole jar of mustard in an attempt to cure a cold. She teased a tiger in a menagerie so much that it grabbed her muff in its teeth and she only just managed to extricate her hand. In everything she did, she exaggerated.

Dangerous rocks, steep mountain roads, speed in all its forms, particularly mettlesome horses, fascinated her. 'The more lively her mount was, the more she enjoyed hurdles. One used to see her arriving at rehearsals in riding-habit, hunting-crop in hand, eyes shining with genius and daring, as dashing and pretty as can be . . .'[10]

Her practical jokes and unconventional behaviour horrified Bériot, who was a paragon of middle-class conformism. Moscheles remembered seeing La Malibran stuff a whole orange into her mouth. 'One must have known De Bériot,' he said, 'to appreciate his amazement and agony at seeing his wife open her mouth wide and discover two beautiful rows of teeth, behind which the orange disappeared. Then she roared with laughter at her successful performance.'[11]

Bériot was not only embarrassed by her eccentricities, but considered himself socially superior to her. He did not conceal this from his friends, and probably not from her, either. One of his friends told Fanny and Sophy Horsley that he very much regretted Bériot's connection with La Malibran, for although he had 'the greatest admiration for her great genius, yet he [Bériot] is a very superior person to herself in point of education and feeling,' and he was sure that Bériot 'would have been so fond of a domestic life.'[12]

Bériot's desire for such a life was thwarted by La Malibran's career and temperament. He seems to have been a loving father, and was devoted to his sister and her family. Having been left an orphan very young, he wanted to re-create the family life which he had barely had. La Malibran was fond of her mother and her siblings, but did not have strongly-developed maternal feelings. A friend in Naples once saw her interrupt Bériot, who was reading aloud to her a letter containing news of their son, in order to tell him some minor theatrical gossip. The same friend was shocked by her 'insensibility even towards her child'; he also noted that their liaison had 'cooled down considerably'.[13]

It certainly had on Bériot's side, and perhaps even on La Malibran's, too. But, having staked everything on a divorce, and by asserting that they were already secretly married, they were caught in a trap. There could be no going back.

Otto Nicolai, the future composer of the *Merry Wives of Windsor*, met La Malibran in Rome when he was twenty-four years old, and was overwhelmed by her charm and 'genius'. In his diary he noted that, at a dinner party, he 'asked Marietta in joke if she would like to marry me, and this seemed to make a considerable impression on her; at least,' he added, 'she turned her head away and rose from the table for a moment.'[14] No one could seriously ask her to marry him, because of the ever-present Bériot; perhaps she sometimes regretted this.

As before, she chose her close friends amongst old men, the closest of these still being General Lafayette, who wrote to her frequently, partly about her divorce, and partly because he was fond of her and missed her. He was indefatigable in his efforts to help her win her freedom, and used his immense prestige with Americans on her behalf, never hesitating to go to the very top. For example, when Edward Livingston, lawyer, US senator and, later, Secretary of State, arrived in France as Minister Plenipotentiary, Lafayette immediately consulted him on La Malibran's behalf.[15] In addition, he kept her informed about the debates on the reform of the divorce laws which were dragging on in the French parliament.

Although most of his letters to her concerned her divorce, this was sometimes just a pretext for writing to her. She did not correspond often enough, he complained, or her letters did not always reach him. He told her about himself, about his family: he was expecting his tenth great-grandchild, a grandson had entered the Ecole Polytechnique, deaths of various relatives had distressed him, and so on. Then he referred lightly and obliquely to the fact that Louis-Philippe, whom he had helped to put on the throne, had turned against him — and, at the same time, paid Maria an elegant compliment; 'My estrangement from the Tuileries has become easier for me to bear since you no longer sing there, for those concerts during which I spent several hours looking at you and listening to you had great charm for me.'[16] 'No matter what my birth certificate says,' he told her, 'my heart remains young, and it loves you most tenderly.'[17] He was seventy-six.

In February, 1834, La Malibran learned from the Naples news-paper that General Lafayette had been taken ill, was better, but was still in bed 'and will not be able to leave the house for some time.'[18] About a month later she received what was probably his last letter to her: 'You have perhaps heard,' he wrote, 'that I was very ill, people even said that I was dead, and I must reassure you, my dear Maria and dear Charles, about the exaggeration of public rumour, and sometimes of prejudice . . .' He ended his letter by recalling with nostalgia the great days of 1830, when he had first met La Malibran, and when he had been the hero of the day: 'We are already very far from that friendly salute from Arsace's sword which touched my heart. Those days will come back, I hope, and no one will enjoy them more than I will . . .'[19]

He died two and a half months later, on 20th May, 1834, without seeing his 'dear ward' again, and before she obtained the divorce over which he had done so much to help her. La Malibran was not in Paris for his funeral — she was singing in Milan — and perhaps it was just as well. 'They buried the old patriot like a criminal,' wrote an American who witnessed the scene:

Fixed bayonets before and behind the hearse — his own National Guard disarmed, and troops enough to beleaguer a city, were the honours paid by the 'citizen king' to the man who had made him! The indignation, the scorn, the bitterness expressed on every side among the people, and the ill-smothered cries of disgust as the two *empty* royal carriages went by, in the funeral train, seemed to me strong enough to indicate a settled and universal hostility to the government.[20]

3

La Malibran finally found her ideal composer, not in Italy but in London, where she was engaged for the summer season, 1833, which opened two and a half months after the birth of her son.

The London season promised to be particularly brilliant that year, and many prominent foreign artists had been engaged to take part in it. By the 27th April they had all arrived, and that evening they all went to see a routine performance of *La cenerentola* at the King's Theatre. In the audience were: Madame Pasta and her husband; Vincenzo Bellini; the tenor Rubini; Paganini; Hummel; Vaccai; Mendelssohn; the pianist Herz; and La Malibran and Bériot.[1]

La Malibran already knew the Pastas, Paganini and Mendelssohn well, and probably all the others, too, with the exception of Bellini. As she was to appear in an English version of his *La sonnambula* in a few days' time, the meeting was important to them both.

Vincenzo Bellini was nearly seven years older than La Malibran, and already recognised as one of the most original and talented composers of his generation. His simple, long-drawn-out melodies, his tender, elegiac music, full of truly Romantic melancholy and poignancy, contrasted sharply with Rossini's more exuberant works, and expressed the spirit of the 1830s more truly than they did. Bellini, fortunate in everything, had been particularly happy in his collaborators: the poet, Felice Romani, his librettist; La Pasta, the first Amina and Norma; and the tenor, Rubini, who had created *Il pirata*. They had all helped him to achieve rapid fame in Italy. By the time he arrived in England for his first and only visit, in 1833, he had written all but one of his operas (*I Puritani*). Having conquered Italy without much difficulty, he had now come to attempt the conquest of England and France.

Certainly the gods loved Bellini. From his birth — on All Saints' Day, as befitted someone born to be the object of a cult — until his death thirty-three years later, he received nothing but favours from nature and from his fellow men. Highly-gifted, charming, sweet-natured, he was exceptionally attractive physically, and even had fair hair and blue eyes which, in his native Sicily, made his appearance not only pleasing, but unusual. His family adored and understood him; his talents were recognised early and given every opportunity to develop; he was always, even in extreme youth, honoured in his native land.

He came from a humble background, and never lost his strong Sicilian accent; but this did not prevent him having a great success in Society. He was too unsophisticated even to conceal the pleasure he derived from invitations, parties, the attentions of beautiful and well-born women. He was vain, and spent a fortune on clothes. With his golden hair impeccably curled, his pink and white complexion, his slim figure elegantly clad, his graceful movements, his languid, sentimental gestures, his beautiful, rather characterless face, 'like milk', he reminded Heine of a beribboned shepherd in some idyllic pastoral.[2] He would have been ridiculous, had it not been for his obvious, naïve good nature and his great talent.

Bellini was, like many Sicilians, extremely superstitious. He was full of premonitions that he would die young, like Pergolesi, the composer whom he most admired. An easy victim of Heine's cruel teasing on that score,[3] he seems to have sensed that he was in some way a predestined victim, too fortunate, too gifted, too beautiful to last. Despite his great success, he was insecure, with a pathetic need for affection. He was irrational, even paranoid, in his mistrust of his colleagues — of Donizetti, for example, and, for a time, of Rossini, who showed him nothing but kindness.

But beneath his vanity, his social aspirations, and his superstitions and suspicions, Bellini was a dedicated artist, a highly professional composer, who knew exactly what he wanted to achieve in the theatre, and he was exacting and demanding of his collaborators.

La Malibran had first heard Bellini's music in 1830 in London. She had gone to a performance of *Il pirata* in order to assess the capabilities of a rival, Madame Méric-Lalande. This singer, 'with the face of a char-woman [...] her middle notes like a stretched wire which would make a little rusty sound . . .', had proved to be no threat, and La Malibran thought that the overture made little effect. But she had seen some originality and beauty in the music, despite 'many weaknesses', and had greatly admired the 'magnificent' trio.[4]

Il pirata was an immature work; but since then Bellini's star had risen very swiftly. His successes in Italy had been great — although there had been some failures, too — and his reputation as a possible successor to Rossini, despite or because of the difference in their style, was growing.

La Malibran had already sung in one of Bellini's operas — *I Capuleti e i Montecchi* (based on *Romeo and Juliet*) — in Bologna in 1832. It was not only the first time she had sung Bellini's music, with which she was later to be so closely associated, but also the first time that she had sung in a contemporary opera of any distinction; *I Capuleti* was then only two years old. In it La Malibran took the part of Romeo, as she had already done in two other operas on the same subject: Zingarelli's *Giulietta e Romeo* (1796) and Vaccai's *Giulietta e Romeo* (1825). In the Bologna performances of Bellini's opera she substituted Vaccai's last act for Bellini's; this showed a lack of tact and taste, and infuriated Bellini and his librettist, Felice Romani, who wrote an article in which he protested about it.[5] However, Vaccai's son maintained that this was not La Malibran's idea, but Rossini's.[6] In any case, the Bolognesi had loved it; the *claque* hired to hiss had applauded, and the scenes of enthusiasm had been unparalleled. In substituting Vaccai's last act for Bellini's, La Malibran set a fashion which lasted long after her death.

In London in 1833 she was not engaged at the King's Theatre, where both opera and ballet companies were headed by the leading international stars of the day. Her place should, by rights, have been amongst them; but she had chosen — for a large fee — to join the much more modest company performing opera in English at Drury Lane.

La Malibran had been engaged for Drury Lane by Alfred Bunn. Bunn, theatrical entrepreneur and bad poet and librettist, had just taken over the management of Covent Garden and Drury Lane theatres. He was an astute business man, proverbially mean, and a tough negotiator. On one occasion, after a stormy rehearsal, La Malibran asked if she might call him 'Good Friday', because he was such a 'hot, cross Bunn'.[7] He was an early advocate of opera sung in English, and also tried, with slight success, to encourage English composers.

Bunn's opening season at Drury Lane was a gamble. Having heard of the great success of *La sonnambula* in Italy, he had engaged La Malibran to sing it in English — she was the only international star able to do this. He had also secured Madame Schröder-Devrient and a German company to perform *Fidelio* and *Der Freischütz*. He had engaged a young and inexperienced tenor, John Templeton, to play opposite La Malibran; she is said to have chosen him herself at an audition. The rest of the company was very second-rate. Henry (later Sir Henry) Bishop, a notorious 'adapter' of other people's music in which he usually interpolated his own, was in charge of the musical direction. None of this boded well; it did not seem likely that Bunn's company would provide any competition to the brilliant, all-star company at the King's Theatre, with its varied programme, including three operas by up and coming Italian composers.[8]

The first performance of *La sonnambula* at Drury Lane proved to be an unprecedented success, thanks entirely to La Malibran. 'We can unhesitatingly say,' the *Morning Post* commented, 'that we never saw a crowded house held with a more potent spell in riveted and breathless attention by the powers of any performer upon any stage . . .' The critic went on to speak of La Malibran's 'intense pathos . . . grace of intellect . . . perfect excellence.'[9] *The Times* was no less enthusiastic: 'Never losing sight of the simplicity of the character, she gave irresistible grace and force to the pathetic passages, and excited the feelings of the audience to as high a pitch as can be conceived.'[10] Both critics praised her pronunciation in English.

The Times concluded its review thus: 'If anything has the power to bring audiences to the theatre we should think that *La sonnambula*, played as it was last night, is more calculated to effect that object than any performance that has lately been seen.'[10] *The Times* was right; *La sonnambula* played to packed houses not only for the rest of that season, but whenever La Malibran appeared in it, which she subsequently did whenever she was in England. Bellini's success there was due more to La Malibran's performance of Bishop's mangled version of *La sonnambula** than to Pasta's performances of *Norma* under his own direction. *Norma* received a rather mixed reception, perhaps because Pasta was increasingly singing out of tune.

The most famous anecdote about Bellini and La Malibran, hallowed by repetition in every biography, is unfortunately probably not true. The story, in a letter allegedly written by Bellini, tells how he went to hear La Malibran sing *La sonnambula* in English. According to this letter, now considered to be spurious or concocted from other, lost letters, Bellini was taken to hear the opera by the

---

* The London version of *La sonnambula*, with some of La Malibran's own embellishments, was revived in San Francisco in the autumn of 1984. Director: Terence McEwen; Amina: Frederica von Stade. (*The Times*, 25th October, 1984).

Duchess of Hamilton; he had never met La Malibran. He scarcely recognised his own music, so much had Bishop 'arranged' it, and he could not understand a word of English. Only when La Malibran was singing did he recognise his *Sonnambula*. At the end of the performance his enthusiasm for her was such that he forgot himself so far as to shout '*Viva, viva, brava, brava!*' in a most un-English way. After some minutes he was recognised by the audience, and was led on to the stage by a crowd of young Englishmen. La Malibran came to meet him and, throwing her arms round his neck, sang: '*Ah! m'abbracia!*' — a quotation from the opera. There was tumultuous applause from the audience; holding La Malibran's hand, Bellini came to the front of the stage to acknowledge the amazing ovation. He is quoted as saying: 'Never in my life shall I feel greater emotion.' From that moment, Bellini and La Malibran became intimate friends, and he promised to write an opera for her.*

This touching scene is not confirmed by any other source, and was not reported in the press; as the first night was very widely covered, it is unlikely that such a scene would have escaped the critics. Bellini, who had anyway already met La Malibran, did attend the first night of *La sonnambula*, and did go back-stage after the

---

* The letter in question first appeared in Francesco Florimo's biography, *Bellini*, p. 137–9. (Florence, 1882). Florimo was Bellini's closest friend; they had been students together in Naples. After the composer's death Florimo devoted his time to keeping the memory of Bellini alive and to collecting material about him. As he was not only Bellini's friend, but also a scholar and a librarian, his biography, which appeared when he was eighty-two years old, was considered authoritative. However, the original manuscript of the letter has never been found — unlike the manuscripts of other letters quoted by Florimo — and experts now doubt its authenticity. (See Pastura, pp. 382–3, and Bellini, *Epistolario* (Cambi) pp. 363–6, and note 1.) Florimo had known La Malibran well, and had very much admired her; one can only suppose that in his old age he came to believe, or wished to believe, that the relationship between her and Bellini had been closer than it was. This letter is not of great importance; we know from other, genuine letters what Bellini's feelings about La Malibran were; but it did probably inspire some other, blatantly spurious letters which imply that a full-scale love affair was going on between them. (For example, those in Vincenzo Ricci's *Vincenzo Bellini* (Catania, 1932). See also Bellini — Cambi, p. 527, note 2.) The myth has been perpetuated in many popular, and some serious, books and articles.

performance to congratulate the performers; La Malibran may have greeted him with *Ah! m'abbrachia!* there, but Templeton, who was present, and who left an account of Bellini's visit back-stage, did not tell this story.[11]

On 16th May, Bellini really did write to his friend Lamperi: 'My *Sonnambula* is being given at Drury Lane Theatre in English. Madame Malibran, who is the protagonist, performs it with great taste; the opera has had a huge and ever increasing success.'[12]

William Macready, the greatest English actor of the day, went to see La Malibran in *La sonnambula*. She 'delighted' him, and he even compared her favourably to Mme Schröder-Devrient, a great actress, whom he had seen in *Fidelio* the day before. But he thought Bellini's opera 'the very excrement of trash'. Macready went on to reflect in his diary on the hypocrisy of the public applauding La Malibran's protestations of purity, as Amina on the stage, which came from 'a wanton's lips'.[13] The public was probably not as censorious as Macready. The comment of Fanny Horsley, a well-brought-up young lady, who was a friend of Mendelssohn, was probably more typical:

> Malibran is the subject of conversation. She calls Bériot 'My Charles' and she says she is divorced from old Malibran and married to Bériot and I am sure I hope she is, it is a pity such love as theirs should [illegible] be in a wrong flow.[14]

There can be little doubt that La Malibran gave such inspired performances of *La sonnambula* because she felt that the part of Amina gave her back her lost innocence, and might convince people that she was not 'a wanton'.

Half-way through the season Bunn suggested to La Malibran that she should appear in *The Devil's Bridge*, the ballad opera she had sung in New York. Here is her reply:

> My Dear Bunn,
>   I cannot promise to play the part of *Count Belino*. The music is exceedingly weak, and after the *Sonnambula* I am not capable of singing *baby's music*; however, I don't say positively *no*, until I have seen both the music and the *pice* again . . .[15]

She did give two performances of *The Devil's Bridge*. 'Her acting,' said *The Times*, 'was remarkably skilful, and infinitely too good for the sad stuff of which the part is composed.'[16] The audience, however, loved it.

While La Malibran was getting good write-ups for singing in third-rate operas at Drury Lane, Bellini was receiving mixed reviews for *Norma*. The *Morning Post*, for example, found it 'lamentably deficient in original ideas', but praised Pasta's performances of this part.[17] It was in London that La Malibran studied Pasta's performances of *Norma* which she was soon to interpret herself.

The season drew to a close; it had been one of the most brilliant for many years. Before it ended, there were numerous benefit nights and concerts. Perhaps the most brilliant occasion was Laporte's benefit, on 27th June, in which 'the four talents of Europe' took part. The future Queen Victoria, just fourteen years old, was present, and described the evening in her diary:

> We came in at the beginning of the second act of *Norma*, in which Madame Pasta sang BEAUTIFULLY. After that Signor Paganini played by himself some variations most WONDER-FULLY; he is himself a *curiosity*. After that was given the last act of *Otello*; Desdemona, Madame Malibran, who sang and acted BEAUTIFULLY. After that was performed *La Sylphide*; Taglioni danced BEAUTIFULLY and looked LOVELY. Fanny Elssler danced also *very well*. We saw the whole of the last act and half of the second. It was Laporte's benefit. I was VERY MUCH AMUSED. We came home at ½ past 1. I was soon in bed and asleep.[18]

Before they parted at the end of the season Bellini promised to write an opera for La Malibran, and she gave him two miniatures which she had painted herself. One was a portrait of Bellini; the other, set in a gold tie-pin or brooch, was a self-portrait; it showed La Malibran with her long hair loose, and her hand raised to touch it. Bellini often wore this pin in the silk cravats which he affected.*

They were only to meet again twice, and fleetingly. Bellini was never to hear her sing again, and never heard her sing his works in Italian. But each was to make the other's name even more famous. Bellini had found his ideal interpreter, and La Malibran her ideal composer. Their names were, from then on, always to be linked.

---

* Both are now in the Museo Belliniano, Catania.

4

In Italy, La Malibran swiftly regained her mythical status, which she had lost in Paris. The French had seen her as literature; the Italians saw her as music. They were not as concerned about respectability as were the French, and anyway her husband and child were not there. Theatrical people were not excommunicate and social outcasts in Italy; and although class prejudice, strongest in Naples, remained, La Malibran to a great extent overcame that, particularly in Milan.

In Italy, she was usually referred to as a genius, and often as 'superhuman'[1] and 'divine'.[2] In Venice she was billed as 'the foremost singer of the Universe'.[3] The scenes of enthusiasm which she evoked were unparalleled. Her performances were prolonged for hours by curtain calls, both during and at the end of the opera: eighteen in Lucca,[4] twenty-four in Bologna,[5] thirty-one in Naples,[6] and at La Scala, Milan,[7] there were sixteen curtain calls after the first act of *Norma*, and thirty at the end. The hysteria of audiences was such that the police frequently had to intervene.[8] People sobbed, screamed and fainted; at the end of performances the stage was littered with flowers, laurels, verses. In Lucca and Naples crowds escorted her back to her hotel; in 1834, twenty thousand people did the same in Milan. When she arrived in Venice, the whole city stopped work and turned out to meet her with bands playing;[9] lithographs of this scene were soon on sale in the streets. In Lucca and Venice she was serenaded. Prices for her performances were often doubled or tripled, but the theatres were always full. In small towns her appearances filled the inns with visitors from outlying districts, and accommodation was almost impossible to obtain.[10] The crowds were such that the Austrian secret police sent reports of her movements to Vienna, for they had discovered that Italian patriotic underground organisations were using the migrations of her fans as cover for their own political activities.[11] Wherever she went lithographs of her were sold, medals struck, laudatory verses published.

Crowned heads and other dignatories showed her their favours. The King of the Two Sicilies forgot protocol and applauded her when she asked him to, and sent her his doctor when she was hurt in an accident.[12] The Queen Mother in Naples was all affability.[13] The Austrian governor of Milan sent her an effusive letter, and a crown.[14] Cardinal Albani, Pius VIII's Secretary of State, wrote her a glowing testimonial;[15] Prince Poniatowski invited her to stay.[16] Some lesser mortals in Neapolitan and London society, however, snubbed her, and this cut her to the quick.[17]

She was fêted as much by the lowest classes as she was by the highest. In Venice the populace considered her of good omen, and followed her around 'like little dogs'.[18] She was known in Italy 'even in the villages. In her usual eccentric fashion, she made the great part of her journeys on the seat with the coachman, and the peasants who knew her would cry out as she passed: Evviva! Viva La Malibran!'[19]

Her divinity was never in question. In Venice, when a group of gondoliers passed round and drank from a cup of wine which her lips had touched, it was said that the cup still remained full — the saint's first recorded miracle.[20] In Venice, too, people began to collect relics; her shawl, her gloves, any article of clothing would be grabbed by the crowd of people who hoped to touch her, and would be torn to shreds by her fans. At her final appearance in Venice, La Malibran slipped on one of the bouquets which were already piling up on the stage; Balfe, who was partnering her, prevented her from falling, but her slipper came off and fell into the pit. There was a violent scramble to get possession of the slipper, or part of it. 'Never,' said Balfe, 'was the game of "hunt the slipper" played before on such a gigantic scale.'[21]

In Bologna the public was so enthusiastic about her performances that, forgetting the strict prohibition of the authorities, it demanded encores, and people clapped and screamed. The Pro-Legato made a complaint to the head of the theatres, who politely replied: 'Ordinary rules cannot apply to the divine.'[22]

Her admirers could see La Malibran's divinity in all she did. In the gardens of the Villa Pamphili in Rome Legouvé witnessed another quasi-religious scene, a kind of transfiguration, when she climbed up on to a platform which made a natural stage above a fountain. Her face, he said, took on a strange, serious expression; she looked heavenwards, and then began to sing *Casta diva* from *Norma*. Her friends who witnessed the scene were profoundly moved. 'Seen thus, above us, framed by leaves, she seemed a supernatural being; when she came down again her face still had an expression both grave and serious, and our own first words of enthusiasm were as if imbued with religious respect.'[23]

La Malibran first appeared as Norma in Naples in 1834. Her success was 'colossal',[24] and from then on many considered it her greatest part. It was one with which she could very easily identify; was she not herself a dedicated priestess, torn between love and her vocation? She had ceased to be Desdemona, the predestined victim, and had become the Druid priestess — or pure Amina in *La sonnambula*, unjustly accused of immorality. La Malibran was no longer a Rossini heroine, but a Bellini heroine.

Therefore, when she faced the greatest test of her career — her first appearance at La Scala, Milan — she elected to appear not in *Otello* which, until then, had always been her choice when facing a new public, but in *Norma*.

It was a challenge; Milan was Pasta's territory. Pasta had been born near Milan, and was considered to be Milanese. *La sonnambula* and *Norma* had been especially written for her, and first performed in Milan with the composer directing;* and Pasta was immensely popular with the Milanese public. News of La Malibran's successes all over Europe had, of course, reached Milan, and had aroused lively interest; but the Milanese were not prepared to accept her reputation on hearsay, nor were they disposed to see their own prima donna displaced by a foreigner. 'I am not afraid of Pasta,' La Malibran declared. 'I will live or die as Norma.'[25]

Even before she had appeared at La Scala, the excitement in Milan reached an hysterical pitch. Although the prices for her first performance were inordinately high, a crowd began to assemble outside the theatre at about mid-day for the evening performance. It was, as someone who was there put it, 'farewell lunch and dinner for that day.'[26] By 3 pm a vast crowd was shouting and screaming at the doors of La Scala, and those who joined the crowd began screaming, too, infected by the mass hysteria. When the doors were finally opened — at 3.15 — the crowd took the theatre by assault with 'a din and an uproar never before heard'.[27] Then, as at the first night of *Hernani* in Paris, the audience had to wait for almost five hours — until 8 pm — for the performance to begin. During that time excitement and boredom mingled to produce abnormal tension in the darkened auditorium.

* *La sonnambula* was first produced on 6th March, 1831, and *Norma* on 26th December of the same year.

Suddenly, the great theatre was illuminated, and the Viceroy, the Vicereine, the entire court and 'a whole company of lovely ladies'[28] filed in. Then everyone turned to look in another direction: Madame Pasta, elegantly dressed, was taking her place in a box. At long last the orchestra struck up, and the curtain rose. The chorus appeared, with Marini, the bass; Reina followed with the tenor's aria; and suddenly La Malibran was on the stage. She was visibly trembling.

'Someone had unwisely told her that a hostile faction would try to bring about her downfall; she had wept for a long time in her dressing-room, refusing even to go on stage.'[29] Always very nervous on a first night, and rarely at her best on such occasions, she had learned in Paris that a hostile audience was not to be trifled with.

> 'The little or nothing that she did on that first evening was all the same enough, for the next day — Friday — no one talked of anything else. People discussed whether La Malibran was comparable to Pasta; hence there were arguments, conflicting opinions, discussions, altercations without end.[30]

This only served to raise the public's curiosity and excitement to a higher pitch.

La Pasta had applauded La Malibran whole-heartedly, and had visited her in her dressing-room in the friendliest manner. But, some time later, she did herself give a few successful performances of *Norma* in Milan, just to show that she had not entirely relinquished her right to her own territory.[31]

In La Malibran's Milanese performance of *Norma* the part of Adalgisa was taken by Josepha Ruiz-Garcia, her half-sister. Although Garcia had always referred to Josepha as his 'niece', many people knew that she was his daughter, and this was openly stated in the press. Josepha had made a fairly undistinguished début in Paris in 1827. Garcia had tried to obtain an engagement for her in Italy; he had written to say:

> She has a very exceptional *soprano sfogato* voice, but I would not like her to make her début here [in Paris] because to follow La Malibran one must be tragic and comic on a high level, and I don't think that my niece is as sublime as her cousin as an actress, although her voice is superior . . .[32]

Josepha was quite favourably received in Milan, but in other cities, such as Bologna, she was not liked, and she failed to make a distinguished career.

The second performance of *Norma* at La Scala was a complete triumph for La Malibran. She was less nervous, and the public was even more excited than before. 'On the second night in the theatre people wept, screamed, howled with inexpressible excitement. They screamed *bis! bis!* even to the recitatives. The last scene was beyond description.'[33] The two performance originally planned caused such a sensation that three more had to be arranged: one of *Norma*, and two of *Otello*. 'After *Otello* the enthusiasm of the Milanese for La Malibran became fanaticism, delirium, idolatry . . .'[34] 'The enthusiasm suscitated by La Pasta in *Norma* two years earlier was changed to delirium for La Malibran.'[35] The box-office receipts were 'fabulous for that time'.[36]

After the final performance (*Otello*, on 24th May), Duke Carlo Visconti di Modrone, then lessee of La Scala, with whom La Malibran was staying, gave a sumptuous party for her in the garden of his palazzo. She was serenaded by the whole orchestra of La Scala. A poem* addressed to her by Felice Romani, the librettist of *La sonnambula* and *Norma* and a very well-known poet, was distributed to the guests.

That same evening La Malibran signed a sensational contract with Visconti for the next two carnival seasons: 1835–6, and 1836–7, and for the autumn seasons of 1835, 1836 and 1837, for a total of 420,000 francs. A separate contract was also signed for the autumn season of that same year (1834).[37]

It is difficult, if not impossible, to give a figure in modern terms for the various fees earned by La Malibran, many of which are quoted in different currencies. It is sufficient to say that she was the highest paid singer of her day, probably the highest paid performer.†

However, Visconti did not feel that she had driven a hard bargain with him — on the contrary, in a letter written on the day on which the contract had been signed he told her that, as she had been generous to him over the contract, he felt that he, too, should be

---

* *De queste a te percosse* . . . The full text of Romani's poem was published in the *Gazetta Privilegiata di Milano* on 25th May, 1834.
† Rosselli (p. 59 and p. 62, Table 4) gives singers' salaries at the San Carlo and Fondo Theatres in Naples, 1785–1892. La Malibran's salary (1834) of 20,730 francs per month is by far the highest. The next highest (C. Ungher) was 12,100 francs per month. See also Bunn, I, pp. 240–2. In 1835 La Malibran received £2,775 in London for 24 performances during May and June. (Grove I.)

generous to her. He therefore offered her free board and lodging in his own house and the use of a carriage, whenever she should be in Milan.[38]

La Malibran had not only found her ideal composer — Bellini — but also her ideal audience — the Milanese.

5

'Opera,' said Bellini, 'through singing, must make one weep, shudder, die.'[1] No one knew better how to do that than La Malibran and, singing Bellini's music all over Italy, that is just what she did. Whole audiences dissolved in tears,[2] people sobbed, fainted, shuddered. When, as Romeo, she slowly realised that Juliet was dead and uttered her name: 'Giulietta!' it had a 'magic' effect on the audience: 'An icy shiver spread over everyone before she pronounced it, and several times, at Bologna, it was necessary to carry ladies out who could not listen to it without feeling ill.'[3] A performance by La Malibran of *Norma* or *I Capuleti* was a shattering experience, and the audience would leave the theatre crushed by emotion, purified by catharsis.

In *La sonnambula* Bellini wanted something different: sensibility, poignancy, melancholy. Again, La Malibran was able to provide it. 'Maria Malibran was the most sublime interpreter of *La sonnambula*,' wrote Bellini's friend, Francesco Florimo:

> She knew how to identify herself so completely with the artless character and sincere feelings of the shepherdess Amina, that she translated perfectly on the stage the tender emotions which move her and which, thanks to a voice mixed with the purest passion, she revealed with the most exquisite truth. She could say that she had made of the part a second creation, and I well remember when she appeared in Naples in the spring of 1833* at the Teatro del Fondo, the impression that she created on people's minds was such, and so great, that one could almost question whether the honours of the triumph belonged to Bellini, the author of the divine idyll, or to the exceptional artist who had known how to interpret it so well . . .[4]

A friend, talking to Bellini about *La sonnambula*, once made what

---

* An error on Florimo's part; she was not in Naples in the spring of 1833. He probably meant autumn, 1834.

he thought was just a complimentary remark, and told him that he thought the music had 'soul' in it. 'This word gave him so much pleasure that he cried out, with his soft Italian accent "*Yes, hasn't it?* SOUL! Oh, I am grateful! Thank you! SOUL, that's the whole of music." '[5] When Bellini later told La Malibran that she had 'three souls'* he was paying her his highest compliment. She fulfilled all his dreams of the perfect interpreter.

La Malibran, too, had been searching for the ideal vehicle for her talents. She once explained to a friend exactly what kind of opera she wanted: 'A sentimental subject, unhappy, tragic, pathetic, mellifluous — and then *another* semi-tragic, that is to say, which ends well . . .'[6] *Norma*, *La sonnambula* and *I Capuleti*, the three Bellini operas which she sang, amply fulfilled all these conditions.

In London in 1833 Bellini had promised to write an opera specially for La Malibran; this was still his dream,[7] and hers. Since then, she had been singing in his operas all over Italy with outstanding success, thus adding to his fame as well as to her own. Bellini himself had heard her only in the garbled English version of *La sonnambula*; but that had been enough to convince him of her genius, and she was constantly in his thoughts. His friends, particularly his closest friend, Florimo, who was in Naples, kept him informed of her stupendous successes and her wonderfully sensitive interpretations not only of Bellini's music, but also of the dramatic conception of his works, which was so important to him.

In the autumn of 1834 Bellini was in Paris, composing *I Puritani* for the Théâtre Italien. This was an extremely important commission, the first he had received from a theatre outside Italy. At the same time, he was in contact with the society in charge of the San Carlo Theatre in Naples, which wanted him to compose three operas. The negotiations were protracted, and Bellini realised that he would not have time to compose a new opera for Naples while he was working on *I Puritani*. He therefore suggested that the first opera for Naples should be *I Puritani*, with the part of Elvira, which he was writing for Giulia Grisi, adapted to La Malibran's lower voice. This was agreed, but the society stipulated that the score should reach Naples by a certain date.

The prospect of La Malibran singing his music excited Bellini, and although he was writing *I Puritani* for Grisi, it was clearly the image of La Malibran that inspired him. Describing the changes

* See p. 191.

which he had made to the score for La Malibran, Bellini told
Florimo: 'I've written a piece for her so curious and so brilliant that
she will be really pleased, as it is of the type she prefers, this piece
is worth ten cavatinas, because it is in the right place — so much
so that I'll give it in Paris, as it makes a great effect.'[8] This was the
famous *Son vergin vezzosa* which, as the composer foretold, never
fails to make a great effect.

Bellini's work on the Paris production of *I Puritani*, and a chapter
of accidents, prevented the revised score from reaching Naples by
the specified date; the society cancelled its contract with Bellini not
only for *I Puritani*, but for the other two as yet unwritten operas as
well. Why the agreement should have been adhered to so strictly is
not quite clear.

La Malibran did everything she could to have this decision
reversed, and to get *I Puritani* performed in Naples. Her friendship
with Bellini and the affinity which she felt with his music made her
doubly keen to add another Bellini opera to her repertoire. But,
despite her considerable prestige in the theatre, she was not
successful; she never performed the 'Malibran' version of *I Puritani*.
It differs fairly extensively from the Paris version.[9]

Bellini took the cancellation of his Naples contract philosophi-
cally, perhaps because *I Puritani* achieved a brilliant success in Paris
and, as a result, he hoped for further commissions there; and also,
perhaps, because to him, as to La Malibran, Milan was more
important than Naples. Even before the Naples contract was broken,
he was thinking of having *I Puritani* performed with La Malibran
in Milan, bypassing Naples.[10]

Bellini's affection for the 'little devil'[11] or 'little angel',[12] as he
called La Malibran, and his admiration for her talents, had always
been great; now, his gratitude to her for trying to do everything she
could to help him — even though she had failed — made him even
more devoted to her. He told Florimo that what pained him most
in the whole unfortunate affair was that La Malibran, 'that dear
lady', had not been able to give the Neapolitans the pleasure of
hearing his opera.[13]

Finally, Bellini wrote to thank La Malibran for her concern for
him and for *I Puritani*. Florimo had told him that 'a mistress could
not have shown more interest. I believe it,' Bellini told her, 'and will
always believe that you love me, because I adore you and your
miraculous talent, as well as your graceful and lively person, not to

mention your *three souls* (because you must have so many, and not just one like all other women).'

He went on to lay down his conditions for their future relationship:

From now on I *want* to write to you from time to time, I *want* you to reply to me, and I *want* our friendship to be fraternal, full of interest and mutual love and based on the most genuine esteem, to become precious. Therefore, from now on, what La Malibran commands, Bellini will do.

Frankness, sincerity — even at the price of causing momentary displeasure, but I do not want consideration — this destroys the most solid friendship, so write to me if with your heart you accept my attachment, born of the highest esteem, fellow-feeling and gratitude.[14]

Prudently, Bellini concluded his letter by sending his regards to Bériot. The correspondence did not flourish, as he had hoped it would. So far as is known, Bellini never wrote to her again, and no letters from La Malibran to Bellini have so far come to light.

In February, 1835, Bellini again asked Florimo to thank his 'dearest Malibran' for her help, and he added:

tell her that I will always love her, even at the risk of earning the hatred of her Charles. Her obliging behaviour in the recent circumstances has made me wish to be in Naples to cover her with kisses in spite of everything; but tell her that I hope to meet her one day, and I don't know what will happen so far as I am concerned.[15]

It was easy to send such messages through a third person; it would have been quite another thing to write them to La Malibran directly. The evidence that Bellini was in love with her — the letters quoted above — is extremely slender. Perhaps, more in keeping with his character, he was in love with the idea of being in love with her. She, at any rate, seems to have given him little encouragement. When she was passing through Paris she did not even bother to contact him.[16] Bériot was always at her side — a fact which Bellini probably did not really mind; he never wanted to be deeply involved. 'I am like that,' he said in connection with another woman. 'I love the woman I don't intend to marry and I'm bored when that prospect arises, if it goes on like that you'll see, I'll never marry. Amen.'[17]

But if Bellini's attitude to La Malibran the woman was ambiguous, his attitude to La Malibran the artist was not; he was very much in love with the artist who knew so well how to bring his works to life. He dreamed of her appearing in his *Beatrice di Tenda*, which had not been a success when first produced in Venice in 1833. 'Oh! If only she would play Beatrice!' he wrote to Florimo, 'not so much for Naples, as for Milan! And then my ill-treated Beatrice would rise again and make the rounds of the theatres like Norma!'[18] La Malibran was of the same opinion; when she heard Madame Persiani singing an aria from *Beatrice di Tenda*, she turned to Florimo, who was sitting beside her in her box, and said: 'I feel that I would know how to sing it divinely!'[19] Bellini also hoped that she would perform *La straniera* and *Il pirata* in Naples; and, in 1835, his dream was that she should introduce *Norma* to Paris.[20]

But only Bellini's premonitions were to come true, not his dreams. He did fleetingly see La Malibran again, but never again heard her sing in the theatre; he never composed an opera specially for her, and his adaptation of *I Puritani*, made for her, was never performed;* she never sang *Beatrice di Tenda*; she never sang *Norma* in Paris, and, indeed, it was not performed there during the composer's lifetime.

* The 'Malibran' version of *I Puritani* was given in a concert performance (billed as 'World Première') at the Barbican Hall, London, on 14th December, 1985, conducted by Raffaello Monterosso. The part of Elvira, adapted by Bellini for La Malibran's voice, was sung by Suzanne Murphy.

La Malibran as Amina in *La sonnambula*, London, 1833. *Crown Copyright Victoria and Albert Museum (Theatre Museum)*

(*Below*) La Malibran as Norma. Lithograph by P. Bertotti, from a French original. *Crown Copyright Victoria and Albert Museum (Theatre Museum)*

(*Above*) A drawing of La Malibran as Desdemona by Princess Victoria, 1833, aged 14. *Windsor Castle, Royal Library* © *1986 Her Majesty the Queen*

(*Above right*) La Malibran as Leonore in the prison scene of Beethoven's *Fidelio*, by John Absolon, 1835. *Crown Copyright Victoria and Albert Museum (Theatre Museum)*

'Facsimile of Made Malibran's Lève toi Jeune Enfant', published with a reprint of the song after her death, London, 1837? *British Library*

Costume sketches by Maria Malibran for *Maria Stuarda*. Photos
Copyright Roger Begine, Machelen, Belgium. Reproduced by
kind permission of the Director, Conservatoire royal de
Bruxelles

Maria de Bériot by Achille Devéria. This is one of the last portraits made of her just before her death; she has signed it 'M. F. De Bériot (ex) Malibran'.

(*Below*) La Malibran's younger sister, Pauline, by Achille Devéria. *Bibliothèque Nationale, Paris*. 'African features with a Parisian expression'. (Cuvillier-Fleury, 15.XII.1838.)

6

La Malibran's astounding successes all over Italy — unparalleled at that time — suggested that she had finally 'conquered' the public; but in fact her old adversary still had to be placated, and did not allow her to forget who was the master. So long as she fulfilled the public's demands she was rewarded with admiration, even idolatry, to say nothing of money. But she had only to take one false step to be called to order.

The public was unpredictable; she could never be sure what would displease it, and she now always faced it with trepidation, sometimes with terror. In Naples in 1833 she hoped to repeat the successes of the previous year by singing the same operas. She announced that she would make her début in *Otello*. '*Otello!*' the dilettanti were heard to exclaim. 'Is it possible? The same operas! The same parts as last year! This woman doesn't know how to do anything else [. . .] You can be sure, she can't do anything except *Otello* and *La gazza ladra*, *La gazza ladra* and *Otello*.'[1] On the first night the attitude of the audience was not particularly friendly. La Malibran was so nervous that her face showed 'the splendid trepidation of a great captain, who finds himself having to do battle on the same field where, on another occasion, he had won his greatest victory.'[2]

Newer operas — Pacini's *Irene* and Coccia's *La figlia dell'arciere*, both written especially for her — were quickly substituted for Rossini; but they, too, failed to please. The public was only placated when La Malibran appeared in Bellini's operas.

In Rome the audience objected to the interpolation of a French song in the music lesson scene of *Il barbiere*. In Naples, in Rossi's *Amelia*, which La Malibran had herself commissioned, everything went wrong: the Neapolitans considered the San Carlo Theatre too grand for an *opera buffa*, and were offended at it being put on there; the scenery and costumes were, according to Bériot, 'horrible';[3] the music, according to Duprez,[4] was too French for the Neapolitans; and, last but by no means least, on the first night La Malibran had the unfortunate idea of dancing a mazurka with a ballet-dancer in the second act. The huge audience, impatient to see her dance, ignored the first act; and when she finally did dance, it was not a success. 'The audience was in a bad mood, and during the rest of the performance it did not hiss her, but it did not applaud.'⁵ She did not dance again at subsequent performances.

This fiasco so frightened La Malibran that at first she refused to appear in Persiani's *Inez de Castro*, and was only finally persuaded to do so by the French tenor, Duprez. This time she obtained a brilliant success.

In Bologna she was very popular; but when she tried to substitute her half-sister for another prima donna who was much liked in Bologna, she was received in 'glacial silence', and 'wept copiously' in her dressing-room as a result. She made it up with the prima donna she had snubbed, and 'reconquered' the public; she was once again received with that 'inebriating applause, which she no longer knew how to renounce without bitter grief.'⁶

Audiences were particularly unpredictable in Naples, and La Malibran never felt at ease there. Nor did Bériot: 'I am waiting for the day when I shall leave Naples for ever as the happiest day of my life,'⁷ he told a friend. Corruption, intrigue and superstition made it impossible to guess how the audience would react. *Claques* could be bought; the king's predilection for a certain singer could deter the audience from applauding her rival. On one occasion La Malibran was unable to perform the last act of *Otello* — the only one with great dramatic effect — because it was considered of ill-omen on an important feast-day. *I Capuleti* also offended susceptibilities because the sight of Juliet's body surrounded by priests on the stage was not only considered of ill-omen, but shocked people's religious feelings. When La Malibran played the old aunt in *Il matrimonio segreto* people disapproved of her make-up as an old woman.⁸ It was impossible to be sure of pleasing such a capricious audience.

The public was, indeed, extremely exacting; and, in those days, theatre directors were equally demanding. Almost always rapturously received in Milan and London, and generously rewarded there, La Malibran certainly had to work hard to obtain both applause and money. In 1836 in Milan she gave thirty performances in two months, twenty of the same opera. In London in 1835 she performed almost every other day — thirteen performances in June alone. According to Bériot, her average day was: a good hour's work at the piano, followed by a 10 am rehearsal; a concert from 1 pm to 4 pm; an opera performance from 7 to 10 pm; then one or two private parties, at which she would often sing, and bed at dawn.[9] No great singer nowadays would contemplate such a programme and, it is now considered, no great voice could survive it. Yet, if La Malibran cancelled one performance, the public was at once irritated, and showed it. She had learned her lesson in Paris and her cancellations were now much less frequent, but they did occur.

Her friends, and theatre directors to whom she was under contract, would implore her not to overtire herself and ruin her voice and her health; but she took no notice. On one occasion, in London, Alfred Bunn went to her dressing-room after a performance and found her preparing to go on to a concert. He remonstrated with her, begging her to send an excuse. She promised to do so, and Bunn drove off to his home in Brompton, then in the country. He was reading in bed at 12.30 am when he heard a bell ring, and then La Malibran's voice saying: 'Tell Mr Bunn not to get up — I am only come for a little fresh air in his garden.' Bunn got up and dressed. He found Maria with Bériot and Thalberg; they told him that she had been to two concerts, had gone home and changed, and had then decided on a trip to the country. Bunn laid on some supper in the garden, and La Malibran enjoyed herself immensely, singing songs until three in the morning. Then she said: 'Now I've had my supper, I will go and steal my breakfast.' She went to the hen-house, took all the eggs, and then drove back to town. Bunn named after her the great walnut-tree in his garden, under which they had had supper.[10]

It could be said — and, indeed, *was* often said — that money was the motive for all this frenzied activity. La Malibran certainly extracted very high fees from concert promoters and theatre directors; she realised that, in the public's view, what is most expensive must always be the best. But, having earned her fee, she gave away her money with a generosity that became legendary. A letter written by her reveals that she anonymously gave 5,000 francs — roughly the fee she was earning for four performances at the time — to a man whose name she did not even know.[11]

Bériot was interested in money, and did not conceal the fact; he did not relish the wandering gypsy life they were leading. In a letter to his brother-in-law he wrote:

This existence would not be bearable any more if it did not have a motive as powerful as money. So we console ourselves by thinking that in a few years, if Providence wills it, we will rejoice at no longer having to part [from you], and that will be no later than 1838 . . .[12]

In theory, La Malibran agreed with Bériot, for she always did everything possible to please him. But, in practice, 1838 was still very far away. It was not easy to think of retirement at the age of twenty-seven. She had reached the top; her problem was, how to stay there. There was really nothing more for her to achieve; but there was the inevitable and alarming prospect of age and decline, of younger rivals supplanting her. La Malibran was walking a tight-rope, and she knew it; the public knew it, too, and much of the excitement that she generated was due to the danger of her vertiginous position, and the public's secret hope that she might make a false step and, in falling, give it a thrill.*

Success was intoxicating, but it was addictive, and bought at a very high price. 'How many women envy me!' wrote La Malibran, in one of her black moods, to Legouvé. 'What makes them envy me? It's this wretched success . . .'[13] The ovations, bouquets, poems, screaming fans, idolatry, had to be paid for with physical and mental exhaustion, a rootless life, stretched nerves and, sometimes, spiritual anguish. What was it all for? Where was she going? Who was she? A goddess or an actress? An outcast or 'the slave they pay to give them pleasure'?[14] Was she Marietta Garcia, La Malibran, Madame de Bériot — or Desdemona, Norma, Romeo, Amina? She was not always sure. The distinction between reality and fiction was becoming more and more blurred. Absorbed by her fantasies, 'she was outside the circle of real life',[15] often carried away 'beyond reality'.[16] At her marriage to Bériot she thought, not of her son, but of Norma's children which, one suspects, were more real to her.[17] Amina's innocence, unjustly suspected, was her innocence, just as Desdemona's terror, when her father was alive, had been her terror. But, although her father was dead, other terrors remained.

La Malibran was afraid — afraid of losing her star status, of losing Bériot, of death. Of these three, the first was the greatest terror, for she believed that only by remaining a great star could she

---

* 'Opera is so much like the circus. People come to watch you flirting with danger, up there on the high wire.' Keith Lewis, New Zealand tenor (Don Ottavio in Sir Peter Hall's Glyndebourne production of *Don Giovanni*, 1982), quoted in the *Sunday Telegraph* Colour Supplement, 5th September, 1982).

hold Bériot's affections and ward off the premature death which she had always expected.

'What she feared most,' said a friend, 'was to find herself divested of her halo of glory.'[18] She was under no illusions about Bériot; she knew that he had allied himself to her because she was famous and capable of earning enormous sums; she believed — and she was probably right — that if she were to lose these assets, his interest in her would evaporate. After five years together, it was obvious, even to outside observers, that his affection for her was cooling. 'She felt instinctively [. . .] that the applause which she elicited was the fuel which fed the flickering flame in De Bériot's heart'; this was the cause of 'the kind of frenzy with which she clung to her fame as an artist.'[19]

She also believed, less rationally, that 'activity and youth alone were capable of warding off death from her, that a pause in her mad habits would signal the end of her life . . .'[20] 'She was convinced that she would die in her prime, and the revulsion which she had from this sad idea which, for her, had all the force of truth, explains several features of her character which, were it not for that, would become insignificant or even ridiculous.'[21]

The Romantics were, as is well known, obsessed by death, and La Malibran was no exception. But, in her case, like Bellini, she does seem to have had a genuine presentiment that she would die young. She believed that her parents would survive her; she wrote to her first husband that she was working as much for them as for herself, as 'the more I'll have when I die, the more there'll be for them'[22] — a curious idea for a girl of just twenty-one. Death was never far from her thoughts; and, like many Romantics, she often personalised death. When she had been seriously ill in Bath in 1830, she had written to a friend to say that she had almost died, 'but the devil said: "She is sensitive, she's unhappy, she must live. *Vivat!*" he turned the bed, and Death was caught; thinking he was at the head of the bed, he found himself, to his great surprise, at the foot . . .'[23] In one of the last songs she composed, *La Morte*,* death is again personalised. Legouvé said of her:

> Although she was life personified, and playfulness might pass for one of the features of her character, the idea of death came to her often. She always said that she would die young.

* See p. 214.

Sometimes, as if she felt some kind of glacial breath, as if the shadow of the other world was projected in her imagination, she used to fall into terrible bouts of melancholy, and her heart would drown in a flood of tears. I have before me these words which she wrote [to me]: Come to see me straight away! My sobs are stifling me! All sorts of funereal ideas are at my bedside, and death is leading them.'[24]

In another letter, written when she was twenty-three, she said that her thoughts were 'cadaverous . . . Death is leading them . . . soon it will be my death.'[24]

Many of La Malibran's sketches[25] contain symbols of death, and she was quick to perceive such signs everywhere. In Venice she insisted, against all tradition, that her gondola should be painted in bright colours: 'I couldn't have brought myself to be buried alive in those gondolas which are black, inside and out,'[26] she wrote. Castil-Blaze remembered saying to her one day, while she was eating her lunch on stage during a rehearsal: 'Marietta, dearest, you won't die!' She replied: 'What shall I do, then? Cruel fate! I'll die like a dog.'[27]

As time went on, and her ability to distinguish between real life and the operas she performed became less and less sure, the idea of death became increasingly familiar to her. Since the age of seventeen she had died a thousand deaths on the stage — as Desdemona, as Romeo, as Norma — and she had had to study death and how to portray it. 'Beautiful in her nightly death',[28] she moved audiences profoundly because she identified so completely with her part, and herself experienced some of the emotions which she acted out on the stage. But these emotions, although they were feigned, marked her; her already unbalanced and morbid nature was not unscathed by her 'nightly deaths'.

In opera, no one dies old or infirm; only heroes, heroines and villains die, always in youth, in their prime. Death is always quick, clean, and relatively painless. In opera, death is usually the solution to an insoluble problem; and, although La Malibran feared death, that is how she increasingly came to see it.

7

It was just before her short but sensational stay in Venice in 1835 that La Malibran was told of the annulment by a Paris court of her marriage to Eugène Malibran.* The news was brought to her by one of her lawyers; when she heard it, she fainted.[1]†

Madame Malibran had, thus, become Mademoiselle Garcia again. It had taken her five years to win her freedom; she could now marry Charles de Bériot. She was only to do so a year later as, according to French law, a certain period had to elapse before she could marry again.

At her wedding party,‡ when her mother reproached her for

---

* The text of the court's judgement is given by Pougin, pp. 188–190. (Tribunal de Première Instance (4ème Chambre), sessions of 20th and 27th February, 1835, in Paris.)

The decision of the court was based on the fact that Maria Garcia and Eugène Malibran had been married by the French consul in New York; as she was a Spanish subject, and Malibran an American citizen by naturalisation, the court decided that the French consul had had no competence to marry them. Since Eugène Malibran had been officially domiciled in France since 1832, a French court had competence to hear the case. The marriage was annulled, and Eugène Malibran was ordered to pay costs, which must have been considerable. The court also decreed that Bériot's and La Malibran's son, Charles Wilfrid, should be deemed legitimate.

† According to Trebbi (*Nella vecchia Bologna*, p. 74) La Malibran heard the news of the annulment of her marriage in Bologna, on her way to Venice, on 19th March; but most other sources say that she heard it in Venice.

‡ Her wedding party, given by Troupenas in Paris on 29th March, 1836, was attended by, amongst others, Rossini and Legouvé. The story of her musical 'duel' with Thalberg at this party (Legouvé, pp. 31–34) may be true; but it is certainly not true that this was the first time she and Thalberg had met. Thalberg — 'the gentleman artist', according to Legouvé, 'a perfect mixture of talent and *respectability*', (*Epis et bluets*, p. 25) — had much in common with Bériot and was his closest friend; he and La Malibran had met earlier, in London.

having sung badly, she replied: 'Ah, what do you expect, Maman! One only gets married once!'[2] Her marriage to Eugène Malibran was indeed annulled, both by the court and in her memory; but it was not annulled by the Catholic Church. Bériot's family maintained that the Church recognised the validity of the 'secret' marriage[3] contracted in 1830; but there is no evidence that the Church voiced any opinion on that subject.

Despite the annulment and, later, her marriage to Bériot, she remained La Malibran. She made some attempts to revert to her maiden name, or to use Bériot's name, but without avail; to the public she was, and always would be, La Malibran. When she saved the fortunes of the Venetian theatre director Gallo, by giving two performances in his theatre,[4] he showed his gratitude to her by re-naming his theatre Teatro Garcia; but he was soon forced to change it to Teatro Malibran.*

At last a free woman, no longer threatened by her father or her first husband, La Malibran could now hold her head high, and her successes that year reflected her new self-confidence. Composers were vying with each other for her talents. Bellini hoped that she would introduce *Norma* to Paris, and still planned to write an opera especially for her. Meyerbeer[5] and Auber[6] also contemplated writing operas for her, and Vaccai was already at work on *Giovanna Grey*. Bunn wanted her to play *Fidelio* in London. In Milan, she was to appear in Donizetti's *L'elisir d'amore* and give the first performance of *Maria Stuarda*. While she was in Venice she met her old friend, the Irish singer and composer, Michael William Balfe, who also wanted to write an opera for her. There was a project that Balfe should write a work based on *Hamlet*, with La Malibran as Ophelia and Donzelli as the Prince.[7] This scheme came to nothing, which was, perhaps, just as well. It is to be doubted that Balfe could have risen to the challenge of *Hamlet*; but Ophelia might have been a great part for La Malibran.

In London that summer La Malibran repeated her usual success in *La sonnambula* in English, and tackled Beethoven's *Fidelio* for the first time. This was a challenge; it was quite unlike any other opera she had sung; the part of Leonore did not really suit her

* Gallo's theatre was the Teatro Emeronitio, formerly the Teatro San Giovanni Grisostomo, founded in 1677. It was restored in 1886, and almost completely rebuilt in 1920. It is still (1984) called Teatro Malibran; there is also a hotel called after her almost next door to the theatre.

voice, and she was inevitably compared, not always favourably,[8] to Madame Schröder-Devrient, who had recently made a great impression in the part in London. Beethoven's opera was not universally acclaimed; some thought it 'of too severe a class',[9] while others thought 'the dullness of the opera was really wearisome'.[10] But when La Malibran made her first entrance, slim — unlike Madame Schröder-Devrient — and androgenous, 'her indescribable look of the profoundest suffering'[11] reduced members of the audience to tears before she had sung a single note.

Macready, who attended a performance of *Fidelio*, thought that La Malibran was superior to Madame Schröder-Devrient only at the end of the second act, but that otherwise she was 'not in her own element'. After the performance, he visited her in her dressing-room and, in his diary, mused on that encounter:

> She saluted me most affectionately, and perhaps, to her I was what she was to me — a memorial of years of careless, joyous hope and excitement; she said I was not altered; I could not say what I did not think of her. I could have loved — once almost did love her, and I believe she was not indifferent to me. It often occurs to me on such recollections: how would my destiny have been altered! I should possibly have been an *ambitieux* — should I have been happier? — should I have had my Nina, my Willie and little Catharine? Left Malibran with a very great depression of spirits.[12]

In his diary, Macready several times[13] referred to having had a nascent romance with La Malibran; but it is difficult to tell when this might have occurred, and there is, so far, no evidence that she was 'not indifferent' to him. They had known each other in Europe and America when she had been little more than a child; Macready had married in 1824, when she was sixteen, and he was not the type of man to have flirted with her after his marriage. He was a strict moralist, although susceptible to women: 'Miss Huddert called in and sat late,' he noted in his diary that same year. 'This is dangerous and ill-advised. A woman's company is always soothing, but it is a perilous indulgence.'[14]

Macready was very jealous of La Malibran, since she earned considerably more than he did. He thought it 'most unjust that a foreigner should be brought into a national theatre to receive enormous sums at the expense of the actors of the establishment.'[15]

Despite her great success and popularity in London, La Malibran was still not a goddess there; and it was in London, in 1835, that, for the first time since Sontag's retirement, she encountered a potential rival. Giulia Grisi, three years younger than La Malibran, very talented and very attractive, was singing the lead in *I Puritani*, which Bellini had composed for her. Grisi was thus already one step ahead, since Bellini had not so far composed the opera he had promised to write for La Malibran. With some daring, Grisi had elected to appear in London in La Malibran's favourite parts, Desdemona and Amina; she was not yet a success in London — for her *Otello* the theatre was half empty[16] — and Bellini did not greatly admire her,[17] but others, notably young Princess Victoria, did. La Malibran and Grisi were seemingly very friendly, and sang duets together at private concerts; but Grisi was a potential threat all the same, and La Malibran knew that, if she were to put a foot wrong and fall from her pinnacle of fame, it was Grisi who would replace her. As a result, her exertions from 1835 onwards became ever more frenetic. She sang even more often, there were more late nights, more hazardous journeys, an even more frantic search for applause.

When La Malibran and Bériot left for Italy at the end of the London season, people there who were fond of her — Bunn, Moscheles — said good-bye to her with misgiving; by now it was obvious to them that the pace of her life was too fast, and that she would not be able to continue like that for much longer. Her brother was of the same opinion.[18]

8

When La Malibran and Bériot arrived in Lucca in August, 1835, they found themselves in the midst of a serious cholera epidemic. People all around were dying, and no one's mind was on opera, even if sung by a goddess. There were intimations of mortality everywhere, and La Malibran was profoundly affected. 'I'm in a very sad mood,' she told a friend, 'for everyone talks only of death, illness, cholera, the devil, hell and purgatory, in which I am up to my neck.'[1]

They left Lucca, and had to make their way to Milan for the autumn season. But the cholera, which had spread to Genoa, made it impossible for them to travel that way. At Carrara, La Malibran decided to risk crossing the Apennines on a mule track through the Spolverino pass; it was a dangerous undertaking, which is probably why it appealed to her. She hired twenty-five men, two carts, eight oxen and six mules; she rode ahead, singing, while Bériot, who did not relish that means of transport, followed in one of the carts. It was a very tough journey, made worse by robbers and the difficulty of finding food, for people feared that the travellers might be infected with cholera, and often refused to have any contact with them. Finally, however, they succeeded in crossing the mountains, and arrived in Milan for the opening of the season.

The Milan season of 1835–6 was to be long — almost seven months. It opened with a series of performances of *Otello*, with La Malibran as Desdemona. The part had lost much of its significance for her, and the Milanese thought the opera old-fashioned; but the magic still worked. She had no difficulty in 'conquering' both her audience and the critics, one of whom compared her to Halley's Comet,[2] due to appear that year on 12th October.

On 23rd September, La Malibran had once again to die as Desdemona. On that same day at Puteaux, near Paris, a real death was taking place which had the greatest significance for her. Unbeknown to her — or to anyone else — Bellini was dying; and by five o'clock, when she was preparing for the evening performance of *Otello*, he was lying dead in an empty house. He was not quite thirty-four years old.

The news of this totally unexpected death reached Milan nine days later; when she heard it, La Malibran broke down and, putting her hand to her forehead, said: '*Sento che non tarderò molto a seguirlo.*'[3] ('I feel that it won't be very long before I follow him.')

La Malibran and Bellini had met fleetingly for the last time a few months earlier, in Paris. He had written to a friend that he had seen his 'dear Malibran' again, 'still with her prodigious talent and her extraordinary madness.'[4] She had then just learned of the annulment of her first marriage, and was full of plans for marrying Bériot; the meeting with Bellini had been of relatively minor importance — at any rate, to her. Their relationship had been tenuous in the extreme: a few meetings, a letter, perhaps a few regrets on Bellini's part, and very little more. But his death — the first of someone of her own generation — shocked her deeply. As artists, they had been made for each other, and he would never now write the opera which he had promised her, which she had so ardently desired; and, as Bellini's presentiments that he would die young had been fulfilled, La Malibran increasingly believed that her own premonitions would be fulfilled, too.

By some irony of fate, on the day when the news reached her, La Malibran was appearing in *L'elisir d'amore*; it was the first time she had sung Donizetti's music, and it was a great success. This would not have pleased Bellini, who was unjustifiably suspicious of, and hostile to, Donizetti. But, following the news of Bellini's death, La Malibran refused to sing his music for three and a half months. She never sang *Norma* again. Instead, she sang comic operas, in which death did not figure — *Il barbiere*, and *L'elisir d'amore*.

Bellini almost certainly died of natural causes — chronic amebiasis and an abscess on the liver, improperly diagnosed and treated.[5] But the circumstances of his death, which shocked the whole of Europe, were bizarre, and immediately gave rise to wild rumours. About ten days before the occurrence, the people with whom he was staying in Puteaux had refused to allow his friends to see him; they may have suspected that he had cholera. So Bellini died alone, and was found later by a friend. Rumours spread that he had been robbed, or poisoned, or both. A post-mortem revealed that he had not been poisoned, but the rumours persisted — indeed, they multiplied. Relic hunters — and relic manufacturers — proliferated. The cult grew so fast that, very shortly after his death, material suitable for mourning garments was being sold in Paris under the name of 'Bellini'; fragments were soon being chipped off his tomb as relics.[6]

In Milan, where Bellini's successful career had started, and where he was well known and well liked, the news of his death was received with consternation. There was a memorial service, and money for a monument was collected; La Malibran contributed both her voice and her money. Donizetti, unaware of Bellini's unjust suspicions about him, composed a *Messa da Requiem*,[7] and also a *Lamento per la morte di V. Bellini*,[8] which he dedicated to La Malibran.

On hearing the news of Bellini's death La Malibran at once wrote a letter of condolence to his closest friend, Francesco Florimo, in Naples, saying that 'the ill-fated day of 23rd September would be of sad memory in the annals of the Italian theatre.'[9] It was the kind of banal phrase that one writes on such occasions; but, like so many incidents in La Malibran's life, it was uncannily prophetic, for she herself was also to die on 23rd September, a year later.

Ferdinando Paer, in Paris, gave a funeral oration in which he said: 'A cruel destiny seems inseparable from those superior spirits who are moved by *the love of art*, and who are animated by the flames of genius. Like luminous and swift meteors [Halley's Comet was expected to appear the next day] they vanish . . . Such were Raphael, Mozart, Hérold and Bellini . . .'[10] This cannot have been of much consolation to La Malibran, who was certainly 'moved by the love of art', who had so often been called a genius, and who had already been compared to Halley's Comet; Hérold, who had died relatively young three years earlier, had been her first music teacher when she had been a child in Naples.

Meanwhile, preparations for the first performance of Donizetti's *Maria Stuarda*, with La Malibran in the title-role, went ahead with some care. La Malibran and Visconti, the director of La Scala, had plans to raise the standards of operatic productions there, particularly the costumes. At that time little attention was paid to the historical accuracy of costumes, especially those for minor characters and the chorus, who were often dressed in costumes taken from some old production of a different opera set in some quite different epoch. When she was in London, La Malibran had gone to Westminster Abbey to make sketches from tombs for the costumes for *Maria Stuarda*,[11]* taking great care to make them historically accurate. She always set great store by her costumes, as Macready had noted in London; he thought them 'admirable', and added: 'Will our actors never learn? Never.'[12]

In Milan the libretto for *Maria Stuarda*† was passed by the Austrian censor, although the subject was a delicate one; any allusion to the execution of a king or queen was, since the relatively recent French Revolution, disturbing to reigning monarchs.

On 3rd December, 1835, Donizetti was in Milan to supervise rehearsals. When he arrived there, he found that the singer chosen to play Elizabeth had resigned in a huff, and the other singers were also in a recalcitrant mood. It was at this juncture, when things were not going well in the theatre, that Donizetti heard that his father had died. He could not go home to Bergamo because of rehearsals, and also perhaps because he could not bring himself to do so. Donizetti, like La Malibran, was abnormally sensitive about death; he could not even bring himself to use the word 'funeral' when writing to ask how much he owed for it.[13]

In this morbid atmosphere — La Malibran mourning Bellini and Donizetti mourning his father — rehearsals for an opera in which death plays a part proceeded uneasily. At the end of December, La Malibran was ill. At the first performance of *Maria Stuarda* (30th December, 1835) she was, according to Donizetti, 'voiceless'.[14] He alleged that she only took part because she did not want to lose her fee of 3,000 francs. She was also in a bad mood because the censor objected to her, as Mary Stuart, calling Elizabeth a 'vile bastard', and kneeling before Talbot in the confession scene. As a result, again according to Donizetti, the audience was cold towards her on the

---

* More than sixty of La Malibran's sketches for costumes have been preserved (in the Brussels Conservatoire), many for *Maria Stuarda*. They are well-drawn, fairly correct historically, show close attention to detail, and include designs for the chorus as well as for the principal singers; they include instructions for shoes, head-dresses, gloves, and so on. One drawing still has a pattern of material pinned to it.

† *Maria Stuarda*, opera in three acts, by Donizetti, libretto by Bardari, after Schiller. Originally produced at the San Carlo Theatre, Naples, as *Buondelmonte* (with the libretto changed by Salatino) on 14th October, 1834, because the original subject — the imprisonment and execution of a queen — was considered to be too sensitive. First produced in its original form at La Scala, Milan, on 30th December, 1835, with La Malibran as Mary, Queen of Scots.

first night, and only applauded on the second and third nights.[15] Donizetti therefore attributed the failure of *Maria Stuarda* — for failure it was — to La Malibran, and his admirers have continued to do so ever since — rather unjustly, for critics at the time praised her performance, while criticising the opera unfavourably.[16] Only six performances — three of them truncated — were given, before the opera was banned by the Austrian authorities.

Years later, Manuel Patricio Garcia described to Delacroix how his sister had played Mary Stuart:

> La Malibran, in *Maria Stuarda*, was taken before her rival, Elizabeth, by Leicester, who entreated her to humble herself before her rival. She finally consented to do so and, going right down on her knees, implored in earnest; but, provoked beyond measure by Elizabeth's inflexible severity, she used to stand up impetuously and let herself go in a fury which produced the greatest effect.[17]

By the middle of January, 1836, La Malibran was singing Bellini's music again, which was what the Milanese really wanted; Vaccai's *Giovanna Grey** had pleased them even less than *Maria Stuarda*. Between 16th January and the end of the season (20th March) she gave nine performances of *La sonnambula* and twenty of *I Capuleti*, which was the success of the season. In *I Capuleti* Bellini and his librettist, Romani, had reduced the whole of *Romeo and Juliet* to just two basic elements: love, and despair. These were emotions which La Malibran knew well, and her performances were overwhelmingly moving.

She also gave one last performance of *Otello*; it was the last time she was ever to play Desdemona, the part with which she was always to be identified in people's memories and in literature. On that same day her friend and employer, Duke Carlo Visconti di Modrone, died.† Bellini had also died on the day she was performing *Otello*; perhaps, after all, the Neapolitans were right, and *Otello* really was of ill-omen; at any rate it was becoming, or perhaps had always been, an opera of ill-omen for La Malibran.

Visconti had been a friend, although not perhaps an intimate one; he was old enough to be La Malibran's father — sixty-five when he

---

* Vaccai's *Giovanna Grey*, especially written for La Malibran, first produced at La Scala, 23rd February, 1836.
† 10th March, 1836.

died — which is, perhaps, why she was friendly with him. They had worked together to improve standards at La Scala, and it was Visconti who had given her a sensational three-year contract. With his death, her future became unsure; would his successor honour the contract?* The sums involved were so enormous at the time that they were enough to frighten any theatre director.

But, if the 1835–6 Milan season had been overshadowed by death, it had also been a season of love — of the Milanese audience's love for La Malibran, and her love for that audience. Ten days after Visconti's death she gave her last performance in Milan: *I Capuleti*, and the last act of *La sonnambula*.† Of all the fantastic ovations which she received, this was perhaps the most overwhelming demonstration of the public's adoration of her. The gardens of Milan and the surrounding country had been stripped of flowers, and La Malibran's slight, fragile figure seemed to disappear beneath the shower of bouquets which were thrown on to the stage. She was recalled over and over again, and the knowledge that she was engaged for the next two seasons and would soon return to Milan again made the Milanese feel that she really belonged to them. The perfect relationship between artist and audience had been achieved; the public had inspired La Malibran, and she had given herself to that public. The ovation was, said an eye-witness, 'not just the homage due to superior talent, but more like a lover's farewell to his beloved.'[18]

---

* La Malibran's death relieved Visconti's successor (Merelli) of this obligation.
† 20th March, 1836.

9

After their marriage in Paris and a short holiday in Belgium, the Bériots arrived in London for the summer season of 1836. Bunn had again engaged La Malibran to sing opera in English: *La sonnambula*, *Fidelio* and, the novelty of the season, a new opera by Balfe, which was as yet un-named.

La sonnambula was always a success. In Beethoven's *Fidelio* La Malibran earned greater praise than she had in the preceding year. Her passionate and unorthodox interpretation of the part of Leonore thrilled the public. 'To attempt to give you an idea of the surpassing beauty of Malibran's performance in *Fidelio* would be vain,' wrote one eye-witness. 'All the rest of the opera is very badly done indeed, but she swallows it all up, you see, you think of nobody but her . . .'[1]

Balfe's project for an opera based on *Hamlet* had come to nothing; but La Malibran had recommended him to Bunn, and the result had been *The Siege of Rochelle*, a great success in London in 1835. As a result, Bunn had commissioned Balfe to write another opera, this time for La Malibran. Balfe's next idea was based on Victor Hugo's *Notre Dame de Paris*.[2] La Malibran had read the novel when it first appeared in 1831, had much admired it, and had felt a strong affinity with the heroine, Esmeralda; so this project must have appealed to her. Balfe or, as he signed his letter to her, 'Billy Balfe the Hirish Potatoe Heater' (sic), wrote to ask her opinion about his idea, as he was very keen 'to write an opera worthy of my little *idol* Marietta Malibran.'[3]

But Bunn had other plans; he fancied himself as a poet, and wrote a libretto for *The Maid of Artois*, a story vaguely similar to *Manon Lescaut*. His verses were atrocious; Balfe seems to have paid as little attention to them as possible, and to have succeeded in composing a work which was, at that time, considered to be theatrically viable and charming, and which contained two hit tunes.*

---

* The hit tunes in Balfe's *Maid of Artois* were: *With rapture dwelling*, which became known as 'Balfe's air'; and *The light of other days*.

When *The Maid of Artois* opened, on 27th May, La Malibran's success was just as great as it had been in *Fidelio* and *La sonnambula*. Balfe's pretty, but weak, music could scarcely compete with that of Beethoven or even of Bellini; but her 'power of exciting the audience'[4] could, and often did, transform an insignificant work into a great theatrical experience. *The Maid of Artois* was the success of the season; it was acclaimed by the press and the public, as well as by serious and discriminating musicians. Moscheles, for example, thought that La Malibran performed it 'marvellously';[5] and Julius Benedict remembered in after years: 'Nothing has ever exceeded the effect she produced in Balfe's *Maid of Artois*.'[6]

However, despite her brilliant successes, she was deeply depressed. In a letter to her publisher and close friend, Troupenas, she told him that her complexion was being ruined by 'the galley-slave's life' she was leading; and she told him, too, that she had lost a lot of weight — always a sure sign with her that she was depressed.[7] The fact was that she was again pregnant; and, if pregnancy in the past had always been a serious inconvenience, this time it was a disaster. In an additional paragraph which Visconti had prudently pinned on to her three-year contract for La Scala, he had stipulated that, in case of pregnancy, she must give him five months' notice, and sing nowhere else.[8] If this pregnancy were to continue, she would be unable to sing in the autumn and spring seasons, 1836–7, in Milan, or anywhere else either. It was small wonder that she told Troupenas that her morale was very low.

A little over a fortnight later, Moscheles gave a concert to a large audience in his own house. At about eleven in the evening, La Malibran and Bériot arrived. Later he commented:

> She looked weary, and, when she sang, one scarcely recognised Malibran, she was so voiceless. We only heard subsequently that she had been thrown from her horse when riding in the park. Although suffering no injury, she had not yet recovered from the violent shock. She was soon herself, however, and sang . . .[9]

She did, indeed, sing: two *scenas* from *Der Freischütz*, an English duet, three Spanish, Italian and French songs, and the duet *Le Songe de Tartini* with Bériot. The evening went on for a long time; at three o'clock in the morning Bériot was still there, gossiping. But, contrary to her usual habits, by then La Malibran had gone home to bed.

Her fall from her horse had been far more serious than Moscheles — or anyone else except La Malibran herself — knew. She had been riding in Regent's Park with her friends, Lord William Lennox and a Mr and Mrs John Clayton. Lennox, the fourth son of the fourth Duke of Richmond, was an old friend — she had met him in Chester in 1828; because of his marriage to the singer, Mary Ann Paton (dissolved in 1831) he moved in theatrical circles, and was portrayed by Disraeli as 'Lord Prima Donna' in *Vivian Grey*. Like all his family, he was a fine horseman, and he provided La Malibran with mounts.

La Malibran had not been well a couple of days earlier, but she insisted on riding despite this, and despite a premonition of some impending misfortune. Bériot, knowing that she was pregnant, had forbidden her to ride,[10] and Lennox and the Claytons also tried to dissuade her.[11] It is probable that she insisted in the hope of provoking a miscarriage.

La Malibran rode ahead with Mr Clayton; Lord William and Mrs Clayton following behind. When they set out, 'her entire conversation with Mr Clayton turned upon the melancholy presentiment.' But suddenly, with her usual gaiety, she said: 'I will have a gallop, and leave dull care behind.'[12]

Lennox has described what happened next:

> On setting off at a canter, she plied her light riding-whip too severely upon the horse's neck. The animal, usually quiet, got his mettle up, and suddenly increased his pace. A clatter of some horses behind added to his excitement, and in a few seconds the rider had lost all control over her steed.
>
> I was a few paces in the rear, and called upon Mr and Mrs Clayton to check their speed at once. Bounding round the inner circle of Regent's Park at an awful pace, Malibran, feeling herself lost, shouted for help, when a policeman rushed forward and seized the horse by the bridle. Unprepared for this sudden movement, the rider was precipitated against the wooden paling, and fell exhausted to the ground.
>
> Upon raising her, we found a contusion on her temple the size of an egg, and she was evidently suffering from some internal injury. A gentleman drove up in an open carriage, and

having offered his assistance, the sufferer was conveyed to her lodgings in Maddox Street.[12]*

Bériot was not at home when she was brought back, but Julius Benedict was there. He remembered that La Malibran was unwilling, indeed afraid, to mention the accident to her husband; she made Benedict promise not to tell Bériot. It was decided that she would say that she had fallen downstairs.[13]

She was very badly bruised and shaken, and her friend and homœopathic doctor, Dr Belluomini, was called. The doctor found her suffering from 'great shock of mind and body, contusions on the head, and an impossibility of moving her left arm at the shoulder.'[14] He administered various homœopathic remedies, and strongly advised her not to sing at Drury Lane that evening; but she took no notice of his advice. She spent the rest of the day trying to conceal her bruises with make-up.[15] When Lennox, on his way to dine in town, called to enquire how she was, he was astonished to learn that she had gone to the theatre.

How long the fiction that she had fallen downstairs was kept up, it is difficult to say, but it was probably for some time. Three weeks later, she was still maintaining to Troupenas that she had fallen 'outside my front door.'[16] In any case, the accident was not reported in the press which, at that time, covered many lesser accidents suffered by much less well-known people. According to Madame Merlin, La Malibran wrote a note to Lennox, asking him not to tell Bériot the true cause of her accident;[17] Lennox may have succeeded in keeping the news out of the press.

The accident happened on 5th July. On 1st July La Malibran's benefit performance had taken place; she had sung *The Maid of Artois* and the last act of *Fidelio*, and had received her customary ovation. That was the end of her contract; but Bunn had re-engaged her for a few more performances. There were none on 2nd, 3rd and 4th July, but she was supposed to sing at a concert on 4th July — she did not do so, as she was 'indisposed'. On 5th July, the day on which the accident occurred, she was due to embark on a gruelling series of four performances on four consecutive nights.

She went through with the four performances; they were: *The*

---

* Countess Merlin (II, p. 67) gives a very different account of the accident, which is repeated in almost all biographies, including Bushnell. But the Countess was not a witness of the accident, whereas Lennox was.

Maid of Artois (5th July); *Fidelio* and the second act of *La sonnambula* (6th July); *The Maid of Artois* (7th July); and *La sonnambula* (8th July). The feat of endurance necessary immediately after her accident was enormous, and had a disastrous effect on her health. She knew this perfectly well herself. On 12th July she wrote to a friend: 'I don't think I'll ever go back [to Paris] again, because I feel very ill. I'm still singing diligently for the English, but my voice is going off. I'm finished.'[18]

Why had she done it? Because it was a challenge? From fear of Bériot? To provoke a miscarriage? For money? Deliberate self-destruction? Perhaps for one or all of these reasons; but, as subsequent events showed, fear of offending the public was probably the principal factor.

In any case, her accident does not seem to have impaired her performances in any way. The public was as enthusiastic as ever. When she appeared for the last time that season, on 16th July in *The Maid of Artois* and the last act of *La sonnambula*, she received an ovation which, even for her, was remarkable. She was visibly very moved by it, and brought the evening to a close by singing *God Save the King*.

The *Morning Post* critic summed up the season and, had he but known it, her whole career. 'The performances of Malibran,' he said, 'will form an era in the history of the stage.'[19] That era was already over; it was her last performance in a major theatre,* and she fittingly ended her stage career by singing Bellini's music.

Just before the Bériots left London for Belgium, Moscheles went to say good-bye to them.

> We found her at the piano, and Costa standing by her. She sang us a comic song that she had just composed: A sick man weary of life invokes death; but when death, personified as a doctor, knocks at his door, he dismisses him with scorn. She had set the subject so cleverly, and sang the music so humorously, that we could scarcely refrain from laughing; and yet we couldn't endure to lose a single note.[20]

La Malibran's friend and colleague, the bass singer Lablache, had

---

* Although she never appeared in a major theatre again, she did give two performances at Aix-la-Chapelle (Aachen)) (see p. 218).

given her the words of this song, *La morte*,* written by a certain Benelli. The song is, indeed, humorous in intent, although it is rather sick humour; but the subject, and the fact that Benelli died suddenly shortly after writing the words, made people consider it a song of ill-omen.[21]

---

* *La morte*. I have not been able to trace a copy of the Italian text. Here is the French version, translated from the Italian by Emile Deschamps:

La Mort

Pan! Pan! qui frappe là? Pan! Pan!
Je suis la mort, la mort eh!
Camarade he! vite ho là!
Ouvre la porte que je t'emporte,
Ouvre à la mort.

Belle santé, tous les jours je t'invoque
L'ingrate qui se moque paraît et puis s'en va.
La santé je t'invoque ah! L'ingrate qui se moque ah!
L'ingrate qui se moque ah!
Paraît et puis s'en va.
Etc., etc.

PART IV

MANCHESTER

Combination of Attractions!
MADAME MALIBRAN,
Mad. JENNY VERTPRE. & Mons. ARNAL

Theatre Royal, Drury Lane.

☞ The Public is most respectfully informed that, the demand for Places to witness the performances of

Mad.ᵉ MALIBRAN

has so exceeded all precedent, that every exertion has been made to effect a Re-Engagement; and therefore **THIS UNRIVALLED ACTRESS** will perform To-Night, and 4 times in the ensuing Week, Being the Last Nights of her Appearance on the English Stage this Year

This Evening, FRIDAY, July 8th, 1836,
Their Majesties' Servants will perform the popular Entertainment of

Turning the Tables

Jack Humphries, Mr. MEADOWS,	Edgar de Courcey, Mr. BRINDAL,
Jeremiah Bumps, ...	Mr. COOPER,
Mr. Knibbs, ... Mr. HUGHES,	Mr. Thornton, ... Mr. BAKER,
Miss Knibbs, Miss LEE,	Mrs. Humphries, Miss SOMERVILLE,
Patty Larkins, ...	Mrs. C. JONES.

After which Bellini's popular Opera of

LA SONNAMBULA!

With the whole of the Music, by the celebrated Composer, BELLINI.

Count Rhodolpho, ... Mr. SEGUIN,
Elvino, ... Mr. TEMPLETON,
Alessio, Mr. DURUSET, Pedro, Mr. HUGHES.
Notary, Mr. TURNOUR, Joanno, Mr. HENRY.
Amina, ... Madame MALIBRAN,
Térésa, Mrs. C. JONES, Liza, Miss FORDE.
Villagers—Messrs. T. Price, Birt, Rakes, Butler, Chant, Atkins, Healy, T. Jones, S. Jones, Miller, S. Tett
Macarthy, C. Tett, Tolkien, White, Lloyd.
Mesdames Allcroft, Boden, R. Boden, Butler, Connelly, East, Goodson, Goodwin, Hughes, Mapleson, Perry, &c. &c.
Peasants—Messrs. Ellar, Gough, Heath, Jenkins, Smith, Hartland, Kirke, Thorne, &c. &c.
Mesdames Ryals, Thomasin, Lydia, Reekie, Hall, Valaucy, Marchant, Foster, Bennett, S. Bennett, Mears
Marsano, Sutton, Vials, Hatton, &c. &c.

After the Opera will be introduced the Comic Duet of
'WHEN A LITTLE FARM WE KEEP,'
By MADAME MALIBRAN, and Mr. PARRY, Junior. (in imitation of a celebrated Comedian)
(As Sung by them with the greatest Success at the different Public Concerts).

To conclude with the popular French Vaudeville, entitled
Mons. et Mad. GALOCHARD!

De Beusrade, Poëte, ... Monsieur LAUTEMAN,
Le Chevalier de Bussy, M. BERTON, Un Valet de Chambre du Roi, M. CHEVALIER,
Monsieur Galochard, by Monsieur ARNAL.
Madame Galochard, ... by .... Madame JENNY VERTPRE.
Suzon, Madame ADELINE. Nanette, Madame COSSARD.

On Monday, **The Siege of Rochelle**. Michel, Mr. H. Phillips, Clara, Miss Shirreff. With **A Musical Melange**, in which Mademoiselle G. Grisi, Signor Rubini, Signor Tamburini, Signor Curioni, Signor Lablache, and Herr Ole Bull will appear. A Grand Pas de Deux, from BENIOWSKY, by Mademoiselle Carlotta Grisi, and M. Perrot. And **Deaf as a Post.**
On Tuesday, **THE MAID OF ARTOIS.** Isoline, Mad. Malibran.

☞ The Free List (except the Press) will be totally suspended

Vivant Rex et Regina.   No Money returned   W. Wright, Printer, Theatre Royal, Drury Lane.

Playbill for La Malibran's performance of *La sonnambula* at the Theatre Royal, Drury Lane, on Friday, 8th July, 1836. This was the last of the four performances which she gave after her riding accident on 5th July. *Le Cesne Collection, Paris*

PROGRAMME.

PART FIRST.

SINFONIA.................. (in D) .... *Mozart.*

AIR, Mr. Machin...... "She wore a wreath".....*Knight.*

DUETTO, Mademoiselle Assandri and **Signor Ivanoff**.. " La ci darem la mano.".. (Il Don Giovanni)..*Mozart.*

AIR, Miss C. Novello........ "Idole de ma vie"........ *Meyerbeer.*

CONCERTO VIOLONCELLO,.................... Mr. Lindley................... *Lindley.*

CANZONET, Mrs. A. Shaw........ "She never told her love"........ *Haydn.*

CANON, Madame Malibran De Beriot, Miss C. Novello, Mr. Bennett, and Mr. H. Phillips, " What joy doth fill my breast" ...... (Fidelio)................... *Beethoven.*

AIR, Mrs. H. R. Bishop...... "Rose softly blooming"...... (Azor and Zemira)...... *Spohr.*

DUETTO, Madame Caradori Allan and Madame Malibran De Beriot ...... "Vanne se alberghi in petto" (Andronico)...... *Mercadante.*

CANTATA, Mr. Braham............. "Mad Tom"............. *Purcell.* (Accompanied on the Piano-forte by Sir George Smart).

QUINTETTO, Madame Caradori Allan, Mademoiselle Assandri, Signor Ivanoff, Mr. H. Phillips, and Signor Lablache...... "Oh guardate che accidente" ..... (Il Turco in Italia)...... *Rossini*

PART SECOND.

OVERTURE TO GUILLAUME TELL, ... *Rossini.*

AIR, Mrs. W. Knyvett...... "Lo! here the gentle Lark"...... Flute Obligato, Mr. Nicholson.... *H. R. Bishop.*

ARIA, Signor Lablache...... " Non piu andrai"...... (Figaro)...... *Mozart.*

QUINTETTO, Madame Malibran De Beriot, Mademoiselle Assandri, Signor Ivanoff, Mr. H. Phillips, and Signor Lablache.... "Sento, Oh Dio!".... (Cosi fan tutte) .... *Mozart.*

ARIA, Madame Caradori Allan...... " Come per me sereno"...... (La Sonnambula)...... *Bellini*

SEPTETTO for Flute, Oboe, Clarionet, Bassoon, Horn, Trumpet and Contra-Basso, Messrs. Nicholson, G. Cooke, Willman, Baumann, Platt, Harper and Dragonetti .... *Neukomm.*

AIR, Mr. Bennett............. "The Exile's Farewell"......... .... *Bennett.*

DUETTO, Signor Lablache and Mr. H. Phillips.. "Se fiato in corpo avete".. (Il Matrimonio segreto).. *Cimarosa.*

AIR, Madame Malibran De Beriot ..... "Le Songe de Tartini" ou " La Cadence du Diable" accompanied on the Piano-Forte by Madame Malibran De Beriot, and Violino Obligato, Monsieur De Beriot.
De Beriot and Penseron.

OVERTURE TO EURYANTHE, ... *C. M. Von Weber.*

Programme of La Malibran's last concert, Wednesday, 15th September, 1836, in Manchester. *Le Cesne Collection, Paris*

(*Above*) Charles de Bériot, with the bust which he made of La
Malibran after her death. Lithograph by Ch. Baugniet, 1838.
Copyright Royal College of Music, London
(*Below*) Engraving by Achille Bertarelli, showing Bellini
welcoming La Malibran to the Elysian fields. *Civica Raccolta
Stampe 'A. Bertarelli' Castello Sforzesco Milano*

Drawing of Manuel Garcia and his daughter Maria as Otello and Desdemona, by Jean-Albert Carlotti, made for the strip-cartoon in *France-Soir*, 13.V.1978 – 15.VI.1978 (in the series *Les Amours célèbres*), text by Paul Gordeaux. *Le Cesne Collection, Paris. Reproduced by kind permission of the artist*

1

La Malibran's family saw a great change in her on her return to Brussels. Not only was she still covered with bruises as a result of her accident, but her character seemed to have altered. She had become very capricious and difficult to please; the alternating manic and depressive moods, from which she had always suffered, now alternated much more rapidly. Her family attributed these changes to her pregnancy. She herself knew otherwise; she told her young sister — swearing her to secrecy — that she knew she was mortally ill, and had not long to live.[1]

Her friend and publisher, Troupenas, had asked her to compose an album of songs, and this she was trying to do during her holiday. The words which he had sent her for a *Ballade* did not inspire her; they were 'pretty', she said, but she needed stronger sensations. 'Send me some [words] which will make my hair stand on end,'[2] she implored him. She planned to dedicate each song in this album to a friend who had been present at her marriage to Bériot; the album was to be a kind of musical testament.*

In a letter written at the end of July she told Troupenas:

I am not at all well. Since my fall, I have frequent headaches and palpitations, which force me to get up 4 or 5 times a night. About three weeks ago, I almost succumbed, when I fell at the door of my house on my way back from the most peaceful *promenade†* — that didn't prevent me from performing, in spite of my disfigured profile and my black and blue forehead. Ask

---

* *Les dernières pensées musicales de M. F. Malibran de Bériot, Recueil de dix romances ou ballades françaises et deux ariettes italiennes avec accompagnement de piano ou de guitare, ornées de superbes Lithographes de Julies (sic) David*, London, n.d., D'Almaine and Co., 20, Soho Square. The songs are dedicated to: Mme Sophie Bertin de Veaux; Virginie Cottinet; Sophie Boutellier; Clotilde Troupenas; the Marquis de Louvois; Baron Paul Pérignon; Rossini; Auber; Nourrit; and Lablache (*La Mort*).
† *Promenade* can mean 'a walk' or 'a ride' in French.

Benedict — *4 evenings running*. So I am paying for my audacity now, and my bravery only served to spoil my future.[3]

She made a little sketch of her 'disfigured profile' on the margin of the letter.

It seems, from this letter, that the myth that she had fallen at home or, as she says, 'at the door of my house', rather than in Regent's Park, was still being kept up almost a month after the event.

In the same letter, she asked Troupenas: 'Is it true that Rossini is writing an opera for me? People assure me that he wants to do it as a surprise for me.* I would give my soul for something like that, at the risk of performing his opera and dying after the first performance.'[3]

Despite her ill-health and her pregnancy, La Malibran's holiday was short; she refused to cancel any engagements. This was, perhaps, because she and her husband had already spent 110,000 francs that year on their properties in Belgium and at Roissy, near Pontoise.[4] Or perhaps it was because journeys, rehearsals and concerts prevented her from thinking too much. On 14th August she gave a concert in Liège, at which her sister Pauline, aged fifteen, appeared with her for the first and only time. A few days later she gave two performances of *La sonnambula* at Aix-la-Chapelle (Aachen), singing in Italian, while the rest of the company sang in German. These were her last performances in any theatre. At the end of August she passed through Paris, and on 7th September she set out for Manchester. She was engaged to sing at the festival there, and intended afterwards to go on to Worcester, Liverpool, Norwich and Dublin.

There had been some rumours in Manchester that La Malibran would not be well enough to take part in the festival. But, to everyone's relief, the Bériots arrived there during the afternoon of Sunday, 11th September. Those who knew La Malibran were struck by her changed appearance; she was hollow-eyed and thin.

The Bériots went first to the Royal Hotel; but, on hearing that some of their friends and colleagues were at the Mosley Arms, they

---

* There seems to be no evidence that Rossini was contemplating writing an opera for La Malibran. His last opera, *Guillaume Tell*, had been produced in 1829; although he was to live for another thirty-nine years, he never wrote another opera.

transferred to that hotel. They were given room No 9, which pleased La Malibran, as she had had room No 9 (in the old Mosley Arms) eleven years earlier, just before she left for America.

But she was not pleased with everything. She was very dissatisfied with some of the programmes arranged for her, and tried, unsuccessfully, to persuade a member of the Festival Committee to change them. His refusal vexed her very much. She complained to him of shivering and a headache; but this did not prevent her from singing fourteen pieces to her friends in the hotel that evening. Bériot, knowing that she had an important rehearsal next morning, tried to restrain her, but she paid no attention to him.

She was not well next day, but she attended a dress rehearsal for the Sacred Concert, and was the centre of an admiring crowd. On the following day, Tuesday, 13th September, the festival opened with a mammoth concert of sacred music in the morning at the Collegiate Church (now Manchester Cathedral). La Malibran did not take part in Haydn's *Creation*, which opened the concert, but she later sang arias by Handel and Cimarosa.

That same evening there was another very long concert, this time of secular music. La Malibran was very unwell, and complained of sickness; but she insisted on performing. She sang an aria from Mozart's *La clemenza di Tito*, which was particularly praised, and also took part in the sextet from *Don Giovanni*.

Her old friend, Mrs Novello, was in Manchester for the festival, accompanying her eighteen-year-old daughter, Clara, who had been engaged to sing. That evening, in spite of feeling very ill, La Malibran gave the young girl some friendly advice about her performance and appearance — she thought that her mother dressed her too plainly. Then she re-arranged Clara's hair for her, and gave her her own double-headed silver hair-pin, saying: 'You will not like it the less because I have worn it in Amina.'[5] Clara kept the pin ever after as a talisman.

Mrs Novello had never seen La Malibran:

... look so lovely, or dressed more tastefully; yet she was in such great pain that when she sang she was obliged to lean for support on the pianoforte, and her feet were so clay cold that I held them for hours in my lap and chafed them with my hands to impart some small portion of warmth to them.[6]

All the same, in a comic duet with Lablache La Malibran 'threw the whole audience into a rapture of laughter.'[7]

The next morning she complained of feeling ill before she got up. She took her usual breakfast of oysters and diluted porter, but was sick. Mrs Richardson, the kindly landlady of the Mosley Arms, said that she thought the porter did not agree with her. La Malibran replied: 'What can I do? I must take something for my voice, and I find this the best thing I can take.'[8] Since the beginning of her pregnancy she had suffered from morning sickness, and had 'an aversion for meat and all nutritious things. She disliked sugar and everything that was sweet, and was fond only of oysters, fruit, anchovies and other slight food, and she sustained her strength with porter and other artificial means.'[9]

She went to the morning concert, another very long programme of sacred music, and in spite of feeling ill she sang particularly effectively. The audience did not know that, on arriving at the church, she had had such a bad headache that she 'had retired to repose in a room at the house of Mrs Hutchinson, a confectioner', before coming back to the church to sing. While she was with Mrs Hutchinson 'she was very ill, and repeatedly exclaimed: "Oh, I am in a fever, and shall surely die!" '[10] But she still did not dare disappoint the public. The *Manchester Guardian* critic considered that 'nothing more magnificent could be conceived, even for this accomplished singer',[11] than her performance that morning of an aria by Pergolesi.

In a duet by Marcello which followed, she was 'all energy and fire'. She sang it with Clara Novello, and was determined that it should create a great effect. She refused to write down the cadence which they were to introduce, saying to Clara: 'You will follow me; I am quite sure of you and of its being encored.' It was. Just before they began it for the second time, Maria caught the eye of Mrs Novello in the audience, and whispered to Clara: 'Look how pleased Mamma looks!'[12]

After the concert, someone congratulated La Malibran on having sung so well, despite feeling ill. ' "Yes," she said, with deep emotion, "My voice is still very good, but it is God alone that gives me strength, and that sustains me." '[13]

She was no better in the evening, but insisted on going to the secular concert. The programme was immensely long — it was to last four hours — and she was to sing two items in the first part, and two in the second, including a duet with Bériot towards the very end of the programme. She first sang in the canon for four voices from *Fidelio*. Then Mrs Bishop and Braham sang arias, and then she came on to the platform again with Madame Caradori-Allan, to sing a duet from Mercadante's *Andronico: Vanne se alberghi in petto.*

By some strange coincidence, Madame Caradori-Allan had made her début in Manchester in 1825 at the same concert at which the 17-year-old Maria Garcia had appeared. They had subsequently often sung together. So they were old friends — or were they? When La Malibran had fallen from favour in Paris in 1831 because of her pregnancy, she had suspected Madame Caradori-Allan of criticising her — it seems, unjustly.[14] But that had probably all been forgotten; they had sung the same duet by Mercadante together the season before, at Madame Caradori-Allan's benefit concert. Immediately after that performance, superstitious people later recalled, Madame Caradori-Allan had been dangerously ill for weeks.

At the rehearsal for the concert in Manchester the two singers had settled how they would perform the duet; but when it came to the actual concert, according to Sir George Smart, who was conducting,

> Madame Caradori-Allan made some deviation; this prompted Malibran to do the same, in which she displayed most wonderful execution. During the well-deserved encore she turned to me and said: 'If I sing it again it will kill me.' 'Then do not,' I replied, 'let me address the audience.' 'No,' said she, 'I will sing it again and annihilate her.'[15]*

There can be no doubt at all that the repeat performance of Mercadante's duet was something quite exceptional; this is vouched for by critics writing next day, who had no idea that it was to be La Malibran's swan song. The *Manchester Guardian* critic reported:

> Mercadante's Duetto by Mesdames Caradori-Allan and de Bériot was decidedly the most marked feature of the evening's performance, and excited an extraordinary sensation. A powerful feeling of emulation seemed to pervade both ladies, and the efforts of each were met by a corresponding exertion on the part of her rival, for rivals in a (we hope friendly) contest for public admiration they certainly were.[16]

Another critic said that the duet would have been

---

* Many biographers — Quicherat, for example — omit the last three words, '. . . and annihilate her', since they show La Malibran in a bad light.

charming, but for a trick of unlovely rivalry in Malibran, who, being second, took it upon herself to oversing the principal in graces and shakes of Caradori's own choosing. This may have been a joke. It looked very like earnest. Malibran's eyes, let us hope, do not always shoot these fires at her friends.[17]

The *Morning Post* critic* wrote that La Malibran's 'exertions in the *encore* of this duet were tremendous, and the fearful shake at the top of her voice will never be forgotten by those who heard it.'[18] But he was writing on 26th September and, unlike his colleagues quoted above, already knew what had happened next.

What happened immediately after the duet was that La Malibran left the stage and collapsed. Most accounts say that she fainted; but more probably she had one of those hysterical fits to which she was prone. She was, in any case, in a highly over-excited state as a result of her duel with Madame Caradori-Allan. According to the *Morning Post* she was 'seized by a nervous paroxysm, in which her shrieks were terrible; they reverberated through the hall . . .'[18] But no one else reported this, and in fact the audience was unaware that she was ill, until there was an appeal for a doctor to go back-stage.

Dr Bardsley, who was sitting in the pit, and Mr Worthington, a surgeon, answered this appeal. Shortly afterwards, one of the stewards announced that Madame Malibran had become so ill that Dr Bardsley had thought fit to bleed her in the arm, and that he did not think it would be safe for her to sing again that evening.

At that moment, Bériot was not there; Lablache, knowing that she was pregnant and believed only in homœopathy, which was opposed to blood-letting, begged Dr Bardsley not to bleed her, and went to look for Bériot. But the doctor said that he could not answer for her life unless he bled her, and he did so.

When the doctor had finished bleeding her, a bystander said, in La Malibran's hearing, that he hoped she would be better shortly, and 'able to resume her duties' that evening. He spoke for her old adversary, the public, which had paid good money to hear her sing, and considered it her 'duty' to entertain it. La Malibran, faint, pale from loss of blood, raised her head and said: 'What, do you think *I* am like your English fighters; that I can lose blood, and go to work again directly?'[19]

The concert continued. Her friends and colleagues went on

---

* The *Morning Post* critic was C. L. Gruneisen.

performing as if nothing had happened; but, when they came off stage, they watched aghast as she was bled, and her life seemed to be slipping away with her blood. Lablache, who loved her like a father, was distraught; but he all the same brought down the house in a comic duet from *Il matrimonio segreto*. At the very end of the concert Bériot played a concerto. Lablache remembered later how he had stood in the wings, trying to attract Bériot's attention, and how the audience, ignorant of what was happening back-stage, relentlessly demanded an encore.* La Malibran was eventually taken back to her hotel where, since she had no maid, she was looked after by the landlady, Mrs Richardson.

The *Morning Post* critic, who was staying in the same hotel, said that 'her agonising cries that night will not be erased from the memory of the writer of this article [. . .] She constantly ejaculated *"Je m'etouffe (sic), O, mon cher ami!"* '[20]

Early next morning La Malibran felt so ill that she decided not to sing at the morning concert. But, from early morning onwards, members of the Festival Committee sent messages, and actually called in person, to enquire how she was, and to ask if she would be singing that day. They probably genuinely enquired from kindness, but they also understandably wanted to know whether they had to alter the programmes; La Malibran was, after all, the principal attraction at the festival. La Malibran took these enquiries in bad part; she realised that, ill though she was, the public would give her no quarter. She said to Bériot: 'Oh dear, say what you will, you see these people will not believe that I am ill.' She told a member of the Festival Committee: 'I will go, lest people should think it is only a sham.'[21]

Then she told Mrs Richardson: 'I have been trying my voice in bed, and it is as strong and clear, and I have as much power as though I were in perfect health; but every note seems to reverberate through my brain.'[22]

In spite of the entreaties of Bériot and Mrs Richardson, she became determined to go to the concert. But she was too ill to dress herself, and Mrs Richardson had to help her; it took a very long time. While her thick, dark hair was being arranged, La Malibran said to Bériot: 'Oh dear! This hair; why should I not get rid of it? I can wear a

* Legouvé's account of Lablache's memories, though probably true in substance, contains several inaccuracies. (*Maria Malibran*, pp. 40–42).

cap? and I am sure I should feel a great deal better if this hair was taken from my head.'[23]

Bériot led his wife into the sitting-room, where she had a violent attack of vomiting; but she was still set on going to the concert, so the Boroughreeve's carriage, inexorably waiting to take her to the church, was lined with sheets and towels. She was almost carried to the carriage, and climbed into it on her hands and knees.

She arrived at the church, but as soon as she heard the first notes of music, she became violently hysterical. Young Clara Novello, who was accompanying her on to the stage, was terrified to see her fall rigid and contorted in a convulsion.[24] But the concert had to proceed; Clara went on to sing, and La Malibran was taken back to her hotel. When she got there, she said: 'Oh! How I wish I could have sung, for I never was in finer voice.'[25]

She was attended by Dr Bardsley and Mr Worthington, who later issued a certificate that she would not be able to sing that day. Next day, a Dr Hull was also called in, and the three doctors issued a further certificate to say that she could not sing.

But it was not only the Manchester Festival authorities who were keen to know when La Malibran would 'resume her duties'. News of her illness had already reached Dublin, where she was booked to sing later that month. Two emissaries were sent over to Manchester to find out if she would be able to fulfil her engagement. When La Malibran heard that they had arrived, and was told the reason for their mission, she became very over-excited — so over-excited, that Dr Bardsley took it on himself to say that she would not be able to sing in Dublin, as it might endanger her life. He and two other doctors signed a certificate to that effect.[26]

That evening, Bériot performed a concerto of his own at a concert. La Malibran was very concerned to know how he had played, and when told that he had been well received and much applauded, she seemed happy. 'If he had had any faults, I should have found them out before now,' she told Mrs Richardson. 'I am certainly blest with a most affectionate husband.'[27]

Dr Bardsley, Dr Hull and Mr Worthington were in constant attendance. Mr Worthington, the surgeon, spent the whole night of Saturday, 17th September to Sunday, 18th September at the Mosley Arms, at La Malibran's request. The doctors saw her again on Sunday morning, found her slightly better, and considered that the danger of a miscarriage had passed and that, with care and rest, she would recover.[28]

Meanwhile, Charles de Bériot had written to Dr Joseph Belluomini, his wife's homœopathic doctor in London:

My poor Maria is seriously ill and in bed. She has been bled, but the complaint has only been augmented by it, and she is today in a state of constant delirium. I do not know what to do, or what will happen. I am in despair. Your presence would restore life to us both.[29]

Dr Belluomini left London by post-chaise on 17th September, and arrived in Manchester the following day at 6.30 pm. That afternoon Mrs Novello had visited Maria; she had found Bériot in tears and, learning that his wife had no woman to look after her, except Mrs Richardson, offered to stay and help. La Malibran was 'very low-spirited'; she told Mrs Novello: 'Manchester will have my bones.'[30]

Mrs Novello was present when Dr Belluomini arrived that evening. La Malibran's 'joy was excessive,' she recalled. ' "I am saved! I am saved!" Maria exclaimed. "He has known me from my youth, and loves me like a child." '

La Malibran asked Mrs Novello to speak to Dr Bardsley and Mr Worthington, who were in the next room, and to explain to them that her own doctor had come from London, and to thank them for their services, which she no longer required. 'Do not let me see them,' she added. 'I am fatigued, and shall only commit some extravagance.' Mrs Novello did as she was asked; the Manchester doctors said that they quite understood the patient's very natural request. They then tried to tell Dr Belluomini what they knew about La Malibran's illness, and how they had been treating it; but Dr Belluomini said that since his system, homœopathy, was totally opposed to theirs, 'he could not derive any benefit from a consultation with them.'[30] This did not endear him to the medical profession in Manchester.

Dr Belluomini examined his patient, and formed the opinion that 'the disease was a nervous fever, of a most dangerous kind . . .' He administered various homœopathic remedies, and the next morning, Monday, La Malibran was very much better. The fever had abated, 'and there was no longer any delirium, except, indeed, a musical movement which seemed constantly to recur to her mind.'[31]

She seemed so much better, that Bériot wrote to Lablache, by then singing at the Norwich festival, to say that she was out of danger, thanks to Dr Belluomini. When the tenor Ivanoff heard this news, he went out and purchased a silver snuff-box, 'splendidly chased', which he wished to send to Dr Belluomini in order to show his gratitude to him for saving La Malibran's life.[32]

Mrs Novello — now Maria's day-nurse, while Bériot and Dr Belluomini nursed her at night — also found the patient much better on Monday, and able to talk a little about Bériot and Lablache: 'I love very few persons,' she said, 'but those I do love, I love.' She spoke, too, about Miss Kelly, an actress whom she greatly admired: 'She makes you feel, because she goes *to the truth*; she does not depend on snippets of ribband [sic] to portray a character.'

Then she suddenly burst out: 'They say I drink; but should I have kept my voice and appearance, with all the fatigue I have gone through, if I had done so?' Mrs Novello tried to console her, by saying that only 'mean minds' would say such things.

'It is of no consequence,' said La Malibran. 'The public will always judge for themselves; although it is rather hard that talent should be exposed to such illiberal attacks — no allowance made for public persons exerting themselves to the utmost, and although requiring more indulgence than any other class of persons. I dare say it will be reported that my illness is a sham.'[33] She was right.

On Tuesday La Malibran was worse, in great pain, often exclaiming: 'Oh, doctor, for the love of God, help me!'[34] But on Wednesday she seemed better again. She asked Bériot to bring her her jewellery, so that Mrs Novello could sort it and put it away for her.

'What a number of rings you have!' said Mrs Novello. 'They are most of them presents from friends,' Maria replied. 'You cannot possibly remember the names of all donors,' suggested Mrs Novello.

Indeed I do [answered Maria], there is not one but I remember. They even recall names and dates which would otherwise escape my memory. This ring was given me by Mrs Knyvett — this one at Naples — my husband presented me this set on our marriage — these were given me at Lucca — but I have nothing half as valuable as many singers. My trinkets are principally endeared to me from circumstances.[35]

That evening, seeing La Malibran so much better, Mrs Novello proposed to Bériot that, after the Worcester festival at which Clara was to sing, she would return to Manchester to nurse Maria, so that he would be able to fulfil his engagement at Liverpool. It was agreed that, if all went well, she would return to Manchester on 1st October.

But the next day, 22nd September, Dr Belluomini began to lose hope. He called in a second opinion, Mr Lewis, an accoucheur; he wanted to know if Mr Lewis thought that the child was dead. Mr Lewis arrived at the Mosley Arms in the evening, and found La Malibran unconscious. He saw at once that she was dying, and said so to Bériot and to Dr Belluomini; the doctor seemed alarmed and surprised. Lewis thought that the child was probably dead, but that by this time it was immaterial; he did not think that La Malibran's illness was connected with her pregnancy, which was still at an early stage. Lewis and Dr Belluomini did not see eye to eye over various medical details. Lewis prescribed some medicaments, and ordered the patient's hair to be cut off. Bériot did this himself. Lewis left; but at midnight he received a message from Bériot, asking him to return immediately.[36]

On arriving at the hotel, Lewis persuaded Dr Belluomini to take some rest, and himself remained with the patient for some hours. He came again the next morning, Friday, 23rd September. There was no improvement, but La Malibran did regain consciousness for a short while, and took a sip of liquid from Bériot.

That morning Mrs Novello was due to leave for Worcester with Clara. On her way to the coach, she called at the Mosley Arms, and was shocked by what she saw: La Malibran half-unconscious, all her hair cut off, her eyes closed, her head turning constantly from side to side. Bériot was 'weeping abundantly'; but even at this late stage, and despite his ardent Catholicism, he did not call a priest.

People waiting at the coach for Worcester saw Mrs Novello arrive in tears. 'Nothing but a miracle can save her!' she said. Everyone was deeply affected, and the coach was held up for a quarter of an hour in order for people to hear the latest bulletin.[37]

That evening Lewis was summoned again. 'Dr Belluomini had thought it fit,' he later recalled, 'to administer the *secolo cornatum*, which had the expected effect, and the result was to produce an impression on the minds of all who had an opportunity of forming an opinion (except probably Dr Belluomini) that the patient was unaffected by her pregnancy.' A miscarriage occurred.[38]

At twenty-five minutes to midnight, on Friday, 23rd September, La Malibran died. She was twenty-eight years old. She died a year to the day after Bellini, and her death, like his, had not been the conventional operatic death — beautiful, swift and painless — which she had so often portrayed on the stage.

Not quite three weeks later, on 12th October, Eugène Malibran died in Paris. He was fifty-five.[39]

2

The next morning Manchester awoke to the shattering news that La Malibran was dead. Many people had recently seen her at the festival, and very few had realised that she was mortally ill. But soon even more extraordinary news began to circulate. La Malibran was lying dead, alone, in room No 9 at the Mosley Arms, and no one knew what to do next. Her husband and her doctor had vanished during the night.

Bériot had not been present when his wife died. He had been in an adjoining room, and the news had been broken to him by Mrs Richardson; on hearing it, he is said to have fainted.

A couple of hours earlier, at 10 pm, Bériot had sent for a Mr Beale, a music dealer and a member of the Festival Committee, whom he did not know, or knew only by sight. He asked Beale to make arrangements for the funeral and burial of his wife. Beale was rather taken aback, since La Malibran was still alive, although obviously dying; he asked if someone might help him in this task, and suggested a Mr Willert, also a member of the Festival Committee; he also asked for written instructions from Bériot, which he received:

> I hereby authorise Mr Beale to superintend to [the] burial of Madame de Bériot. I wish her to be interred in a respectable manner, in a situation he approves of. Also a small tablet to be erected to her memory. It is my desire that *no persons may be* admitted to take likenesses, or cast, or *otherwise*.
>
> C. de Bériot

Manchester, 24 7bre, 1836.[1]

This document, dated *after* La Malibran's death, but requested *before* she died, was given to Mr Beale the following morning. Bériot had particularly stressed to Beale the night before that there should be no post mortem, and that no cast of the face or head should be taken.[2]

After he had been told of his wife's death Bériot did not go into her room to see her again. He lay on his bed, in a state of apathy, while Mrs Richardson and his servant packed his and his wife's possessions. At half past one in the morning — an hour and forty minutes after La Malibran died — he came out of the Mosley Arms assisted by Mrs Richardson, and got into a carriage with Dr Belluomini. Before leaving, he gave Mrs Richardson a ring of turquoise set in black enamel, which had been worn by his wife, and a locket containing some of her hair. Then he and the doctor drove off in the direction of London.

Bériot's departure — it almost looked like flight — so soon after his wife's death, and the laconic instructions which he had left concerning her burial, shocked the people of Manchester, and put Beale in a difficult position. At first he did not even know what La Malibran's religion had been, and according to what rites she should be buried. He consulted the Festival Committee as to what he should do, and a general meeting of the Committee was called to discuss the matter on 26th September.

Meanwhile, La Malibran's death and Bériot's disappearance had created an enormous impression in Manchester; ordinary people were deeply shocked, and some sections of the community had more precise reactions. Members of the Festival Committee certainly felt a little guilty — had they harassed La Malibran too much about her appearances at the festival? They had not realised how ill she had been. All the same, they had behaved generously, by paying her her full fee — 600 guineas — although she had only appeared in half the scheduled concerts. Bériot, on receiving her fee, had donated £25 to Manchester charities.[3]

The medical profession in Manchester considered the recent events, and found cause for concern. Dr Bardsley, Mr Worthington and Dr Hull had all attended La Malibran, had looked after her most devotedly and, before they had been summarily dismissed by Dr Belluomini, had been of the opinion that she had been on the way to recovery. And they had been dismissed in favour of whom? A foreigner, who was also a homœopath, in other words, a quack. A good many people in Manchester — including, at a later date, Mr Lewis, the accoucheur called in by Dr Belluomini — thought that an inquest and a post mortem should have been held.[4] The fact that Bériot had expressly said that there should be no post mortem, and that Dr Belluomini had disappeared, made people even more suspicious.

The Festival Committee duly met, and decided that it would be responsible for La Malibran's funeral; a sub-committee was appointed to make the necessary arrangements. But the Festival Committee also issued a careful report[5] on La Malibran's illness and death, partly aimed at showing that the Committee and its members had behaved in a proper manner, and partly in order to dispel the numerous wild rumours which were already circulating in the city. The report stated that Dr Belluomini appeared to have behaved properly, whatever system of medicine he may have used.

On one thing everyone agreed: Mrs Richardson, the landlady of the Mosley Arms, had behaved impeccably throughout, and she continued to do so after La Malibran's death. The hotel was besieged by sightseers, journalists and relic hunters; Bériot had expressly asked that no one should see his wife's body, and that no portraits or death masks should be made. Mrs Richardson defended La Malibran dead with the same zeal and affection with which she had nursed her while alive, and refused to admit anyone to room No 9. But apparently, unbeknown to her, some morbid sightseers did succeed in bribing the servants in order to get a glimpse of the corpse.[6] ' "Her features," wrote one admitted to this exhibition of departed genius, "are placid and her last moments must have been without pain." '[7] A death mask was, apparently, made — there are several copies extant* — but there is no way of telling if they are genuine. They do, however, seem to confirm the description of La Malibran's face after death by those who saw it.

---

* Death Mask. Although Bushnell claims that the existence of a death mask of La Malibran was 'a secret so well kept that until the present day' it was 'all but unknown' (Bushnell, pp. 224–5), this is incorrect. Several death masks have been well known in Europe and America for many years. There is one in the Brussels Conservatoire; La Malibran's grand-daughter owned one; one was exhibited at a concert at l'Hostel de Sagonne, Paris (Les Soirées du Marais) on 11th January, 1941. According to Bushnell, there is also one in the Theatre Collection of Princeton University; this is reproduced in Bushnell's book, in which it is suggested that it may have been made by the sculptor, William Bally. See also Laurence Hutton, 'A Collection of Death Masks' (*Harper's New Monthly Magazine*, London, New York, 1892, Vol XXIV, pp. 618–31; there is a photograph of La Malibran's mask on p. 626). Her friend, Edmond Cottinet, wrote on seeing the photograph: 'It is she! [. . .] It is she with her slightly African type, containing perhaps a little negro blood . . .' This mask came perhaps from the collection of the phrenologist, George Combe, who visited America in 1838–9.

The public desire to see La Malibran's body, and the supposition that some people paid for this sight, is said to have inspired Feydeau's novel, *Le Mari de la danseuse*[8] in which a ballerina's corpse, dressed in her stage costume, is exhibited for money.

Preparations for the funeral went ahead. At first, everyone expected Bériot to return from London to attend it. But it was soon learned that he had not stayed in London, but had pressed on and embarked for Belgium on Sunday, 25th September. This news astounded Mancunians; how could a man abandon his wife's body to strangers and not even attend her funeral? Although those who had seen Bériot during his wife's illness — the doctors, Mrs Richardson, Mrs Novello, members of the Festival Committee — insisted that he had behaved admirably, and had been grief-stricken, people in Manchester would not believe it. To most Mancunians he had become, at best, a cold, heartless man and, at worst, a villain. Rumours circulated that there had been something suspicious about La Malibran's death, and also that Bériot had rushed to Belgium in order to get his hands on her money. This latter accusation was possibly true. She left 700,000 francs.

All that can now be said with certainty about Bériot's behaviour is that he had lost his head, either from grief, or from tiredness — he had, after all, nursed his wife almost continuously for nine days. Mr Lewis and Mrs Richardson had tried to persuade him to stay for the funeral. Dr Belluomini, a good friend to Bériot, later came to his defence, and took the whole blame for Bériot's flight on himself. He stated that it was he who had persuaded Bériot to leave Manchester immediately after his wife's death. This may have been true; but one can hardly believe that 'He [Bériot] was so powerfully affected, that it was necessary, in order to save his life, to divert his mind by a sudden journey.'[9] The doctor does not seem to have realised that their precipitate departure had also been extremely damaging to his own reputation.

Bériot had lived through a terrible experience, and his immediate reaction had been, as it was in all important events in his life, to turn to his sister, who meant more to him than anyone else, and who usually organised his life for him. On this occasion, too, she took matters into her own hands.

In the meantime, the news of La Malibran's death began to spread beyond Manchester. As she had died at the weekend, it did not appear in the London papers until Monday, 26th September; but it reached Worcester, where the festival was in full swing, on Sunday.

Many of her friends and colleagues, including the Novellos, were there, and the news cast a gloom over the whole festival: 'many of the veterans of the orchestra shed tears.' When Madame Caradori-Allan, La Malibran's partner in the last, fatal duet, heard the news 'she went into violent hysterics.'[10]

On 26th September Alfred Bunn was sitting in his garden in Brompton, under the walnut tree which he had named after La Malibran, when the news of her death was brought to him. He was 'stunned at first'; he had seen her in Paris only three weeks earlier, and his forthcoming season at Drury Lane depended on her. But he alone of her London friends reacted spontaneously and in the spirit of friendship: he postponed the opening of Drury Lane Theatre for a week, and set off for Manchester on 29th September to attend the funeral.[11]

On 26th September the London papers reported the news, but it had been so unexpected that they were unable to comment on it at once. *The Times* published La Malibran's obituary — two full columns, an unprecedented length in those days — on 30th September. The *Morning Post*, unlike *The Times*, had had a correspondent — G. L. Gruneisen — in Manchester for the festival; he had gone on to Worcester, and had a certain amount of inside information, some of it incorrect. The *Morning Post* was, from the beginning, extremely hostile to Bériot, and was later to be very unfair to him and his family.

On 26th September Princess Victoria learned the news from the *Morning Post*. She recorded the details in her diary, and then added: 'There is something peculiarly awful and striking in the death of this great Cantatrice, undoubtedly the *second in the world* (Grisi being the *first* in *my opinion*) to be thus cut off in the bloom of her youth and the height of her career suddenly is dreadful!'[12]

When Ole Bull heard the news, he was deeply affected. 'Ah! I remember how I wept in Bologna when I saw her as Desdemona in "Othello"!' he commented. He also remembered how La Malibran had once said to him: 'The public will kill you, either by their neglect, or their exactions.'[13] But he had little time to mourn; he was asked to take La Malibran's place at the Liverpool festival. He postponed some concerts, and at once set off for Liverpool. The advertisements had already been printed, with La Malibran's name on them.

Balfe heard the news in a friend's house. Willert Beale, a child at the time, remembered that Balfe had been 'completely overcome', and had remained in their house for hours, 'unable to control his grief.'[14]

On 27th September Macready was in Shrewsbury. He returned to his inn, as usual in a bad temper, irritated by some actors at rehearsal, and asked for a newspaper. He had read most of it when he suddenly saw the headline: *Malibran is no more!*

> I felt as if my mind was stunned [he wrote in his diary]. It was a shock which left me no power to think for some little time. I read on, when recovered from the horror and surprise of the news, and was quite restored by the stuff — the *newspaper sentiment* and string of falsehoods [...] I once could have loved her, and she has since said that she loved — 'was in love with' — me. Had I known it for certain, I might have been more miserable than I am. Latterly, she had decreased in my regard, and in my esteem she had no place. This world is a sad loss to her, and she to it. Poor Malibran![15]

Princess Victoria returned to the subject of La Malibran's death in her diary on 30th September. After recording all the details, she added her own comment:

> It is the most melancholy end that could be imagined! To come to an inn in a foreign land with nobody to nurse her, and *die* there! What a sad and tragical end to her bright career! I can still hardly believe it possible that she, whom I can see before me as she was at our own concert, dressed in white satin, so merry and lively, and whose pathetic voice when speaking I can hear, is now in the silent tomb; for the funeral was to take place at 10 o'clock this morning with great splendour. And so today all, all is over with poor Malibran![16]

But Princess Victoria was wrong; the funeral was to take place the next day (1st October); and all was not yet quite over with poor Malibran.

3

Alfred Bunn arrived in Manchester on 30th September, and went straight to the Mosley Arms, where Mrs Richardson admitted him to room No 9.

> [It was] a very small room, lighted by two windows looking out upon a dull wall. In it was a bed of narrow dimensions, and rather mean furniture, (green stuff edged with black worsted binding, if I remember rightly), and in the centre of the bed lay a coffin covered with common black cloth.[1]

Bunn was so overwhelmed by the impression made on him by this scene that he took out some paper and, writing on the lid of the coffin, composed a long *Monody*. It was not great poetry, but it was deeply felt.[2]

During the previous week preparations had been going ahead for the funeral. The Festival Committee had decided that if it was worth doing, it was worth doing well, and no expense or trouble had been spared. The pathos of the situation had touched every heart, and the city fathers, the Festival Committee and the ecclesiastical authorities were all working together with a will.

It had been decided that La Malibran should be buried in the Collegiate Church (now Manchester Cathedral), where she had so lately sung. The Warden and Fellows of the church decided not to take their usual fees, and a vault belonging to the Walton family was put at the Committee's disposal, since it had always been a Catholic grave; the last person to have been buried in it, some fifty years earlier, had been a Roman Catholic priest.[3]*

As no members of La Malibran's family and only two personal friends — Sir George Smart and Alfred Bunn — were planning to

---

* This priest was John Walton, the last of the family to be buried in the vault before La Malibran. It also contained the remains of Edward FitzHerbert, brother-in-law of the famous Mrs FitzHerbert, morganatic wife of George IV.

attend the funeral, many distinguished men from Manchester and the surrounding country had volunteered to be official mourners; these included John Macvicar, the Boroughreeve of Manchester, as Chief Mourner; the Earl of Wilton; and many members of the Festival Committee.

By Friday evening, 30th September, all was prepared for the funeral next day. It was at this juncture that Mr Willert, a member of the Festival Committee, received a letter from Dr Belluomini in London, dated 29th September, and stating that he had received a letter signed by Bériot's sister in Belgium, saying that her brother had changed his mind and now wished his wife's body to be transferred to Belgium for burial there. Mr Willert was horrified; it was too late to cancel the funeral, scheduled for early the next morning, and it was too late that evening to ask anyone's advice. Very early the next morning he conferred with other members of the Festival Committee; it was decided that only a letter signed by Bériot himself could override the written instructions which he had given to Mr Beale, and that a letter signed by his sister and addressed to Dr Belluomini was not sufficient. A reply to this effect was sent to the doctor on Saturday afternoon, and he was informed that the funeral had already taken place.[4] By Friday afternoon it had certainly been too late to cancel the funeral — a mammoth civic function, with several hundred people involved.

On Saturday, 1st October, the people of Manchester awoke to pouring rain; in Paris, exactly a year less a day earlier, rain had poured all day at Bellini's funeral. It was a year to the day since La Malibran in Milan had heard the news of Bellini's death, and had said that she would soon follow him to the grave.

The people of Manchester were not deterred by the weather, and at a very early hour crowds already lined the route which the procession was to take. The Beadles of Manchester, their staves covered with crape, were stationed outside the Mosley Arms. The bells of Manchester tolled.

First of all, a service according to the Roman Catholic rite was conducted over the coffin in room No 9 of the Mosley Arms, by the Rev. James Cook of St Augustine's Chapel, Granby Row, assisted by the Rev. Randolph Frith.[5]

When it was over, a very long procession began to form: the Deputy Constable of Manchester and the four Beadles; sixty members of the Festival Committee, on foot, three abreast; six mourning coaches containing the chief mourners, including Sir

George Smart, Alfred Bunn, and Mrs Richardson; and twenty-six private carriages — the whole line stretching from the front of the hotel in Market Street, along Piccadilly, and the entire length of Lever Street. The 'richly-plumed hearse' was drawn by 'four fine black horses'. The procession took a rather circuitous route — it was market day — through streets lined with crowds, to the Collegiate Church, where it was joined by about five hundred 'gentlemen, all in deep mourning', who would probably have walked in the procession, but for the pouring rain. Ladies waited in the church.

The coffin bore a brass plate with the inscription:

Maria Felicia de Bériot
Died 23rd September, 1836
Aged 28 years.

Only in death did Maria finally lose the name of her first husband.

The coffin of the woman who had been so small and light was carried into the church by eight men, and the lengthy service began. The church, draped with black, was packed full; and the huge crowd of men and women, all in dark clothes or full mourning, gave it an even more sombre appearance. 'Many of the principal merchants and manufacturers of the town and neighbourhood [. . .] and most of the foreign merchants' were present. Charles Kean the younger, whose father La Malibran had known in America, was in the crowd.[6]

The music included the *Dead March* from *Saul*, and Handel's *Holy, holy*, which La Malibran had so lately sung in that same church, and which was now played as a dirge on the organ.

When the coffin had been placed in the vault, which was in the south transept, the official procession of mourners filed past and left the church; then 'the thousands of people who, by this time, had quitted their seats, and thronged to the gates of the choir and transept, were admitted to see the grave.'[7] Finally, the crowds who had not been in the church were admitted to file past the grave, coming in at one door, and leaving by another. They continued to do so from 12.15 pm until after 3 pm; many thousands of people must have paid their last respects to La Malibran that day. The crowd was reverent, and deeply moved; people were silent, except for the occasional 'God rest her', or 'Poor thing', murmured as they passed.[8]

That evening, members of the Festival Committee and everyone in Manchester could feel well satisfied with the day's events. A young and talented foreigner had had the misfortune to die in their city, and had been abandoned by her husband and friends; Manchester had risen to the occasion, and had given her a funeral fit for a queen. The Committee there and then set about discussing how to raise funds in order to erect a suitable monument to La Malibran. Next day, Sunday, all the principal mourners and many other people attended another service in the Collegiate Church. The Rev. Richard Parkinson preached a sermon on the theme of La Malibran's death.[9]

But, that very afternoon, a courier arrived in Manchester from Brussels. He was bearing a letter from Bériot, written on 27th September; on 29th September, the day on which the courier had left Brussels, the British Minister had authenticated Bériot's signature with his seal. The letter stated that Bériot had decided to have his wife's body buried in Belgium; that he was too ill to come to England himself, but was sending two of his relations to supervise the transfer of the body.[10]

This letter caused consternation in Manchester; and from that moment public opinion there, never very sympathetic to Bériot, hardened against him. Bériot did not, of course, know about the splendid funeral which Manchester had given his wife, and probably imagined that Beale had carried out his instructions in the most modest manner, or that his wife was not yet buried. Presumably, on his arrival in Belgium, his sister and mother-in-law had been shocked by what had happened and by the way Bériot had behaved, and had urged him to make good his mistake. But he had acted too slowly; and, as a result, an immense and damaging misunderstanding between La Malibran's family and the authorities and people of Manchester was to develop.

No action was taken in Manchester for a few days. But Dr Belluomini, who had become Bériot's representative in England, wrote several letters to British newspapers,[11] giving his version of what had happened at the Mosley Arms and taking on himself the blame for Bériot's flight. No doubt he hoped, by so doing, to make matters better; but in fact he achieved the opposite effect. The matter of an inquest was raised again by the *Morning Post*,[12] and Dr Belluomini's credentials were also questioned, mainly by the medical profession. Homœopathy, a recent development, was then considered to be fringe medicine, and the medical profession took the opportunity, afforded by La Malibran's death, to berate it. *The Times*,[13] hitherto rather aloof from the fray, reprinted an article from the *Medical Gazette*: 'Homœopathy and its late doings', which was extremely hostile to homœopathy in general, and to Dr Belluomini in particular. The *Medical Gazette* regretted that there had not been an inquest. The affair was also discussed at length in *The Lancet*,[14] and controversy raged about the medical details of the case. Lewis, the accoucheur who had been present when La Malibran was dying, and who had also always been hostile to Dr Belluomini, wrote to the press to say that there should have been an inquest.[15]

On 3rd October the Boroughreeve of Manchester received a letter from the Belgian Chargé d'Affaires, asking that the question of the transfer of Madame de Bériot's body to Belgium should be expedited. The Boroughreeve replied that he had no power to intervene, since the matter now came under the jurisdiction of the ecclesiastical authorities.[16]

A few days later, Bériot's cousin, Monsieur de Fiennes, a lawyer, arrived in Manchester and put up at the Mosley Arms; he was to stay there for some time. He transmitted messages to and from Bériot who may, or may not, have been ill, but whose presence in Manchester would certainly have aroused great hostility.

By this time, a great many people were involved in the affair. The Belgian Chargé d'Affaires appealed to the Home Office; Lord John Russell wrote to the Manchester Stipendiary Magistrate, asking him to intervene with the civil and ecclesiastical authorities. The Festival Committee met, and decided that it had done its duty by burying Madame de Bériot, but that it had no authority to disinter her; it expressed the view that public opinion in Manchester would be very hostile to such a move. Finally, it was established that a corpse could not legally be disinterred from a church without a faculty from the chancellor of the diocese (in this case, Chester), but that this faculty was usually granted unless someone should lodge a *caveat*.[17]

The affair dragged on. In a letter, Bériot appealed to the better feelings of Mancunians, tried to justify his conduct on the fatal night, and demanded his wife's body.[18] By now, responsible public opinion was beginning to sympathise with Bériot, and when his cousin made an application to the Ecclesiastical Court at Chester for a faculty to disinter the body, most people hoped that it would be granted. The bishop himself assured Monsieur de Fiennes that it would.

On 26th November, Bériot was able to write to his friend Parola in Milan:

I am at last on the eve of seeing my heart's dearest wish realised. The court at Chester has just consented to the exhumation, you will doubtless have learned from the newspapers all the infamous calumnies which a few individuals wish to heap on me in order to keep the remains, doubtless for some *interested* motive, there could be none other for such conduct. It will not be long before I discover the whole of this abominable plot. I believe I am already on the track of *everything*.[19]

But Bériot had been misinformed. A few people in Manchester, led by Mr R. C. Sharp, Senior Churchwarden of Manchester, were entirely opposed to Bériot and to the transfer of the body to Belgium. When the case went to the Consistory Court for the Diocese of Chester, Sharp lodged a *caveat*. The court did grant Bériot the faculty to remove the body, but Sharp decided to appeal against this decision to the Metropolitan Court at York.[20]

Sharp had also managed to get over seven hundred signatures to a document, a *Memorial to the Warden and Fellows of the Collegiate Church*, praying them not to grant any faculty for the disinterment of the body of Madame Malibran.[21]

By now most decent people in Manchester, including most members of the Festival Committee, had changed their minds. The quarrel had become undignified. People realised that they had been unfair to Bériot, and there were letters to the press to that effect.[22] But Sharp and his supporters, known as the Memorialists, became more and more extreme, digging up old gossip, suggesting that Bériot had not been legally married to La Malibran, and so on. The *Morning Post*, too, printed a good deal of scurrilous gossip;[23] but the *Manchester Guardian* was restrained, and the *Manchester Times* was very hostile to the Memorialists.[24] On the other hand, two other Manchester papers were very hostile to Bériot. Manchester was split into two factions; the majority were now pro-Bériot; but a small and very vociferous minority was against him.

These arguments had been going on for more than two months when suddenly, on 8th December, an event occurred which brought everyone to his senses: La Malibran's mother arrived in Manchester.

Joaquina Garcia had come to claim her daughter's body. Bériot had realised that he was so unpopular in Manchester that it would be very unwise for him to appear there, and someone — Charles's sister? — had hit on the brilliant idea that Madame Garcia should go instead. She was now fifty-six years old, and not highly educated; but she was courageous and intelligent, and had right on her side, for it would be difficult to deny a mother's right to her daughter's remains.

And so it turned out. The day after her arrival in Manchester Madame Garcia had an interview with Bériot's chief opponent, Mr Sharp. He immediately began to climb down, but said that he was not acting on his own, but on behalf of a number of other people, the Memorialists. He asked Madame Garcia to put her request in writing, so that the Memorialists might discuss it. Madame Garcia then wrote the following letter:

> Sir, having had the inexpressible sorrow to lose at Manchester my beloved daughter, Madame de Bériot (née Garcia) and also the deprivation of not being able to weep upon her tomb, nor yet to fulfil the duties prompted by my heart and my religion, if she is not removed into her adopted country, which is also mine, — I come to intreat you, Sir, to grant me this favour, and to use your influence with your fellow-townsmen, that they raise no more obstacles to the disinterment of the mortal remains of my poor daughter; and that they may be removed with me into the bosom of her family.
>
> Accept, Sir, and believe the expression of my profound gratitude.
>
> Joaquina Garcia
>
> Manchester, 9th Dec. 1836.
> Mr Robert C. Sharp.[25]

A meeting of the Memorialists was held, and it was generally agreed that, whilst La Malibran's husband had behaved very badly, her mother had done nothing wrong, and that it was impossible to refuse her request. A resolution was passed that the Memorialists would no longer oppose the disinterment of Madame de Bériot.[26]

Madame Garcia and Monsieur de Fiennes travelled to Chester. Bériot's application for the faculty to disinter the body was withdrawn, and Sharp withdrew his *caveat*. The faculty was granted to Madame Garcia on 17th December.[27] Bériot was charged £1,200 for the funeral expenses.

At about 5 o'clock in the morning on 20th December, some twenty-five people assembled in the Collegiate Church to superintend the disinterment of La Malibran's coffin. An early hour had been chosen so that there should be no curious onlookers. It was bitterly cold, and dark; lights placed on the chancel floor by the grave threw strange shadows, illuminating from below the faces of those present. The moon could be seen through the windows. Apart from the grating of the grave-diggers' spades, there was no other sound, until a cord, placed round the coffin in an attempt to raise it, broke; the coffin fell back with a dull thud. This happened three times. Eventually the coffin was carried out through the north door of the church, through which it had been brought in two and a half months earlier.[28] A hearse was waiting to take it back to the Mosley Arms. When it arrived there, Madame Garcia and Monsieur de Fiennes took leave of Mrs Richardson, and drove off to London, preceded by the hearse.

The party went to the house of a friend in Finsbury Square, where many friends and musicians came to pay their last respects to La Malibran. After a couple of days, the coffin was taken to St Katharine's Dock, and embarked in a 'small open boat', as 'there was not a regular boat which would accept the charge'; although the hour of its removal to St Katharine's Dock had been kept secret, a crowd was waiting to witness the scene. Early on 22nd December the boat sailed for Antwerp.[29]*

Charles de Bériot was waiting at Ixelles for the arrival of his wife's body. Since her death, he had been in 'a state of torpor'.[30] He seems to have been incapable of taking any action, and his sister and other members of the family had made all the necessary arrangements for him. He told a friend:

> All that I've suffered and all that I am still suffering is beyond comprehension. Poor Maria! You know how I loved her! Why did Providence give me an angel in order to snatch her away from me so soon? At the most brilliant moment of her glory ... If you knew how much I miss her ... in spite of all the care and tenderness of my family, I feel that she has left me alone in the world. I only live now to think of Maria and to weep ... .[31]

---

* Although both Fétis and Pauline Viardot maintained that Madame Garcia embarked on an open boat, the *Morning Post* of 24th December, 1836, reported, more credibly, that she embarked 'on a steamer'.

But he eventually recovered, and married again four years later.*
Bériot waited all through Christmas for the arrival of his wife's
coffin. Although the boat in which Madame Garcia was travelling
with the coffin had left St Katharine's Dock on 22nd December, the
weather had been so bad that it had not been able to cross the
Channel until after Christmas, and had very nearly been lost off
Flushing. It was not until New Year's Day that La Malibran's coffin
finally arrived at the Bériots' house at Ixelles.[32]

Even then the long journey was not quite over, nor was the
rancour which seemed to pursue poor Maria's remains. The Pro-
testants of Manchester had seen to it that Roman Catholic priests
had performed the last rites over the coffin; but the Roman Catholic
Archbishop of Malines refused to allow La Malibran a church burial
in Belgium. According to her family, this was because the Archbishop
believed that she had only had a Protestant funeral in Manchester,
and refused to accept the declaration of the English Roman Catholic
clergy.[33] It is possible, however, that the Archbishop would not grant
an actress Christian burial, and also that he knew that, in the eyes
of the Church, Maria was the wife of Eugène Malibran.

---

* Bériot remarried in July, 1840. His second wife was Marie Hueber, of
Vienna. It has sometimes been suggested that she was the sister or half-
sister of Bériot's close friend, the pianist Sigismond Thalberg, who was the
illegitimate son of Prince Moritz Dietrichstein and Baroness Wetzlar; but
this question remains obscure. Bériot's son by his second wife, Franz-
Charles, was born in 1841. From then onwards Bériot played rarely in
public, but he continued to teach, to compose, and to travel; in 1843 he
was appointed professor at the Brussels Conservatoire. He complained
frequently of bad health, and his eyes, which had always been weak, gave
him increasing trouble; his elder son therefore helped him with his work.
In 1858 his second wife died when she was only thirty-six, and Bériot
became completely blind. In 1863 his younger son died. Bériot lived on,
still very active mentally despite his blindness and the personal tragedies
which beset him, until 1870; he died on 8th April, at the age of sixty-eight.
He was buried in the same grave as his second wife. His influence on the
Belgian school of violin playing was very considerable, and a few of his
compositions are still occasionally played today.

La Malibran's son, Charles-Wilfrid, was originally destined for a military
career, but he became a pianist and composer, and lived mainly in Paris,
where he gave some lessons to Ravel. He died on 22nd October, 1914,
leaving only daughters; thus, with him the Bériot name died out, but there
are descendants of Bériot and La Malibran through the female line.

This was a bitter blow to the Bériot family. Because of the Arch-bishop's ruling, priests tried to persuade parents whose children were to sing at the civil funeral to forbid them to take part, and many did so. But Fétis, then Director of the Brussels Conservatoire, whose own *Miserere* was to be performed, put a notice up in the Conserva-toire to the effect that anyone who failed to take part in the ceremony would no longer be admitted to the Conservatoire.[34]

On the day of the funeral, a vast crowd assembled outside the Bériots' house. Just before the coffin was carried out everyone, including the family, left the house. Charles turned back, to have one last look at his wife's coffin; his sister accompanied him.[35]*

Then the procession moved off to the cemetery at Laeken, some miles away. It was bitterly cold, and the snow was so deep that a special passage had to be cut to allow the procession to pass. There was music, there were vast crowds, but there were no priests.

Fétis, who had known La Malibran from birth, made a moving funeral oration. After comparing her to Raphael and Mozart, who had also died young, he said:

> If it were necessary to invoke today some evidence of the world's admiration for her for whom we weep, we would find it, gentlemen, in that stubborn struggle which you have witnessed for possession of these remains which are displayed before you. Never has a treasure, no matter how precious, been contended for like these relics. It is, perhaps, a fact unique in history, that there should be such a cult for the memory of a great artist. And do not be mistaken; there is in it more signifi-cance than in all the successes of a brilliant career.[36]

---

* In a letter to her husband (n.d., Wauwermans, pp. 196–7), Constance de Francquen implies that her brother was present at La Malibran's second funeral; but *Le Monde dramatique* (an undated cutting in the Bibliothèque de l'Opéra) states that Bériot had left home several days earlier, to stay with an uncle. If this is true, it means that Bériot was unable to face either of La Malibran's funerals.

4

What killed La Malibran? In his old age Legouvé, with admirable common sense, affirmed that she had died as the result of a riding accident.[1] But this did not satisfy her contemporaries, and it cannot fully satisfy posterity.

La Malibran had always courted danger and perhaps, like so many Romantics, she had also courted death. After her riding accident she had insisted on singing so as not to offend the public, had refused all medical treatment, and had ignored the advice of her doctor and friends, although she herself knew that her accident had caused serious damage to her health. There can be little doubt that her attitude hastened her death, and that she realised that it would. Why did she behave like that? Was it a fatalistic acceptance of what she believed to be her destiny — to die young? Or was it because she could not face the future? Her behaviour, from the moment she was thrown from her horse until her last concert in Manchester, could be interpreted as a kind of slow suicide.

A century and a half after the event, we cannot say with certainty what killed her. The medical and psychological evidence is inconclusive, and difficult to interpret properly today. At best we can hazard a guess that it was the terrible penalties of success, the relentless demands of the public, and her inability to reconcile her public and private lives — the twin Romantic aims of love and art — which drove La Malibran to self-destruction.

Her death caused a greater sensation amongst her contemporaries than any other death of that epoch.[2] This was particularly so in France, where she had personified the ideals of a brilliant and precocious generation. Her friends mourned the loss of a charming woman and a fascinating companion; but even people who had only seen her on the stage or knew her only by hearsay took her death as a personal grief. La Malibran's death marked the end of an epoch; her contemporaries felt that their own youth had died with her. It was their first *memento mori*.

As to the reasons for her death, her contemporaries were agreed on only one thing: that she had not just died as a result of a riding accident. Although the medical evidence was published very fully in England, and less fully on the Continent, the public knew better than the doctors. Everyone knew that La Malibran had been a goddess; and goddesses do not die from such prosaic things as a riding accident or a miscarriage. The public believed that there must have been more to it than that.

'The emotion felt in Paris was immense,' said her friend Edmond Cottinet. 'The grief of her friends was violent, bitter, indignant; this death was an assassination.'³

An assassination? By whom? The public knew in its heart of hearts that it was not completely blameless. It had driven her too hard, asked too much of her, expected her to bear its own frustrations, emotions and fantasies, and to expiate them. The public knew subconsciously that it had helped to kill what it loved. To make amends, it would soon canonise La Malibran; but its first reaction, no doubt in order to smother its own feelings of guilt, was to look round for a scape-goat. Everyone tried to lay the blame on someone else.

In Manchester, where people felt guilty at having pestered La Malibran 'to resume her duties' during her last illness, the blame was laid on Bériot and Dr Belluomini — both foreigners — and on homœopathy, a foreign 'fringe medicine'. Three days after her death 'public opinion had already sentenced both of them.'⁴

In Paris, another scape-goat was found. In a long obituary, the influential critic Jules Janin laid the blame squarely on England and on Manchester, 'the gloomiest town of gloomy England'. La Malibran had, he wrote,

> aroused truly French enthusiasm in that dismal England which is so difficult to arouse; she had made the pale English understand all the transports of music; what efforts! What work! What indefatigable zeal! That woman was like Alexander; she was bent on universal conquest; she even wanted to subdue England, and it cost her her life [. . .] It is England which killed her for us, it is the English fog which weighed down the whole of her exhausted genius. She killed herself because she wanted to animate that statue of iron and coal, which one calls England . . .

And so on. France, on the other hand, had known how to appreciate her. 'She trusted us [French] as a child trusts its father [. . .] How proud and happy we were to give her glory and fortune!'⁵ The fact that La Malibran had left France because the French public had turned against her when she was pregnant and unable to satisfy all its whims, was conveniently forgotten.

Gautier was probably nearer the mark when he said that La Malibran died crushed by the applause of the public, but this was not an explanation which her audiences could be expected to accept; a more convenient explanation had to be found.

Jules Janin eventually found it. He was one of the first, if not the first, to express a belief which was almost universally held by La Malibran's contemporaries. 'It was not only England which killed her,' he admitted. 'Her soul killed her, as a hidden fire kills a noble oak tree [. . .] She burned with an inner fire which no one suspected, she was consumed by a double passion, drama and song, which she obeyed unto death.'⁶

Two weeks later, Alfred de Musset published his *Stances à La Malibran* — the greatest elegy of French Romanticism — in *La Revue des deux mondes*.⁷* In it Musset, too, expressed the same idea:

* The myth of a love-affair between La Malibran and Alfred de Musset began to grow soon after her death. Musset's *Stances à La Malibran* made the public imagine that he had been in love with her, or even that they had had a love affair. The belief was so widely held that, after the poet's death, his brother, Paul de Musset, felt it necessary to deny it in his biography, (p. 177 and note 1). Paul de Musset had been annoyed by overhearing strangers in a train discussing his brother's love affair with La Malibran; he maintained that his brother had seen her only once off-stage, when she was singing at a party, and had never spoken to her. Paul de Musset is not always a reliable source — a brother can be even less objective than a best friend — but there is no reason to doubt this statement. But, after the poet's death, when he could no longer deny it, his name was frequently linked with that of La Malibran; his admirers felt that she would have been a more appropriate choice for his love than George Sand, considered by many to be a wicked, emancipated and debauched woman. Lamartine also appears to have expressed this view, and to have believed that there had been a nascent love affair between Musset and La Malibran, and to have regretted that it had come to nothing. (Séché, *Lamartine* pp. 257–8, and Lamartine, *Cours familier de littérature*, III p. 466.) If, as Paul de Musset maintained, they had never spoken to each other, this was nonsense; yet Lamartine had known both La Malibran and Musset well. Edmond Cottinet, son of close friends of La Malibran, in his reminiscences of her (1889, pp. 98–9) stated that she and Musset had known each other, and that he, as a boy, had witnessed a meeting between them. There is, at the

C'est le Dieu tout puissant, c'est la Muse implacable
Qui dans ses bras en feu t'a portée au tombeau.

And, addressing La Malibran, he asked:

Que ne l'étouffais-tu, cette flamme brûlante,
Que ton sein palpitant ne pouvait contenir!

This explanation of La Malibran's death satisfied everyone; it was poetic, Romantic, and it stopped people from feeling guilty. No one was to blame; it was her dedication to Art, 'the implacable Muse', and the 'sacred fire' which had killed her. And, once Musset had said it, and said it in unforgettable poetry, everyone believed it. Many years later, Legouvé tried to bring common sense to bear on the subject, but it was far too late; the myth was well-established, the cult was flourishing, and Musset's *Stances* were very well known.

The idea that 'whom the gods love, die young' was also inevitably invoked in connection with La Malibran. Musset had put it as a tentative question in his *Stances*:

Ou faut-il croire, hélas! ce que disaient nos pères,
Que lorsqu'on meurt si jeune on est aimé des dieux!

But had the gods loved La Malibran? Certainly they had given her many gifts: 'Youth, beauty, kindness, genius'; she had been, said Lamartine, 'favoured amongst expressive souls.'[8] But happiness? She herself had not felt loved by the gods; when she was twenty-three she had told Legouvé that the 'stream of tears' in her heart would water the flowers on her grave, and perhaps recompense her in the next world. 'Come and tell me that you are sorry for me,' she begged him.[9]

Another famous French elegy of an earlier age was also invoked in connection with her death:

Mais elle était du monde, où les plus belles choses
Ont le pire destin.
Et, rose, elle a vécu ce que vivent les roses,
L'espace d'un matin . . .

---

moment, no way of disproving this account, but it somehow does not ring true. This question is further complicated by the fact that Musset did fall in love with, and court, La Malibran's younger sister. (See FitzLyon, *The Price of Genius*, pp. 48–61.)
* From *Consolation à Monsieur du Périer* (1599), by François de Malherbe (1555–1628).

Many people felt that La Malibran had been lucky to die in her prime, that she had had 'the genius to die very young, in the spring-time of her talent and her beauty, before her crown had lost a single pearl, her halo a single ray.'[10]

Four years later Liszt, writing to a friend from the same hotel room in Manchester in which La Malibran had died, echoed the same thought: 'Poor Malibran [...] *She was an abundant woman* (as Victor Hugo said to me one day) who was, perhaps, right to die young. Who knows? She might very well have finished up by going to St Petersburg and singing out of tune like la Pasta.'[11]

Gautier, a dramatic critic, remembered that La Malibran had been an actress: 'To stop at the right time, to make a timely exit — very few people have known how to do this,' he wrote; and then, in a typically Romantic phrase, he said: 'Intelligent death sees to it for a few favoured people: Alexander, Raphael, Lord Byron, Malibran.'[12]

5

The apotheosis of La Malibran occurred as soon as she was dead and her cult, like all true cults, arose spontaneously. It had anyway existed while she lived; but her death — which some people saw as martyrdom — made her status as saint or goddess unimpeachable. There could no longer be any question of reality intervening to spoil her image; imagination could run riot.

Most of the symptoms that usually accompany a cult occurred: La Malibran had been exceptional before her death, and had been venerated by thousands; her death was premature, sensational, and happened in mysterious circumstances; the possession of her remains was disputed; rival claims to her origin were soon to be made; relics and icons were to be sought after and venerated; hagiographies were to be written; legends about her qualities and virtues were to grow; 'miracles' were to be attributed to her; her grave was to become a place of pilgrimage, and ex-votos were to be placed on it.

The cult was certainly spread by the swift appearance of numerous hagiographies, but it was not engendered by them; they fulfilled an already existing need.

The body of a saint is always the object of curiosity and veneration, often accompanied, at the popular level, by a tinge of necrophilia. We have seen how people bribed the servants at the Mosley Arms in order to see La Malibran's body.[1]

The quest for relics began even before she was buried. 'Ladies from all parts of Manchester applied to Mrs Richardson of the Mosley Arms for some relics of little intrinsic value in themselves, which had belonged to Malibran. One lady, in particular, offered ten guineas for a sandal, but not a single article was to be procured.'[2] So, instead, people cut pieces from the funeral pall.

Shortly before her death, La Malibran's long hair had been cut off; Bériot took it to Belgium with all his wife's possessions. He later handed out locks of hair to chosen friends and these became much sought after — hair is always a significant relic. Like the death masks to be found in public and private collections, it is not possible to tell if all the locks of hair are authentic, but they may well be.

In Italy, La Malibran and Bellini were immediately linked after her death. If they had not had a love-affair in this world, the public decided that they would certainly have one in the next. In Bologna,[3] in Milan,[4] and probably in other Italian cities, there were performances of popular works — probably songs or small cantatas — in which La Malibran's meeting with Bellini in the Elysian Fields was described; the authors of these works clearly considered La Malibran to be a goddess, rather than a saint. From then on, the legends of the two cult figures were to be inextricably mixed. These first popular manifestations were quite without guile; but, later on, less innocent attempts were made to link the pair, which caused — and still cause — confusion.

Other signs of the growing feeling were quick to appear. Poems, usually but not always doggerel, appeared in the press in England, France, Belgium and, especially, Italy, where the popular cult seems to have been particularly widespread.[5] Crude drawings were printed in newspapers, or on broadsheets, showing La Malibran in her tomb, or angels carrying her up to heaven, or Bellini leading her into the Elysian Fields.

The faithful wanted icons, and commerce supplied them. Even before her death La Malibran's portraits had been reproduced and sold in quantities wherever she sang. Now, the demand for likenesses greatly increased. Lithographs — some good copies of well-known portraits, but often crude and barely recognisable — caricatures, scenes from La Malibran's life, busts and medallions, were in great demand. Pictures of the funeral sold well in England. In Naples two years later, Madame Nourrit wrote: 'Here everything is imbued with the memory of Madame Malibran. There is a portrait of her in almost every house, and I, who am in a furnished flat, have her bust before my eyes.'[6] Before La Malibran's death, Marie Dorval had had an icon of her in her dressing-room;[7] years after her death, Alfred de Musset had one in his study.[8] In the twentieth century, Maria Callas always had a portrait of La Malibran with her; it was the only picture, apart from a photograph of her teacher, found with her when she died.[9]

Objects incorporating a portrait were also made and sold; for example, an ornate nineteenth century clock,[10] with a model of Decaisne's portrait of La Malibran as Desdemona surmounting it;

Staffordshire figurines;* and, in the twentieth century, mass-produced ash-trays.

Artists went on painting La Malibran long after her death. For example: Théodore Chassériau's portraits of her as Desdemona (1849 and 1852),[11] and the portrait by Hermann-Maurice Cossman,[12] who was only fifteen when she died. It is customary for saints' likenesses to be painted over and over again, and they may sometimes be confused or identified with other saints; Lamartine identified La Malibran with Saint Cecilia,[13] and it is obvious from the many portraits of her with a harp or a lyre that artists, either consciously or unconsciously, did the same.

Apart from the numerous and lengthy obituaries in the British, French, Italian, American and Belgian press, pamphlets and books began to appear very soon after her death, some within a week.[14] The literary quality of these hastily concocted, often anonymous works was not high: 'Adieu! Nightingale of the nations — thy requiem will ring through the world, and the responsive sighs of myriads shall attend thy departure.'[15] The sermon preached at her funeral in Manchester was reprinted as a pamphlet with some additional details.[16] Most of the information in these publications was inaccurate, much of it reprinted from articles in the daily press.

A biography of La Malibran had already appeared before her death.[17] Immediately afterwards, during the last three months of 1836, at least two more appeared in Italy[18] and one in England, by Isaac Nathan, composer and friend of Byron. The latter was so popular that it had gone into three editions by the end of the year, and there was a German translation in 1837.[19]

Nathan's book was the first true hagiography, although it is far more moderate and restrained and less inaccurate than some later books. Nathan, who had probably known La Malibran, recognised her apotheosis — 'The illustrious Malibran has prematurely winged her flight to join the seraph voices of a higher world'[20] — and he tentatively ascribed saintly qualities and powers to her:

. . . we were almost inclined to believe that, like singers of

---

* After Queen Victoria's accession to the throne on 20th June, 1837, a large demand for figurines of her was anticipated; some of the Malibran figurines were adapted to portray the queen. See P. D. Gordon Pugh, *Staffordshire Portrait Figures* (London, 1970), p. 177, and plates A2, 3; E86, 87, 130, 148, 149.

ancient days, she could transport the mind into sublimity —
infuse the spirit of benevolence — inspire divine energy —
arouse the slumbering conscience — restore social sympathies
— regulate moral feelings — restrain the fury of ambition —
unlock the iron grasp of avarice — expand the liberal palm to
deeds of charity — breathe the sacred love of peace into the
bosom of the turbulent, and the mild spirit of forbearance and
toleration into persecuting bigotry and prejudice.[21]

Other hagiographies soon followed. The most notable — or
notorious — was by Countess Merlin; although the first editions
(Paris and Brussels, 1838) were relatively sober, the English editions
(1840 and 1844) included ever more fantastic stories, and are true
hagiography. All subsequent biographers have, inevitably, drawn
heavily on Countess Merlin, since she knew La Malibran well; but
Fétis, who was also a close friend, said that 'most of this biography
is fiction.'[22]*

Rival claims are often made for the possession of a saint — not
only of his or her relics, but also for the honour of having bred him
or her. Nathan was the first to stake a claim to La Malibran, by
stating that her father was Jewish[23] — something that cannot be
substantiated; we know, at any rate, that Garcia was baptised.[24]
Nathan, an English-born Jew, also put in a word for England, saying
that La Malibran was 'an Englishwoman by education'.[25] These
claims were far less fantastic than those put forward in the same
year by an anonymous native of Lucca. He asserted that La Malibran
had been born near Lucca of Italian parents, from whom Garcia
had bought her when she was a child. He gave quite circumstantial

---

* Bunn, too, maintained that everything in Madame Merlin's book
concerning him was wrong (Bunn, II, pp. 95 and 112–14). Madame Merlin
wrote to people who had known La Malibran, and asked them for their
reminiscences; but her book is written as if all the reminiscences in it were
her own; as she only saw La Malibran in Paris, and infrequently after
1832, much of her book was inevitably based on hearsay. Lord William
Lennox alleged that Mme Merlin's publisher incorporated his reminiscences
of La Malibran in the Countess's book without permission. This is unlikely,
as the details of — for example — La Malibran's riding accident in the
Countess's book are different from Lord William's account. It is impossible
now to sift fact from fiction, particularly in the later editions of Madame
Merlin's book. She probably never saw the later, English editions, which
were very likely printed without her knowledge.

evidence: her name was Domenica Carmina; she was the daughter of Francesco Paolinelli, known as 'Il Pampinaro'; she was born at San Lorenzo della Cappella. La Malibran was not, therefore, 'a genius who had gone from France to Italy, but an Italian genius who had gone to France.'[26]

Saints must perform miracles, and the hagiographers provided them for La Malibran. The cup from which a crowd of gondoliers drank her health, but which always remained mysteriously full, has already been mentioned.[27] According to one writer, when crossing the Atlantic from America to France La Malibran calmed a terrifying storm by standing on deck and singing Mozart's *Alleluia*;[28] it is unfortunate that we know, from her own letters, that she was so sea-sick on the crossing that she could not leave her cabin. Several sources tell us how, by singing the *Willow Song* from *Otello*, she restored a lunatic to his right mind; after her performance he was able to leave the asylum and return to his family.[29] She is also said to have saved the life of a child, dying of convulsions, by getting into a bath with him; as a result, the child was immediately calmed, and was soon sleeping peacefully.[30] Her acts of charity — some of them probably true — are repeated with embellishments in all the hagiographies.[31]

From the moment of her death La Malibran's frailties and peccadillos — her avariciousness, her marital irregularities, her illegitimate children, her competitiveness — were suppressed, or forgotten and forgiven, and scarcely ever referred to again. For example, her last words to Sir George Smart before she sang her final fatal encore with Madame Caradori-Allan: 'I will sing it again and *annihilate her*', are almost always omitted. La Malibran had not been a particularly sinful woman, but she had been human — a fact which no one any longer admitted.

In 1843 Bériot erected a small mausoleum over La Malibran's grave at Laeken. It is in the form of a little temple, with a very undistinguished statue of La Malibran as Norma, by the Belgian sculptor Geefs, inside it. Lamartine, at the request of the Viardots,[32] contributed four lines of equally undistinguished poetry,* which

---

*   *Beauté, génie, amour furent son nom de femme,*
Ecrit dans son regard, dans son coeur, dans sa voix,
Sous trois formes au ciel appartenait cette âme.
Pleurez, terre, et vous cieux, accueillez-la trois fois.

Had Lamartine knowledge of Bellini's description of La Malibran as a woman with three souls (see p. 191), or is this just another coincidence?

were inscribed on the tomb. This shrine gave a further impetus to the cult, and at once became a place of veneration and pilgrimage. The mausoleum has a decorative iron door — usually kept closed — and through the spaces in the metal-work people deposited, and still do, flowers, cards, coins, ex-votos.

Belgium owned La Malibran's shrine and relics, but the rest of Europe, particularly France, also felt the need for some form of temple or centre for the cult. In 1857 a grandiose project was drawn up for 'a vast edifice, a MONUMENT' to La Malibran, to be constructed on the Boulevard de Sebastopol in Paris. Shares were offered for sale by a certain A. Malibran — perhaps one of Eugène Malibran's nephews. The monument was to consist of a huge concert-hall, foyers, balconies, terraces, gaming-rooms and galleries capable of holding 2,400 people. There were also to be restaurants, cafés, grottos, waterfalls, and 'a Turkish room, where people will be served in the oriental manner, and where hookahs will be smoked.' This Romantic dream seems to have remained a dream, perhaps because the estimated cost was almost two million francs.[33]

But the true shrine of a saint is where his or her mortal remains rest, and Brussels continued to be the centre of La Malibran's cult. Sixty-five years after her death, the devotion of the faithful had not diminished, although probably no one who had known her — except Legouvé, then ninety-four years old — still remained alive.[*] In 1901 a Belgium journalist wrote:

> Once a year the chapel is opened, and the bouquets, wreaths, innumerable cards which people continue to put there with fervour are removed ... At the cemetery at Laeken, on All Souls' Day, the crowd throngs round the mausoleum of the unforgettable Desdemona. Uneducated people believe that the little chapel harbours the remains of a saint.[34]

That belief continues to this day, and tributes are still deposited at the shrine. In 1950 Maria Callas made a special visit to La Malibran's tomb.[35] In 1982, 146 years after she died, there was a special

---

[*] Legouvé went to see Mme de Grammont when he was writing his biography of La Malibran, probably in the 1880s. 'He talked to me about La Malibran, the latest of his reminiscences,' she recalled. 'He had been very much in love with her, she had sung for him in Naples, this doddery old man had galloped by her side on mettlesome horses in the woods of Passy. Malibran ... Musset ... The *Willow Song*.' (cit. Morgulis, p. 378).

gala opera performance at the Théâtre de la Monnaie in Brussels, at which all the ladies were given a pink rose; early next morning, several of these roses had already been deposited at the shrine of La Malibran.

6

Can any general conclusions be drawn from the life and death of La Malibran and of other secular cult figures? Why does one person, rather than another, become a cult figure? Why La Malibran? Why not Pasta or Sontag? Why Valentino? Why not Douglas Fairbanks Senior?

First of all, we should perhaps define precisely what we mean by a cult figure, since the term is now often loosely used to describe someone who is merely very famous and popular. Cult figures must be the focal point for a form of religious worship, with shrines, relics and so on. Thus, La Malibran was a cult figure, but her sister, although just as successful, was not; Napoleon is a cult figure — even today, and outside France — but the Duke of Wellington is not; Jimi Hendrix is a cult figure, but not Brian Jones.

Secular cult figures seem to have at least three features in common: they are exceptional in some way during their lifetime; they represent the mood of their own generation; and they die young. A few — Napoleon, Paganini, Elvis Presley — survived into early middle age; but the vast majority died before they had time to age visibly or go out of fashion. Those who were on the way to becoming cult figures, but survived to be middle-aged or old, lost their cult status; Liszt and Taglioni are examples. An interesting case is Nizhinsky, who died at the age of sixty-two, but became mentally ill and ceased to communicate with the world when he was thirty-one; he may there-fore be said to have 'died' young; his cult was suspended during the years he spent in asylums, to be revived again after his actual death.

During their lifetime, many cult figures feel, as La Malibran did, that they are somehow predestined victims; Byron, Bellini, Marie Duplessis ('*La dame aux camélias*') and, in this century, Valentino, Carole Lombard, Gérard Philipe, James Dean, Buddy Holly, Jimi Hendrix and Janis Joplin all had premonitions about their early deaths.

Perhaps, because of this, such people seem to live at a faster pace than other people do; they cram more into their short lives than other people do into a normal lifetime; 'they hurry to live.'[1] They are attracted by things which speed life up: before the twentieth century, fast horses; in this century, fast cars, motor-bikes, aeroplanes; drink; drugs. These are often the cause of their deaths.

Secular cult figures also have some things in common with what we know, from history or legend, about religious saints, who did not necessarily die young but who often suffered martyrdom, and legends about their deaths proliferated, especially on the popular level. The deaths of secular cult persons, too, are almost always surrounded by drama, controversy, or suspicion — which is often unfounded, but nevertheless persists. Although some of these people die ordinary deaths, the public will not believe it. Pergolesi — an eighteenth century cult figure — died from tuberculosis at the age of twenty-six, but his contemporaries believed that he had been poisoned. Bellini, who felt an affinity with Pergolesi and admired his music, believed that he, too, would die young, 'like Pergolesi'.[2] After his death, rumours that he had been poisoned circulated, as they had about Pergolesi. Valentino died after an operation for appendicitis; but it was rumoured that he had been poisoned, or stabbed, or that he had not died at all — a rumour which also circulated about Bruce Lee, Jim Morrison and James Dean. 'During the three years after his death, letters addressed to Dean continued to outnumber the fan mail of any living star.'[3] 'Che lives' is written on many walls; and, in the USSR, posters are displayed, announcing that Lenin (an officially imposed cult figure) 'lived, lives, and will live'. It is hoped, and sometimes believed, that such people are immortal.

There was controversy about the deaths of Jean Harlow, Marilyn Monroe, Jimi Hendrix and, still periodically revived, about the death of Napoleon. Some cult figures, like La Malibran, died as a result of a violent accident: Carole Lombard, James Dean, Buddy Holly. Some — President Kennedy, Martin Luther King, John Lennon — were assassinated. Many, including La Malibran, Marilyn Monroe, Elvis Presley, Jimi Hendrix and Janis Joplin, were probably killed by their own life-styles. Such people are often self-destructive; but they have to face the public, which is inexorable, and subjects them to intolerable stresses.

Like the funerals of religious saints, the funerals of secular cult persons are often accompanied by extravagant scenes. 'People were [. . .] especially anxious to have contact with or to gain possession of the corpse of reputed saints.'[4] We have seen how true this was in

La Malibran's case. The scenes at Valentino's funeral were probably
the most extraordinary, when 40,000 people ran amok while trying
to see his body, which had to be hastily removed for fear that it
would be torn to pieces. At the funeral of Elvis Presley armed police
struggled to control an estimated 100,000 mourners, and three heli-
copters hovered overhead. The scenes at the funerals of James Dean
and Eva Peron were scarcely less dramatic. Such funerals generate
mass hysteria, people scream, faint, and are trampled underfoot;
many were injured at Valentino's funeral, and at Elvis Presley's two
people were killed. On the other hand, Che Guevara's body was
incinerated in great secrecy by those who had shot him, because
they rightly realised what an important relic and rallying point his
body might become for his admirers.

Because religious saints' remains were such valuable relics, their
bodies were often moved about, fought over, or even stolen.
Attempts were made to steal the bodies of both Valentino and
Elvis Presley. There are also many legends of saints' bodies — both
Christian and Islamic — choosing their own burial site.[5] Legend has
it that St Denis, for example, after he was decapitated, picked up
his own head and walked five miles with it under his arm to his
preferred resting-place.[6] Although such legends do not yet seem to
be attached to modern secular saints, it is a striking fact that the
bodies of a number of such people have not been allowed to rest in
peace, but have been moved around and reburied in a different
place. Amongst those who, like La Malibran, were buried, then
exhumed and reburied, or whose remains were moved about, usually
for perfectly logical reasons, were: Napoleon, Paganini, Bellini,
Marie Duplessis, Nizhinsky and Maria Callas. But perhaps the most
peripatetic corpse was that of Eva Peron which, after her husband
fell from power, was taken from Argentina to Italy, secretly buried
in Milan, then exhumed and taken to Madrid, and finally back to
Argentina again.

When, in 1876, Bellini's remains were transferred from Paris to
Sicily, extraordinary scenes occurred all along the route followed by
the train bearing his coffin. As in 1926, when Valentino's body was
taken from New York to California, huge crowds assembled at the
railway stations through which the train passed, and there were
many highly emotional demonstrations.[7] Much of this emotion can
be attributed to Italian and Sicilian patriotism; but the most extraordinary act of devotion to Bellini's memory was not performed by
an Italian or a Sicilian, but by an American. When the cortège

arrived in Catania, an autopsy was carried out, probably in order to dispel the rumours still circulating that he had been poisoned. Bellini's body had been embalmed when he died in Paris; but he had been dead for forty-one years and, according to the medical evidence,[8] parts of his corpse had badly deteriorated. While the autopsy was taking place, a young American woman, Maria Luisa Swift, somehow gained admittance, and asked permission to kiss the corpse. Permission was granted, and Mrs Swift not only kissed Bellini's remains 'with a lover's kiss, long and resonant', but also managed to steal two hairs from his embalmed chest.[9]

Fans' quests for relics can go to amazing lengths. People tried to chip pieces off Valentino's tomb — a custom often connected with religious saints[10] — and, three years after his death, 44,000 chunks of marble from a tomb in which Elvis Presley's body had temporarily rested were being sold by mail order at £44 a piece.[11] One thousand pairs of Valentino's socks were insufficient to satisfy relic hunters and to stock the shrines which soon grew up all over America. People sold — and bought — paper wrappings from chewing-gum which James Dean may — or may not — have chewed.[12]

Some Christian saints were subject to states of ecstasy, and this was taken as an additional sign of their sanctity. Many writers referred to having seen La Malibran 'in ecstasy'.[13] In her case, it is probable that these witnesses saw or heard about the hysterical fits to which she was prone, and that the cause of her 'ecstasy' could best be explained by doctors. But, as we have already noted,[14] some Catholic writers believe that the art of the actor has something in common with the experiences of mystics. La Malibran's contemporaries, who saw her as a mythical figure even in her own life-time, often applied religious or mythical terms to her, and this is true of other secular cult figures. In the twentieth century the use of psychedelic drugs can produce states of heightened consciousness, which the users claim are akin to ecstasy, and several secular cult figures were users of such drugs.

Saints have always been a good commercial proposition; in the Middle Ages monasteries with an important saint's relics made a large income out of pilgrims — the tourists of that time — and out of the sale of images, medallions, and so on. Today it is hoped that a new multi-million pound Beatle shrine in Liverpool — the Cavern Walks complex — will revive the city's flagging economy. The Elvis Presley industry in Memphis is very big business indeed, and has a vested interest in keeping his cult alive.[15] It will be interesting to see how long it will do so; cults arise spontaneously, but they can also spontaneously wither away. In the case of La Malibran, commercial interests did not support her cult for very long, yet it has lasted for a century and a half, probably, in French-speaking countries, because of Musset's *Stances*, which every educated Frenchman knows by heart; but it is also durable in Italy, particularly in Venice, where she only spent a fortnight.

It may be that the cults of people who died before the invention of photography and sound recording are particularly durable. Such people are truly mythological; it is impossible for later generations to know what they looked or sounded like, we can only imagine perfection. But, in the twentieth century, we can see old films of the dead gods and goddesses of a previous generation, listen to their records and form our own opinion. To later generations, such people are often disappointing, unattractive, or even ridiculous. La Malibran has escaped that fate.

Secular cult figures, like religious saints, can be debunked, but they still cannot be fully explained. They often have certain propensities — their premonitions, their peripatetic corpses, the odd coincidences which were such a feature of La Malibran's and other cult figures' lives — for which there is no logical explanation. There are more male than female cult figures, just as, apparently, there are more male than female religious saints.[16] This does not seem to be because women are more prone to hero-worship than men are — on the contrary, most true cult figures, even Valentino and Marilyn Monroe, seem to appeal equally to men and women. What is more, although probably few female cult figures were virgins like their saintly sisters, few were married women with children; if, like La Malibran, they had children, they kept it dark. Maternity, except in the case of the Virgin Mary, St Anne, and one or two other Christian saints, does not seem to inspire cults.[17]

'Those who have examined the sociology of saints,' says Stephen Wilson, 'are agreed that they reflect the structure of the societies which produce them.'[18] La Malibran reflected France in the 1830s; just as we, in the twentieth century, have had the secular saints who reflect our society, and whom we deserve.

THE LEGACY OF LA MALIBRAN

'La Malibran,' said the *Athenaeum* critic H. F. Chorley, 'passed over the stage like a meteor, as an apparition of wonder, rather than as one who on her departure left her mantle behind for others to take up and wear.'[1] It is true that her temperament and style of performance were too eccentric to be copied by other singers, and probably only her sister had a comparable voice and technique. But, although it was impossible to imitate her, she revolutionised opera, as Taglioni and Marie Dorval revolutionised the ballet and the French theatre; after her career, opera was never to be quite the same again. There was no going back to the Classical restraint of a Pasta; and, although La Malibran's baroque performances would probably be quite unacceptable nowadays, great singing actresses of the twentieth century are her descendants. Maria Callas, for example, was proud to be considered a reincarnation of La Malibran; her interpretation of *Norma* was in the same tradition.

Unlike her sister, Pauline Viardot, La Malibran had little direct influence on composers; no major work by a major composer was written for her. Those operas which were specially composed for her, such as Halévy's *Clari*, Persiani's *Inez de Castro* and Balfe's *The Maid of Artois*, did not long remain in the repertoire after she had ceased to perform them. The 'Malibran' version of Bellini's *I Puritani* did contain an aria specially composed for her, but she never sang it. Several composers — Bellini, Auber,[2] Meyerbeer[3] and, perhaps, Rossini[4] — contemplated writing an opera for her, but never did so. The only major composer who acknowledged a small debt to her was Chopin, whose playing, according to one of his pupils, was 'entirely copied from the vocal style of Rubini, of La Malibran, of La Grisi etc.; he says so himself.'[5]

But, although no major work was written for her, she nevertheless opened up new possibilities to composers, librettists and singers, and created new expectations in audiences. Romantic operas written towards the end of her career and after her death — by Donizetti, the young Verdi and other lesser composers — owe something to her.

For example, the mad scenes, which were for a time so fashionable, probably derive from her frenetic acting, although she never played a mad scene proper herself. *Carmen* (in which Bizet uses one of her father's songs) is an obvious example of her legacy.[6] It is not too difficult to see Puccini's heroines as her artistic grandchildren.

La Malibran was herself one of the few women of the epoch who wrote music. Like her father and sister, she was a talented composer, mainly of *romances*, that specifically French and Romantic type of song.[7] These rather naïve drawing-room songs were immensely popular from the mid-eighteenth to the mid-nineteenth centuries, and the fashion for them reached a peak in the late 1820s and 1830s. Thousands of copies were sold in albums, 'keepsakes', or as sheet music, and they were performed by amateurs, often with harp or guitar accompaniment. The subject matter was usually either sentimental, heroic, or fantastic; La Malibran wrote many examples, and published several albums during her lifetime. After her death a last album, *Les dernières pensées musicales de M. F. Malibran de Bériot*, enjoyed a great vogue and became a best-seller. When she sang her own *romances*, or her father's songs, such as *El contrabandista*, accompanying herself on the harp, they were always a great success; her sister sometimes performed them, too. But audiences were probably captivated by the singers rather than the songs, and La Malibran's *romances* are hardly ever performed today.* Yet she was considered an outstanding composer of this type of work, was dubbed '*La Sévigné de la romance*',[8] and her songs were praised by such exacting critics as Berlioz,[9] Schumann[10] and Debussy.[11] Poets — Marcelline Desbordes-Valmore, Emile Deschamps — were proud to collaborate with her.

Many artists painted or drew La Malibran's portrait, but she is said to have complained that they represented her as ten times uglier than she really was. This we cannot judge. There exist some delightful portraits and busts of her, but mostly, it must be said, by rather minor artists. A portrait still in the possession of her family is attributed by family legend to Delacroix; but Delacroix did not admire her, and there is no record of his having painted her. Horace

---

* On 9th April, 1982, at the Teatro Malibran in Venice, in the series of concerts 'Omaggio a Venezia', Joan Sutherland and Richard Bonynge gave a concert dedicated to La Malibran, during which music by Mozart, Balfe, Rossini and Donizetti was performed, as well as compositions by La Malibran and Bériot.

Vernet painted her, but the portrait's whereabouts are not now known.[12] The mould of Dantan's caricature was destroyed by the artist after her death; it was said to have been particularly cruel, and that Dantan had made it against his will, at La Malibran's own request.[13] There is, or was, a charming portrait by Léon Viardot, Louis's brother.[14] Henri Decaisne's very well-known portrait of La Malibran as Desdemona (1830) was given by her mother to the Musée Carnavalet in Paris, where it still is. L. Pedrazzi's fine portrait is in the Theatre Museum of La Scala, Milan. There is a bust by Baruzzi in the Liceo Musicale, Bologna, one by Pompeo Marchese in Milan, and another by Sangiorgio at La Scala. A bust by Giungi, executed in Bologna in the spring of 1834, is in the Brussels Conservatoire. After her death Bériot made a bust of her and gave copies to her friends.[15] There were portraits by Jean-Hilaire Belloc,[16] Tony Johannot[17] and Achille Devéria,[18] and probably by many other lesser artists. There are several caricatures and drawings by A. E. Chalon;[19] there are numerous lithographs of portraits by John Hayter, F. Spagnuoli, H. Grevédon, O. Tassaert, A. Albert and many others.* In some of these portraits, even in those by very minor artists, La Malibran's melancholy charm is apparent — very few portraits show her smiling. But Pauline Viardot maintained that the only portrait which really resembled her sister was the unfinished one by François Bouchot.[20]

La Malibran was, above all, reflected in literature. At that time 'the fever of literature was everywhere',[21] and La Malibran's personality and art immediately appealed to writers and poets of the epoch. 'Poets have always treated me kindly,'[22] she told a friend, and she was right. Alfred de Musset's *Stances à La Malibran*, written a fortnight after her death, have assured her of immortality; but long

---

* At least three oil paintings which have sometimes been described as portraits of La Malibran cannot be positively identified as such. A portrait in the National Gallery, London (No. 2218 in the 1973 catalogue), was, at one time, considered to be an American study of La Malibran, but is now classed as a French portrait of an unknown woman. A portrait belonging to the Royal Academy of Music in London and one in Ixelles (supposed to be La Malibran ill) have no reliable *provenance*, and although they look vaguely like the singer, cannot be positively identified until it is known who painted them, and when. La Malibran's fame is such that people were — and are — so keen to own portraits of her that their enthusiasm is not always tempered by caution.

before she died her contemporaries saw her as 'a poet'[23] or simply as 'poetry',[24] or as a poem: *'cette femme-poème'*.[25] And poets major and minor, from Lorenzo da Ponte (born 1749)[26] to Christine Alan[27] writing in the 1970s, have paid their tributes to her.

The number of poems addressed to her was vast, and most of them have been lost. It was the fashion at that time, when every self-respecting young man could string a few lines of verse together, to throw poems on the stage to an admired singer at the end of the performance. This practice was widespread in America, France and Italy. Much of this ephemera has disappeared, although a few poems, mostly of no distinction but sometimes with a charming period flavour, survive in contemporary newspapers or as broadsheets; the earliest examples are American.[28]

It was not until she reached Paris in 1828 that La Malibran began to make an impact on Romantic writers. Ludovic Vitet's numerous articles in *Le Globe* (unsigned) were the first comments about her by a well-known writer with a Romantic bias. Inevitably, her influence took some time to filter through into published works. She is frequently mentioned in novels from about 1830 onwards; by then her name was synonymous with 'great star' and had become a household word. Most of these references are of little interest, merely showing how famous she had become; Balzac, an assiduous opera-goer, mentions her in this way.[29] Some novelists went a little further and discussed her performances, and one — R. de Beauvoir — wrote a typically Romantic (and muddled) hymn to the reigning goddess: 'Our inimitable Desdemona, pale daughter of Garcia and of Shakespeare, with the look of an angel, whose singing trembles and prays. Beautiful in her nightly death, and making us hate Othello — she, our only poet, our only theatre: Malibran.'[30]

We have already discussed La Malibran's influence on Legouvé — a minor writer but the first to devote a full-length novel to her — and on George Sand. Alfred de Musset, apart from celebrating her in his *Stances à La Malibran*, also wrote about her in elegant and eloquent prose, and her performances as Desdemona are reflected in several of his poems.[31] Lamartine also wrote about her in prose, and in one rather feeble poem.[32] Gautier much admired her, but only refers to her directly in his dramatic criticism. Jules Sandeau shared his enthusiasm for her with George Sand while they were collaborating, and later wrote about her on his own.[33] Among the foreigners who saw her in Paris was Hans Christian Andersen; her performances had given him 'some of his most sublime impressions . . . in the world of art,' and she is reflected in his first novel, *Improvisatonen* (1835).[34]

The impact made on Romantic writers by La Malibran's personality, her style of performance, her life-style and her premature death was very great, as shown by innumerable references to her in letters and memoirs of the period. Not all of them referred to her directly or mentioned her by name; but the images of the tortured soul, the pale and melancholy heroine condemned to an early death, the artist who abandons all for art or love, the frenetic, passionate outsider, the Spanish gypsy, the predestined victim, and so on, to be found in so many Romantic works, probably owe much to her.

In Italy, too, an enormous number of poems were addressed to her, mostly by rather minor poets,[35] and many Italian artists and sculptors made her portrait. One German — Otto Nicolai — commemorated her with a memorial cantata.[36] Italians had always seen her as music; it was, therefore, fitting that five of the best-known Italian composers of the day — her friends Donizetti, Pacini, Mercadante, Coppola and Vaccai — should have collaborated in composing a memorial cantata to her.[37]* She is, however, chiefly remembered in Italy as the incomparable interpreter of Bellini's operas, and thus of Italian Romanticism.

As we have seen, immediately after La Malibran's death an enormous number of poems and articles were published about her in French, Italian and English. Eventually these popular expressions of grief diminished; but poets — Heine,[38] Villiers de l'Isle Adam,[39] Théodore Banville[40] — still sometimes invoked her, and she became one of the patron saints of the self-styled Nouveaux Romantiques in France in the 1970s.[41]

Nor have prose writers, dramatists, script-writers and librettists

---

* This cantata was performed for the first time in England in *The Last Days of Malibran*, a music theatre piece for opera singers by Michael Rennison, at County Hall, London, on 20th and 21st November, 1986.

Other events, also organised by Michael Rennison, to mark the 150th anniversary of La Malibran's death, included a performance of Rossini's *Otello* at St John's, Smith Square (2nd November, 1986), and a Memorial Service, held in Manchester Cathedral on 23rd September, the actual date of her death. During this service some of the music which La Malibran had sung, or which had been performed at her funeral service in that same church, was included; and the Dean of Manchester, the Very Reverend Robert Waddington, read extracts from the sermon preached by Canon Parkinson on October 2nd, 1836, the day after her funeral. (See p. 237.)

neglected her. At least two operas[42] about her have been composed; there have been numerous plays[43] — one was running in Paris in 1983 — films[44] and radio and television programmes.[45] There has even been a strip cartoon about La Malibran in a French newspaper.[46]

In most of these works, and in biographies — often hagiographies or romantic fiction, or a combination of the two — the principal characters in La Malibran's story have become stereotypes: La Malibran and Bériot are romantic lovers; Eugène Malibran is the villain — and in one play, at least, was dressed and made up to look like a pantomime villain;[47] Sontag is the wicked rival, and so on. La Malibran, who spent the whole of her short life performing opera, has now herself become the heroine of innumerable soap operas.

She has, however, retained her mythical status. In Jan Morris's fictional Balkan town of Hav there is a Cinema Malibran.[48]

NOTES

PART I, CHAPTER 1

1 Pauline Viardot to Rietz, 21.I.1859. *Musical Quarterly*, I, p. 533.
2 Jewish: Nathan, p. 2. Moorish: Merlin, p. 13.
3 Pauline Viardot to Rietz, 21.I.1859, *Musical Quarterly*, I, p. 533.
4 Subira, p. 179. Cotarelo, p. 61, n. 1, and p. 536.
5 Cotarelo, p. 148.
6 *Ibid*, pp. 190, n. 2.
7 G. No. 009793, Parish of San Martín, Madrid. Book 52, Folio 422.
8 Pauline Viardot to Louis Viardot, Berlin, 28th Feb. [1867]. Ms., Bibliothèque Nationale, BN N.a.f.16274, fol.319.320.
9 Pauline Viardot to Rietz, 1.I.1859, *Musical Quarterly*, I, p. 371.
10 M. S. Mackinlay, p. 13.
11 See note 7, above.
12 As note 8, above.
13 *Ibid*.
14 Cotarelo, p. 267.
15 *Ibid*, pp. 61–2, n. 2; however, not all the information in this note is correct. See also family tree by André Le Cesne in: Ivan Tourguénev, *Nouvelle correspondance inédite* (Paris, 1971). Planche XV.

PART I, CHAPTER 2

1 Mackinlay, pp. 35–6, and other sources.
2 Michotte, *An Evening at Rossini's*, p. 126. See also the first Rosina's account of the first night fiasco of *Il barbiere*, Geltrude Giorgi-Righetti, *Cenni di una Donna cantante sopra il Maestro Rossini, etc.*, Bologna, 1823.
3 Mackinlay, p. 42: 'some years'. Grove I ('Malibran'): 'two and a half years'. Hogarth, II, p. 408: 'eight or nine years' — which is obviously wrong.

4 See FitzLyon, *The Price of Genius*.
5 Merlin, I, pp. 12–16, etc. Ella, II, p. 330. Escudier, p. 274. Bouilly, III, pp. 382–5. Héritte-Viardot, p. 4.
6 Bouilly, III, pp. 382–3.
7 Pougin, pp. 11–12.
8 Merlin, I, p. 16.
9 *Ibid*, pp. 13–14.
10 *Manchester Guardian*, 5.X.1836.
11 *The Times*, 15.VI.1825.
12 *The Times*, 1.VII.1825.

PART I, CHAPTER 3
1 *New York American*, 10.XI.1825.
2 *Ibid*, 28.XI.1825.
3 *Ibid*, 18.XI.1825.
4 *Ibid*, 7.XI.1825.
5 See FitzLyon, *Lorenzo da Ponte*.
6 See *New York Review*, December, 1825, pp. 78–83.
7 Lorenzo da Ponte, *Memorie*, II, p. 76.
8 *Ibid*, II, p. 127.
9 See, for example, *Impromptu*, by E. L., (in French), *New York American*, 3.I.1826, and an unsigned poem in Italian, *New York American*, 17.IV.1826.
10 Maria Garcia to Giuditta Pasta, [14.II.1826], Ferranti-Giulini, p. 38.
11 *Otello* (Garcia) 7.II.1826. *Othello* (Kean), 8.II.1826.
12 Maria Malibran to her mother, 26th January [1827]. Ms., Le Cesne Collection.
13 *Evening Post*, 9.II.1826.
14 As note 10, above.

PART I, CHAPTER 4
1 Letter from Maria Garcia to Giuditta Pasta, *cit.* Bushnell, p. 10. See also Giulini-Ferranti, pp. 66–9.
2 Owen, p. 231.
3 *Ibid*.
4 *Ibid*, p. 230.
5 See Bushnell, p. 26.
6 Legouvé, *Maria Malibran*, p. 13.
7 Merlin, I, p. 45.

PART I, CHAPTER 5

1 See Tissot, p. 512, n. 1. Malibran was naturalised in New York, 31.III.1818. (Pougin, p. 189).
2 Bouilly, III, p. 385. Moscheles, I, p. 242. Hogarth, II, p. 415. Fétis, *Biographie universelle*. Anon, 'Madame Malibran's marriage', and many other sources.
3 Maria Garcia to Eugène Malibran, n.d., Teneo, p. 446.
4 *Ibid*, p. 447.
5 Ms., Bibliothèque de l'Opéra.
6 Tissot, pp. 513–4. Malherbe (p. 247) gives the marriage contract; but this is an unreliable source.
7 *New York American*, 25.III.1827.
8 The manuscripts of these letters are now in the Bibliothèque de l'Opéra.
9 Manuel Garcia to Giuditta Pasta, n.d., Ferranti-Giulini, p. 63.
10 *New York American*, 30.III.1826 and 3.IV.1826.
11 Maria Malibran to 'Dear Milady', n.d., but written from 36, Liberty Street (in English). Ms., Bibliothèque de l'Opéra.
12 Performance of 7.VIII.1826. *New York American*, 8.VIII.1826.
13 *New York American*, 7.IV.1826.
14 *New York American*, 26.IV.1826.
15 L. da Ponte, *Memorie*, II, p. 77.
16 *New York American*, 1.VI.1826.
17 *New York American*, 29.V.1826.
18 *Albion*, 27.V.1826.
19 On 16.X.1826.

PART I, CHAPTER 6

1 Father Malou to Maria Malibran, 9.V.1827. Teneo, pp. 448–9.
2 John, Bishop of New York to Maria Malibran, 12.V.1827. Teneo, pp. 449–50.
3 22nd June, 1826, in aid of the Orphan Asylum.
4 Barnard Hewitt, *Theatre U.S.A., 1668–1957* (New York, 1959), p. 103.
5 *Albion*, Jan. 27th, Feb. 10th and 17th, 1827.
6 Maria Malibran to her mother, 24th Jan. [1827]. Ms. written in a mixture of Spanish and Italian. Le Cesne Collection.
7 Da Ponte to Montresor, New York, 1.VIII.1831. *Memorie*, II, p. 219.
8 *Albion*, 20.I.1827.
9 *Albion*, 17.II.1827.

10 As note 6, above.
11 Maria Malibran to Eugène Malibran, Philadelphia, 17.VI.1827. Teneo, p. 450.
12 *Ibid*, 'Lundi soir', [18.VI.]1827. Teneo, p. 451.
13 *Ibid*, 20.VI.1827. Teneo, pp. 451–2.
14 As note 6, above.
15 Bushnell, p. 40.
16 See, for example, Francis, p. 258.
17 *Albion*, 3.XI.1827.
18 *American*, 30.X.1827.
19 *New York American*, 30.X.1827 and *Albion*, 3.X.1827.
20 *Albion*, 3.XI.1827.
21 *Ibid*.
22 Maria Malibran to Eugène Malibran, 20.XI.1827. Teneo, p. 453.
23 *Ibid*.
24 Maria Malibran to Eugène Malibran, 13.XII.1827. Teneo, p. 454.

PART II, INTRODUCTION
1 Berlioz, *Mémoires*, (Paris, 1969), I, p. 125.
2 *Ibid*, I, p. 137.
3 Musset, *Confession d'un enfant du siècle*, *Oeuvres d'Alfred de Musset*, Paris, 1866, VII, p. 2.

PART II, CHAPTER 1
1 Maria Malibran to Eugène Malibran, 29.XII.1827. Teneo, p. 455.
2 *Ibid*, 13.XII.1827. Teneo, p. 454.
3 *Ibid*, 29.XII.1827. Teneo, p. 455.
4 Bauer, II, p. 171.
5 Grove, I, article on Sontag.
6 Hogarth, II, p. 406.
7 *Revue et gazette musicale*, II, 1827–8, p. 589.
8 *Ibid*.
9 *Morning Post*, 18.VII.1836.
10 *Ibid*, 22.IV.1829.
11 *Il giornale delle Due Sicilie*, 13.X.1834.
12 Chorley, pp. 8, 10–11.
13 *cit*. Tiersot, *Lettres de musiciens*, II, p. 28.

14 Florimo, *Cenni storici sulla scuola musicale di Napoli, cit.* Pougin, p. 248.
15 Bellini to Lamperi, 29.IV [1835], *Epistolario*, p. 546.
16 Moscheles, I, p. 243.
17 Fétis, article on Malibran in *Biographie universelle.*
18 Verdi to Arrivabene, Genoa, 27.XII.1877. Alberto Annibale, *Verdi intimo*, p. 205.
19 Michotte, *An Evening at Rossini's*, pp. 121–2.
20 Scudo, *Henriette Sontag*, New York, 1852, translated from an unidentified article in a French publication.
21 Maria Malibran to Eugène Malibran, 7.II.1828. Teneo, p. 480.
22 *Ibid.*

PART II, CHAPTER 2
1 F. Soulié, *Deux séjours, cit.* Bailbé, p. 24. For an analysis of this 'need and passion', see Bailbé, pp. 23–33, and Guichard, pp. 98–103.
2 Legouvé, *Soixante ans de souvenirs*, I, p. 287.
3 *Ibid.*
4 Delacroix, *Journal*, 12.X.1822. p. 29.
5 Philothée O'Neddy, *Feu et flamme, Nuit septième, Dandyisme* (1833).
6 Bauer, II, p. 269. Legouvé, *Maria Malibran*, p. 6. Chorley, p. 6.
7 Legouvé, *Maria Malibran*, p. 6.
8 Chorley, p. 6.
9 Fétis, *La Revue et gazette musicale*, 3 (1828), pp. 268–71.
10 Maria Malibran to Eugène Malibran, 8.V.1828. Teneo, p. 464.
11 *Le Globe*, 13.X.1828.
12 Dumas, *Mes mémoires*, II, p. 419.
13 Stendhal to Sutton Sharpe, 23.III [1828]. *Correspondance*, II, p. 139.
14 Delécluse, *Journal, 1824–28*, pp. 488–9.
15 Liszt to Maria Malibran, n.d. Ms. written from rue Montholon. No. 7 bis. Brussels Conservatoire.
16 Juste Olivier, (1,VII.1830), p. 164.
17 Gautier, *Histoire de l'art dramatique, 2ème série*, p. 282.
18 Dumas, III, p. 249.
19 George Sand to Casimir Dudevant, [28? Jan. 1831] *Correspondance*, I, pp. 789–790.
20 Séché, *Lamartine*, p. 257. Lamartine, *Cours familier*, III, p. 466.
21 Legouvé, *Maria Malibran*, p. 7.

22 Gautier, *Histoire du romantisme*, p. 62.
23 J. de Saint-Félix, *Mlle de Marignan*, *cit.* Bailbé, p. 31, and Jules Sandeau, *Le Concert des pauvres*, Olivier, p. 94.
24 Gounod, *Mémoires d'un artiste*, p. 42.
25 Heine, *Lutèce*, p. 249, *cit.* Bailbé, pp. 31, 76.
26 M. A. Bazin, *L'Epoque sans nom*, II, p. 123, *cit.* Bailbé, p. 25, n. 51.
27 Jules Sandeau, *Le Concert des pauvres*, Olivier, p. 94.
28 A. Arnould et A. de Lavigne, *Tout chemin mène à Rome*, I, p. 28, *cit.* Bailbé, p. 33.
29 As note 24, above.
30 Blaze de Bury, *cit.* Lafôret, p. 211.

PART II, CHAPTER 3
 1 Stendhal, *Life of Rossini*, p. 216.
 2 Musset, 'Débuts de Mlle. Garcia', *Revue des deux mondes*, 1.XI.1839.
 3 See Edmond Estève, 'De Shakespeare à Musset. Variations sur la romance du saule', *Revue d'histoire littéraire de la France*, XXIX, 1922, pp. 288–315.
 4 As note 2, above.
 5 *Le Saule*; *Lucie*; *Stances à la Malibran*; *Sonnet à George Sand*.
 6 For mentions of it in novels, see Bailbé.
 7 See Guichard, pp. 65–8.
 8 Forneret, *Un Crétin et sa harpe*, in Steinmetz, p. 544.
 9 *Ibid.*
10 As note 2, above.

PART II, CHAPTER 4
 1 Maria Malibran to Eugène Malibran, 20.XI[1827]. Teneo. p. 453.
 2 *Ibid*, Paris, 13.XII.1827. Teneo, p. 454.
 3 *Ibid*, [Paris], 29.XI.1827. Teneo, p. 455.
 4 *Ibid*, Paris, 15.I.1828. Teneo, p. 457.
 5 *Ibid*, [Paris], 7.II.1828. Teneo, p. 461.
 6 See p. 50, and Merlin I, p. 118.
 7 Maria Malibran to Eugène Malibran, [Paris], 6.II.1828. Teneo, p. 459.
 8 Maria Malibran to Mme. Chastelain, Paris, 19.II.1828, Teneo, p. 461.
 9 Maria Malibran to Eugène Malibran, 3.III.1828. Teneo, p. 463.

10 See p. 44 and p 51, footnote.
11 Maria Malibran to Eugène Malibran, 8.V.1828. Teneo, p. 464.
12 *Ibid*, p. 463.
13 Maria Malibran to Mrs Wainwright. Ms., Bibliothèque de l'Opéra.
14 Maria Malibran to Eugène Malibran, Haut Brizay, 2.VIII.1828. Teneo, pp. 468–9.
15 *Ibid*.
16 Maria Malibran to Eugène Malibran, [Paris], 11.X.1828. Teneo, p. 472.

PART II, CHAPTER 5
1 Paul Foucher, *La Malibran*, *La Chronique musicale*, May–June, 1874, p. 262.
2 Bauer, II, p. 171.
3 Francis, p. 258.
4 Castil-Blaze, *Revue de Paris*, Oct., 1836.
5 Merlin, I, p. 16.
6 Lamartine, *Cours familier de littérature*, Vol. III, p. 464 (*Entretien XVIII*).
7 Quicherat, I, p. 275.
8 Gautier, *Histoire de l'art dramatique*, 6ème série, p. 149.
9 *cit.* Villiers, *La Psychologie du comédien*, pp. 214–5.
10 François Mauriac, *Journal* (Paris, 1940), III, p. 114. See also Villiers, *Le Cloître et la scène*, which examines this subject in depth.
11 Legouvé, *Maria Malibran*, p. 13.
12 Nathan, p. 7, quoting *The Atlas*.
13 Blaze de Bury, *Meyerbeer et son temps*, p. 78. *Manchester Guardian*, 28.IX.1836.
14 Merlin, I, p. 58.
15 Bull, p. 60.
16 Cottrau, pp. 17 and 18.
17 Diderot, *Le Paradoxe sur le comédien*, 1773, published 1830.
18 For example, Vitet in *Le Globe*, 28.VI.1828 and 3.V.1828; Legouvé, *Maria Malibran*, pp. 9–10, 14, etc.
19 Willis, III, p. 2.
20 Tito Gobbi, *My Life*, pp. 49–51.
21 Legouvé, *Maria Malibran*, p. 13.
22 *La Patrie*, 11.V.1860. Article signed SAM.
23 Legouvé, *Maria Malibran*, p. 14, and *Le Globe*, 4.X.1828.

24 Delacroix, *Journal*, January (1847), pp. 170–3.
25 Musset, 'Concert de Mlle. Garcia', *Revue des deux mondes*, 4.XI.1839.
26 Merlin, I, p. 208.
27 Mendelssohn to his family, London, 25th April, 1829. Hensel, I, p. 180.
28 See J. Lucas-Dubreton, *La Restauration et la Monarchie de Juillet*, (Paris, 1926), p. 110.
29 Meyerbeer, *Briefwechel und Tagebücher*, Band II, pp. 116, 119, 138, 362, etc.
30 Gautier, *Histoire du romantisme*, p. 2.

PART II, CHAPTER 6
1 *Morning Post*, 22.IV.1829.
2 *The Times*, 3.VIII.1829.
3 *The Times*, 27.IV.1829.
4 Mendelssohn to his family, 25.IV.1829. Hensel, pp. 179–80.
5 Hogarth, II, pp. 411–2. See also Devrient, p. 83.
6 Delacroix, *Journal*, p. 173.
7 *Athenaeum*, 1.V.1830.
8 *Ibid*, 8.V.1830.
9 *Bath Journal and General Advertiser*, 16.VIII.1830.
10 *Morning Post*, 10.V.1830.
11 Maria Malibran to? London, 30.IV.1830. Wauwermans, p. 62, and Pougin, p. 97.
12 Disraeli to his sister, 20.VII.1833. *Home Letters Written by Lord Beaconsfield, 1830–52*, (London, 1928), p. 124.

PART II, CHAPTER 7
1 Gautier, *Histoire du romantisme*, p. 62.
2 Merlin, I, p. 98.
3 Stendhal, *Souvenirs d'égoïsme, Oeuvres intimes*, p. 1454.
4 Fontaney, 7.IX.[1831], p. 28.
5 Maria Malibran to Eugène Malibran, 25.VI.[1828]. Teneo, p. 468.
6 Mérimée to Albert Stapfer, 16.XII.1828. *Correspondance générale*, I, p. 33.
7 See Maurice Parturier, Introduction to *Lettres de Mérimée à Ludovic Vitet*, (Paris, 1934), XXIII–XXIV.
8 See, for example, Barbey d'Aurevilly, *Memorandum*, 29[Sept. 1836], (Paris, 1927), p. 33. Chopin, *Korespondencja*, I, p. 206.

9 *The Times*, 1.VI.1829; see also *Morning Post* of same date.
10 Fétis, quoted by Wauwermans, p. 7.
11 Wauwermans, p. 5.
12 Bauer, II, p. 170.
13 Moscheles, II, p. 6.
14 Liszt to Marie d'Agoult, 30.XI.1839. *Correspondance de Liszt et de la Comtesse d'Agoult*, (Paris, 1933), II, p. 308.
15 Charles de Bériot to 'Mon cher Eugène,' Paris, 9.VIII.1821. Ms., Brussels Conservatoire.
16 Maria Malibran to Eugène Malibran, 27.VI.1829. Teneo, p. 476.
17 Bauer, II, p. 170.
18 Maria Malibran to Eugène Malibran, 8.IV.[1829]. Teneo, p. 475.
19 On 23.XI.1829.
20 *Journal des débats*, 6.XI.1829. *Le Globe*, 20.X.1829.
21 *Journal des débats*, 7.XII.1829.

PART II, CHAPTER 8
1 Merlin, I, pp. 110–11.
2 Maria Malibran to Constance de Bériot, n.d., Wauwermans, p. 51.
3 Maria Malibran to ? [London], 30.IV.1830. Pougin, p. 97.
4 Wauwermans, p. 64.
5 Dr Belinaye. *Morning Post*, 24.X.1836 (copied from the *Medical Gazette*).
6 Wauwermans, p. 64.
7 *Ibid*. pp. 64–5.
8 *Ibid*, p. 65.
9 *Ibid*, pp. 65–9.
10 *Ibid*, p. 65.
11 *Ibid*, p. 66.
12 *Ibid*.
13 *Ibid*.
14 *Ibid*, p. 67.
15 *Ibid*.
16 *Ibid*.
17 *Ibid*, pp. 68–9.
18 Moscheles, I, pp. 242–3.
19 *Manchester Guardian*, 28.IX.1836.

20 Maria Malibran to Baron Denié, Bath, 11.VIII.1830. Wauwermans, pp. 67–8.
21 Robert to Severini, 5.IX.1830, 22.IX.1830 and 29.IX.1830. Soubies, pp. 44 and 46.

PART II, CHAPTER 9
 1 Michotte, *An Evening at Rossini's*, pp. 121–2.
 2 Maria Malibran to Lamartine, Bath, 11.VIII.1830. *Lettres à Lamartine*, p. 108.
 3 She is compared to Corinne in several sources, including the Philadelphia edition of Merlin, II, pp. 27–8. Dante and Goethe: *Manchester Guardian*, 5.X.1836. Byron: Legouvé, *Maria Malibran*, p. 29.
 4 Escudier, pp. 288–9.
 5 Dumas, *Mes mémoires*, III, p. 78.
 6 Berlioz, *A travers chants*, p. 5.
 7 Letter from Vigny to a friend, 30.III.1831. *Correspondance*, I. pp. 40–1.
 8 Cottinet, p. 94. See also: J. Janin, *Deburau*, (Paris, 1881), p. 204.
 9 Harriet Smithson to Maria Malibran, Dec., 1830. Ms., Brussels Conservatoire.
10 For example, on 23.II.1829 at the Opéra, and on other occasions.
11 Pulver, p. 12.
12 Chopin, *Korespondencja*, I, p. 202.
13 *Ibid*, p. 206.
14 George Sand to Casimir Dudevant, [28? I.1831]. *Correspondance*, I, p. 789.
15 See Legouvé, *Maria Malibran*, pp. 46–7.
16 Escudier, pp. 28–9.
17 Merlin, II, pp. 89–90.
18 Legouvé, *Maria Malibran*, pp. 17–19.
19 Bauer, II, p. 171.
20 Kalkbrenner to Maria Malibran, n.d. Ms., Brussels Conservatoire.
21 Blaze de Bury, p. 79.
22 *Ibid*.
23 Philarète Chasles, p. 259.
24 *Ibid*.
25 Marie d'Agoult, *Mes souvenirs*, p. 304.
26 Escudier, p. 288.

27 Legouvé, *Maria Malibran*, p. 21.
28 Maria Malibran to Lamartine, Bath, 11.VIII.1830. *Lettres à Lamartine, 1818–1865*, pp. 105–11. It is clear that she wrote quite frequently to Lamartine; but this is the only letter which has so far come to light.
29 *cit.* Marix-Spire, *George Sand*, p. 27 and n. 53.
30 Bouilly to Maria Malibran, Paris, 8.VIII.1834. Ms., Brussels Conservatoire.
31 Legouvé to Maria Malibran, 7.II[1830]. Ms., Brussels Conservatoire.
32 *Ibid.*
33 Lamartine, *Cours familier de littérature*, Vol. III, pp. 463–4.
34 As note 31, above.
35 Maria Malibran to Legouvé, April, 1831. Legouvé, *Maria Malibran*, p. 45. See also *Max*, p. 186.
36 As note 31, above.

PART II, CHAPTER 10

1 Legouvé, *Soixante ans de souvenirs*, Vol. I, pp. 234–72. There is also a separate edition of his reminiscences of La Malibran, Paris [1880], which is the edition I have used. For example, compare: *Max*, pp. 177 and 186, with *Maria Malibran*, p. 45; *Max*, p. 218–9, *Maria Malibran*, p. 46; *Max*, p. 178, *Maria Malibran*, p. 46; and see *Max*, pp. 158–62, which is clearly based on La Malibran.
2 For example. *Max*, p. 134 and Bouilly, III, p. 402.
3 *Max*, pp. 222–3, 232, 246.
4 *Max*, p. 160.
5 *Max*, pp. 158–9; *Maria Malibran*, p. 25.
6 *Max*, p. 123; *Maria Malibran*, p. 20.
7 *Max*, p. 146.
8 *Ibid*, p. 250.
9 Merlin, II, p. 88.
10 See, for example, Léonard de Géréon, *La Rampe et les coulisses*, (Paris, 1832), p. 58: 'Son père (*infandum!*) seduit par sa grâce et sa gentilesse, conçut dit-on l'affreux projet de la retenir auprès de lui afin de satisfaire une passion qui révolte le coeur.'
11 *Manchester Guardian*, 28.IX.1836.
12 *Max*, p. x.
13 Alfred de Musset, *Lettres de Dupuis et Cotonet, Oeuvres*, IX, p. 118.

14 Legouvé, *Maria Malibran*, pp. 47–8.
15 *Journal des débats*, 12.XI.1829.

PART II, CHAPTER 11
  1 Merlin, I, p. 106.
  2 See André Villiers, *La Prostitution de l'acteur*, (Paris, 1946).
  3 Maugras, pp. 35 and 44.
  4 *Ibid*, pp. 140–1.
  5 *Ibid*, p. 208.
  6 *Ibid*, p. 221.
  7 *Ibid*, p. 139.
  8 *Ibid*, p. 469.
  9 *Ibid*, pp. 473–4.
 10 *Ibid*, pp. 140–1.
 11 Prod'homme, *Musical Quarterly*, July, 1920, p. 387.
 12 Maria Malibran to Eugène Malibran, 28.IX.1828. Teneo, p. 471.
 13 Maugras, pp. 162–9, 172.
 14 *Ibid*, pp. 243–4.
 15 *Ibid*, p. 458.
 16 Maria Malibran to Valentine? London, 6.V.1830. Ms., Bibliothèque Royale, Brussels.
 17 Devrient, pp. 77–8.
 18 Marie d'Agoult, *Mes souvenirs*, pp. 303–4.
 19 Merlin, I, pp. 106–7.
 20 Quicherat, I, p. 477.
 21 Escudier, p. 288.

PART II, CHAPTER 12
  1 George Sand to Jules Boucoiron, [Paris], 4.III.1831. *Correspondance*, I, p. 818.
  2 George Sand to Casimir Dudevant [Paris, 26.I.1831]. *Correspondance*, I, pp. 789–90.
  3 *La Prima Donna*, (signed Jules Sand), *Revue de Paris*, April, 1831.
  4 *La Fille d'Albano*, (signed J.S.), *La Mode*, 15.III.1831.
  5 *La Marquise*, *Revue de Paris*, December, 1832.
  6 *Rose et Blanche*, (signed Jules Sand), 2 vols., Paris, 1833.
  7 *Pauline*, (signed George Sand), *Revue des deux mondes*, 15.XII.39 and 1.1.1840. The first part was written in 1832.

8 Sandeau: *Le Concert pour les pauvres, La Sylphide*, 19 and 26.II.1842.
9 *Revue de Paris*, April, 1831, p. 239.
10 *Ibid.*
11 *Ibid*, pp. 242–3.
12 See note 18, below, and Hensel, I, p. 180.
13 *Revue de Paris*, April, 1831.
14 *Ibid*, p. 244.
15 *La Mode*, 15.III.1831, p. 165.
16 Karénine, *George Sand*, I, p. 355.
17 For details of Pauline Viardot's life and career see: FitzLyon, *The Price of Genius* (London, 1964).
18 Alfred de Musset: 'Sur les débuts de Mlles. Rachel et Pauline Garcia', *Revue des deux mondes*, 1.I.1839.
19 George Sand to Pauline Viardot, n.d., (June, 1842), *Correspondance Sand-Viardot*, p. 159.
20 *Revue et gazette musicale*, 1.I.1837.
21 Liszt. *Rondeau fantastique sur un thème espagnol ('El Contrabandista')* 1836. Published Vienna, 1837. Dedicated to George Sand. S252.R.88.
22 *El poeta calculista*, first performed 28th (or 29th?) April, 1805, Madrid.
23 Gilbert Chase, *The Music of Spain* (2nd ed., New York, 1959), pp. 210–11.
24 Séché, *Le Monument d'Alfred de Vigny*, p. 210.
25 *Revue et gazette musicale*, 1.1.1837.

PART II, CHAPTER 13

1 Abraham Mendelssohn to his wife, Paris, 27.VIII.1830. Hensel, Vol. I, p. 258.
2 Maria Malibran to Legouvé, Norwich, August, 1830. Legouvé, *Maria Malibran*, pp. 46–7.
3 Bériot to Maria Malibran, Brussels, 1.XI.1830. Wauwermans, pp. 73–4.
4 *Le Figaro*, 6.XI.30 (*Otello*).
5 See, for example, *La Revue et gazette musicale*, 9, 1830.
6 Maria Malibran to Eugène Malibran, 2.XII.1830. Teneo, p. 480.
7 Lafayette to Maria Malibran, 5.XII.1830. Ms., Brussels Conservatoire.
8 Stendhal, *Souvenirs d'égoïsme, Oeuvres intimes*, pp. 1418–9.

9 Cuvillier-Fleury, *Journal intime*, 23.III.1831, I, p. 316. See also Merlin, I, p. 121.
10 Pougin, p. 94.
11 Lafayette to Maria Malibran, 6.III.1834. Ms., Brussels Conservatoire.
12 Lafayette to Eugène Malibran, 2.I.1831. Teneo, pp. 480–1.
13 Merlin, I, p. 119 and other sources.
14 Charles de Bériot and Maria Malibran to Constance de Bériot, nd., [December, 1830]. Ms., Brussels Conservatoire.

PART II, CHAPTER 14
1 Cuvillier–Fleury, *Journal intime*, Wednesday, 2nd [March], 1831. I, p. 285.
2 Philarète Chasles, *cit.* Séchan, p. 192.
3 Fontaney, *Journal intime*, 22nd November [1831], p. 83.
4 Maria Malibran to Eugène Malibran, 8.IX.1828. Teneo, p. 470.
5 Reparaz, pp. 166–7 (no source given), and Merlin, I, p. 190.
6 Merlin, I, pp. 190–1.
7 *Ibid.*
8 Mérimée to Stendhal, 1.XII.1831. Stendhal, *Correspondance*, I, p. 883.
9 Maria Caradori-Allan to Maria Malibran, 18.XI.1831. Ms., Brussels Conservatoire.
10 Merlin, I, pp. 185–6.
11 Mendelssohn to Carl Immermann, Paris, 14.I.1832. Felix Mendelssohn-Bartholdy, *Letters from Italy and Switzerland* (London, 1862).
12 Ms. draft letter, nd., Le Cesne Collection.
13 *cit.* Pougin, p. 193.
14 Merlin, I, p. 199.
15 Maria Malibran to Constance de Francquen, nd., Wauwermans, pp. 85–6.
16 Adolphe Adam, *Souvenirs d'un musicien* (Paris, n.d., 1901?), XXIII.
17 Véron, *Mémoires d'un bourgeois de Paris*, III, p. 270.

PART II, CHAPTER 15
1 *The Times*, 10.V.1836.
2 Fétis, *Biographie universelle*, article on Malibran.
3 Mérimée to Stendhal, 1.III.1831. Stendhal, *Correspondance*, II, p. 883.

4 Merlin, II, pp. 9–10.
5 As note 2, above.
6 See Hensel, pp. 301–2; Clarke, *The Life and Times of Vincent Novello*, pp. 36–9; Moscheles, I, p. 243 and II, pp. 7–9.
7 Pougin, pp. 114–16.
8 Bauer, II, p. 169.
9 Wauwermans, pp. 81–2.
10 Bull, p. 89.
11 See pp. 138–9.

PART III, CHAPTER 1
1 Bériot to his sister, Chiavanna, 26.V.1832. Ms., Bibliothèque Royale, Brussels.
2 Legouvé, *Maria Malibran*, pp. 26–9; *Revue de Paris*, 12.VII.1832. There is a ms. note from Horace Vernet to La Malibran, Rome, 20th Feb., 1834, in the Brussels Conservatoire, which shows the warmth of his friendship for her.
3 Merlin, I, p. 205.
4 Maria Malibran to Louis Viardot, Rome, 21.VI.1832. Pougin, pp. 109–10.
5 *Ibid.*
6 Séchan, p. 15.

PART III, CHAPTER 2
1 Ms. letter from Maria Malibran to a male friend (Troupenas?), Rome, 21st June, [1832]. This letter was formerly in the possession of Alice Viardot; present whereabouts unknown.
2 *Vospominaniya A. N. Abarinovoy, Istoricheskiy Vestnik* (St Petersburg), LXXXIII (1901), p. 221.
3 Monaldi, p. 32.
4 Moscheles, I, pp. 242–3.
5 *Ibid.*
6 Bull, p. 65.
7 *Ibid.*
8 Moscheles, I, p. 243.
9 Abraham Mendelssohn to his wife, London, 7th July, 1833. Hensel, pp. 301–2.
10 Blaze de Bury, p. 79.
11 Moscheles, II, p. 7.
12 Sophy to Lucy Calcott, [1835]. Horsley, pp. 226–7.
13 G. Cottrau to his brother, Naples, 13.I.1838. Cottrau, p. 56.

14 Nicolai, *Tägebucher*, 9.XI.1834, p. 36.
15 Lafayette to Maria Malibran, 7.I.1833. Ms., Brussels Conservatoire.
16 *Ibid.*
17 *Ibid.*
18 *Il giornale delle Due Sicilie*, 26.II.1834.
19 Lafayette to Maria Malibran, Paris, 6.III.1834. Ms., Brussels Conservatoire.
20 Willis, III, p. 58.

PART III, CHAPTER 3
 1 *Morning Chronicle*, 29.IV.1833.
 2 Heine, *Florentinische Nächte, Samtliche Schriften*, I, pp. 570–4.
 3 *Souvenirs de Madame C. Jaubert* (Paris, 1881), pp. 288–90.
 4 Maria Malibran to ?, London [April, 1830]. Pougin, p. 76.
 5 *Gazzetta Piemontese*, 18.I.1836.
 6 Vaccai, pp. 143–5.
 7 Crowest, *A Book of Musical Anecdotes* (London, 1878), II, pp. 287–8.
 8 Donizetti's *Anna Bolena*, Bellini's *Il pirata* and *Norma*.
 9 *Morning Post*, 2.V.1833.
10 *The Times*, 2.V.1833.
11 Husk (editor), *Templeton and Malibran*, p. 7.
12 Bellini to Lamperi, London, 16.V.1833. *Epistolario*, p. 368.
13 Macready, *Diaries*, 7.V.1833. I, p. 31.
14 Fanny Horsley, 7.VII.1833. Horsley, p. 37.
15 Maria Malibran to Alfred Bunn, n.d., Bunn, II, pp. 114–15.
16 *The Times*, 22.V.1833.
17 *Morning Post*, 24.VI.1833.
18 Princess Victoria in her diary, Thursday, 27th June [1833]. Lord Esher, *The Girlhood of Queen Victoria*, I, pp. 79–80.

PART III, CHAPTER 4
 1 *Teatri, arti e letteratura*, 19.II.1835.
 2 *Ibid*, 14.II.1835.
 3 *L'Apatista*, 18.III.1835.
 4 1834.
 5 1832.
 6 1832.
 7 La Scala, 1834.

8 Milan and Bologna, 1834. Naples, 1835 (Duprez, pp. 117–18). Milan, 1835 (Pougin, pp. 201–2).
9 Maria Malibran to ?, Venice, 28.III.1835. Pougin, pp. 178–9.
10 For example, Bologna, 1834.
11 Morgulis, pp. 379–82.
12 *Il giornale delle Due Sicilie*, 1.VIII.1832. Merlin, II, p. 9. Pougin, pp. 114–16.
13 Bériot to his sister, 31.VIII.1834. Wauwermans, pp. 119–21.
14 Count de Hartig to Maria Malibran, 21.III.1836. Ms., Brussels Conservatoire.
15 Cardinal Albani to Marquis Zappi, Senigallia, 22nd July, 1834. Ms., Brussels Conservatoire. See also Wauwermans, pp. 113–17.
16 Bériot to his sister, 31.VIII.1834. Wauwermans, pp. 119–21.
17 Merlin II, p. 74.
18 As note 9, above.
19 Prod'homme, *The Baron de Trémont*, p. 388.
20 Merlin, II, p. 74.
21 Kenney, p. 102.
22 Trebbi, pp. 54–5.
23 Legouvé, *Maria Malibran*, pp. 29–31.
24 G. Cottrau to his brother, 4.III.34, *cit.* Pougin, p. 151.
25 Mackinlay, p. 108.
26 Monaldi, p. 35.
27 *Ibid.*
28 *Ibid.*
29 *Ibid*, p. 36.
30 *Ibid.*
31 Gatti, p. 85.
32 Pougin, pp. 99–100. (But Pougin did not believe that Josepha was Garcia's daughter.)
33 Monaldi, pp. 36–7.
34 *Ibid.*
35 Gatti, p. 84.
36 *Ibid.*
37 The ms. contracts are in the Brussels Conservatoire.
38 Letter from Visconti to Maria Malibran 24.V.1834, Milan. Ms., Brussels Conservatoire.

PART III, CHAPTER 5

1 Bellini to Count Pepoli, n.d. (early 1834). *Epistolario*, p. 400.
2 *Norma*, in Milan. *Teatri, arti e letteratura*, 28.V.1834.

3 Merlin, I, pp. 218–9; II, p. 6.
4 Florimo, *Bellini*, p. 136.
5 *cit.* Quicherat, I, p. 193.
6 Maria Malibran to Troupenas, post-marked 20.IV.1832 (in connection with Auber's unfulfilled desire to write an opera for her). Ms., Le Cesne Collection.
7 Bellini to Florimo, 30.XI.1834. *Epistolario*, pp. 486–7.
8 *Ibid*, 21–22.XII.1834. *Epistolario*, p. 489.
9 See Weinstock, *Bellini*, Appendix Q, *Versions and Variants of I Puritani*, pp. 448–55.
10 Bellini to Florimo, 21–22.XII.1834. *Epistolario*, p. 493.
11 *Ibid*, 5.I.1835. *Epistolario*, p. 497.
12 *Ibid*, 18.II.1835. *Epistolario*, p. 519.
13 *Ibid*.
14 Bellini to Maria Malibran, Paris, 27.II.1835. *Epistolario*, pp. 526–7. The manuscript is in the Brussels Conservatoire.
15 Bellini to Florimo, Paris, 18.II.1835. *Epistolario*, p. 521.
16 *Ibid*, 30.XI.1834. *Epistolario*, p. 486.
17 *Ibid*, pp. 486–7.
18 *Ibid*, and see also letter to Florimo, 4.X.[1834], *Epistolario*, p. 441.
19 Monaldi, p. 158.
20 Bellini to Florimo, 1.VII.1835. *Epistolario*, p. 574.

PART III, CHAPTER 6
1 *Il giornale delle Due Sicilie*, 3.XI.1833.
2 *Ibid*, 14.XI.1833.
3 Bériot to Parola, Naples, 13.I.1835. Ms., Bibliothèque Royale, Brussels.
4 Duprez, p. 116.
5 As note 3, above.
6 Trebbi, pp. 57–60.
7 Bériot to Parola, Naples, 3.III.1835. Heron-Allen, pp. 8–9.
8 *Otello*: Anna de Brémont, *The Great Singers* (London, 1892), p. 123. Merlin, I, p. 224. *I Capuleti*: Merlin, I, p. 226. Foucher, p. 262. *Il matrimonio segreto*: Merlin, I, p. 226.
9 Merlin, II, p. 56.
10 Bunn, II, pp. 93–4.
11 Maria Malibran to ? 29.XI.1829. Ms., Bibliothèque de l'Opéra.
12 Bériot to his brother-in-law, 25.II.[1834?]. Wauwermans, p. 123.

13 Maria Malibran to Legouvé [April, 1831], Legouvé, *Maria Malibran*, p. 45.
14 Merlin, I, pp. 106–7.
15 *Ibid*, I, p. 70.
16 *Ibid*, I, p. 16.
17 *Ibid*, I, p. 55.
18 *Ibid*, I, p. 107.
19 Gronow, I, p. 317.
20 Merlin, II, p. 84.
21 *Ibid*, pp. 80–1.
22 Maria Malibran to Eugène Malibran, 8.IV [1829]. Teneo, p. 475.
23 Maria Malibran to Baron Denié, Bath, 11.VIII.1830. Wauwermans, pp. 67–8.
24 Legouvé, *Maria Malibran*, p. 38, and letter from Maria Malibran to Legouvé (April, 1831), pp. 45–6.
25 Mostly in private collections.
26 Maria Malibran to ?, Venice, 18.III.1835. Pougin, pp. 178–9.
27 Castil-Blaze, *L'Opéra italien*, p. 451.
28 R. de Beauvoir, *L'écolier de Cluny*, I, p. 20. *cit* Bailbé, p. 100.

PART III, CHAPTER 7
 1 Wauwermans, p. 146.
 2 Legouvé, *Maria Malibran*, p. 32.
 3 Wauwermans, p. 159.
 4 For an account of this, see Pougin, pp. 181–5 (based on Venetian sources), and Kenney, pp. 101–2.
 5 Meyerbeer, p. 138, and p. 591, n. 79.
 6 Maria Malibran to Troupenas, post-marked 20.IV.1832. Ms., Le Cesne Collection; and letter from Auber to Maria Malibran, Paris, 14th March, 1832. Ms., Brussels Conservatoire.
 7 Kenney, p. 100.
 8 Moscheles, II, p. 5.
 9 *Morning Post*, 13.VI.1835.
10 Macready, I, p. 236.
11 Von Raumer, *England in 1835*, *cit*. Bushnell, p. 196.
12 Macready, p. 236.
13 *Ibid*, pp. 343–4.
14 *Ibid*, p. 243.
15 *Ibid*, p. 337.
16 *Morning Post*, 6.V.1835.

17 Bellini to Florimo, 1.VII.1835. *Epistolario*, pp. 573–4.
18 Delacroix, *Journal* (27.I.1847), p. 123.

PART III, CHAPTER 8
  1 Maria Malibran to the Marquis de Louvois, Lucca, 2.IX.1835. Pougin, pp. 198–9.
  2 *Gazzetta privilegiata di Milano*, 13.IX.1835.
  3 Pougin, p. 202.
  4 Bellini to Lamperi, 29.IX.[1835]. *Epistolario*, p. 546.
  5 See Weinstock, *Bellini*, pp. 202–8.
  6 Pougin, *Bellini*, p. 177, n. 1.
  7 Donizetti, *Messa da Requiem*, for soloists, four voice chorus, and orchestra, 1835.
  8 Donizetti, *Lamento per la morte di V. Bellini, 1835(?)*. Setting of verses by Maffei.
  9 Maria Malibran to Florimo; n.d. Florimo, *Bellini*, p. 63, and n. 1.
 10 Quoted in *Gazzetta privilegiata di Milano*, 11.X.1835.
 11 Ashbrook, *Donizetti*, p. 175, and Wauwermans, pp. 104–6, 111–12, 121–2.
 12 Macready, p. 236.
 13 Ashbrook, p. 102.
 14 Donizetti to Dolce, 3.I.1836. Zavadini, p. 394.
 15 *Ibid.*
 16 Lambertini in *Gazzetta privilegiata di Milano*, 31.XII.1835.
 17 Delacroix, *Journal* (27.I.1847), pp. 122–4.
 18 G. Barbieri, pp. 39–40 (quoting an anonymous journalist).

PART III, CHAPTER 9
  1 From Fanny Horsley, 29.VII.1835. Horsley, p. 220.
  2 Balfe to Maria Malibran, London, 18th November, 1835. Ms., Brussels Conservatoire.
  3 *Ibid.*
  4 *The Times*, 10.V.1836.
  5 Moscheles, II, p. 11.
  6 Beale, II, p. 201.
  7 Maria Malibran to Troupenas, 21.VI.1836. Ms., Le Cesne Collection.
  8 The original document is in the Brussels Conservatoire.
  9 Moscheles, II, pp. 9–10.
 10 Wauwermans, p. 163.

11 Lennox, II, pp. 207–9.
12 *Ibid.*
13 Edwardes, p. 263. Wauwermans, p. 165.
14 *Manchester Guardian*, 8.X.1836.
15 Wauwermans, p. 165.
16 Maria Malibran to Troupenas, post-mark 16.VII.1836. Ms., Le Cesne Collection.
17 Merlin, II, p. 69.
18 Maria Malibran to a French publisher (Troupenas?), 12.VII.36. Monaldi, pp. 37–8.
19 *Morning Post*, 18.VII.1836.
20 Moscheles, II, pp. 11–12.
21 Wauwermans, p. 176. Merlin, II, p. 78.

PART IV, CHAPTER 1
 1 Interview with Pauline Viardot, *Musical Courier*, 12.I.1898.
 2 Maria Malibran to Troupenas, post-mark 26.VII.1836. Ms., Le Cesne Collection.
 3 *Ibid.*
 4 *Ibid.*
 5 M. S. Novello, 'The Last Days of Malibran', *Manchester Guardian*, 15.X.1836.
 6 *Ibid.*
 7 *Manchester Times*, 17.X.1836.
 8 *Manchester Guardian*, 28.IX.1836.
 9 Dr Belluomini in the *Morning Post*, 5.X.1836.
10 *Manchester Times*, 1.X.1836.
11 *Manchester Guardian*, 15.IX.1836.
12 M. S. Novello, *op. cit.*
13 *Manchester Times*, 1.X.1836.
14 See pp. 153–4.
15 Smart, p. 283.
16 *Manchester Guardian*, 15.IX.1836.
17 cit. *Manchester Guardian*, 28.IX.1836.
18 *Morning Post*, 26.IX.1836.
19 *Manchester Guardian*, 18.IX.1836.
20 *Morning Post*, 28.IX.1836.
21 *Manchester Chronicle*, 1.X.1836.
22 *Manchester Guardian*, 28.IX.1836.
23 *Ibid.*
24 Mackenzie-Grieve, p. 38.

25 *Manchester Chronicle*, 1.X.1836.
26 *Ibid.*
27 *Manchester Guardian*, 28.IX.1836.
28 *Manchester Chronicle*, 1.X.1836.
29 *Cit.* Dr Belluomini in a letter of 4.X.1836, *Manchester Guardian*, 8.X.1836 and other papers.
30 M. S. Novello, *op. cit.*
31 *Manchester Chronicle*, 1.X.1836, Statement by the Festival Committee, see also Dr Belluomini's letter, note 29, above.
32 *Morning Post*, 24.IX.1836.
33 M. S. Novello, *op. cit.*
34 *Ibid.*
35 *Ibid.*
36 *Manchester Times*, 1.X.1836. Mr Lewis's statement: *Manchester Guardian*, 16.XI.1836, quoting *The Lancet*, 12.XI.1836.
37 M. S. Novello, *op. cit.*
38 *Lancet*, 12.XI.1836, *Manchester Guardian*, 16.XI.1836.
39 Eugène Malibran died at 18, rue Saint-Fiacre, Paris. On his death certificate (*3ème arrondissement*), he was described as a '*rentier*', and '*célibataire*'.

PART IV, CHAPTER 2
 1 *Manchester Chronicle*, 26.IX.1836. See also *Manchester Guardian*, 1.X.1836 (Report of the Festival Committee), and 28.IX.1836.
 2 *Manchester Guardian*, 28.IX.1836.
 3 *Ibid*, 1.X.1836.
 4 *Ibid*, 16.XI.1836.
 5 *Ibid*, 1.X.1836.
 6 H. Sutherland Edwardes, II, p. 265.
 7 *Manchester Guardian*, 1.X.1836.
 8 *Le Mari de la danseuse*, by Ernest Feydeau (Paris, 1863 and several subsequent editions).
 9 Dr Belluomini's letter of 29.IX.1836, quoted in the *Manchester Guardian*, 5.X.1836.
10 *Worcester Herald*, 1.X.1836.
11 Bunn, II, pp. 94 and 96.
12 Princess Victoria's diary, Monday, 26th September [1836]. Lord Esher, *The Girlhood of Queen Victoria*, I, pp. 168–9.
13 Bull, pp. 89–90.
14 Beale, p. 28.

15 Macready, *Diaries*, 27.IX.1836, pp. 343–4.
16 Princess Victoria's diary, Friday, 30th [September], 1836. Esher, I, pp. 170–1.

PART IV, CHAPTER 3
1 Bunn, II, pp. 96–7 and 127–130.
2 *Ibid*, pp. 128-9.
3 *Manchester Guardian*, 5.X.1836, and *Manchester Times*, 1.X.1836.
4 *Ibid*.
5 *Ibid*.
6 *Ibid*.
7 *Ibid*.
8 *Ibid*.
9 *A Sermon preached on the Second Day of October 1836, being the day after the Public Funeral of the late Madame M. de Bériot in the Collegiate Church of Manchester by the Rev. Richard Parkinson, M.A., Fellow of the Collegiate Church.* Appendix: Statement by the Festival Committee. John Macvicar, Chairman. (Manchester, 1836).
10 *Manchester Guardian*, 5.X.1836.
11 See *Morning Post*, 3 and 5.X.1836, *Manchester Guardian*, 5.X.1836.
12 *Morning Post*, 3.X.1836.
13 *The Times*, 10.X.1836.
14 *The Lancet*, 8th, 15th, 22nd October, 5th and 12th November, 1836.
15 *The Lancet*, 12.XI.1836 and *Manchester Guardian*, 12.XI.1836.
16 *Manchester Guardian*, 12.X.1836.
17 *Ibid*, 12, 19 and 22.X.1836.
18 *Ibid*, 2.XI.1836.
19 Bériot to Parola, 26.XI.1836. Ms., Bibliothèque Royale, Brussels.
20 *Manchester Guardian*, 2.XI.1836. *Morning Post*, 19.XI.1836.
21 *Manchester Guardian*, 16.XI.1836, *Morning Post*, 20.XI.1836.
22 For example, letter from Joseph Ewart, *Morning Post*, 21.XI.1836.
23 For example, *Morning Post*, 14.XII.1836.
24 For example, *Manchester Times*, 26.IX. and 24.XII.1836.
25 *Manchester Guardian*, 17.XII.1836.
26 *Ibid*.

27 The original document is in the Brussels Conservatoire.
28 *Manchester Guardian*, 21.XII.1836.
29 Interview with Pauline Viardot, *Musical Courier*, 12.I.1898, and *Morning Post*, 24.XII.1836.
30 Wauwermans, p. 191. Bériot to E. Stevens, n.d., ms. Bibliothèque Royale, Brussels, in which he asks Stevens to make all the funeral arrangements.
31 Bériot to Parola, 26.X.1836. Ms. Bibliothèque Royale, Brussels.
32 Wauwermans, p. 195, and *Le Courrier Belge*, 2.I.1837.
33 Wauwermans, pp. 195–6.
34 *Ibid*, p. 197.
35 Letter from Mme. de Francquen to her husband, *cit.* Wauwermans, p. 197. *Le Courrier belge*, 3.I.1837.
36 *Ibid*, 6.I.1837.

PART IV, CHAPTER 4
1 Legouvé, *Maria Malibran*, pp. 34–5.
2 See, for example, F. Lammenais, *Correspondance générale*, Letter of 18.XI.1836 to Marion (Lettre 2589, Vol. VII), in which he states that La Malibran's death caused a far greater sensation than the death of Charles X, who died in November, 1836. Comments on La Malibran's death in letters, diaries and newspapers are legion.
3 Cottinet, pp. 99–100.
4 William Archer Shee, *My Contemporaries, 1830–1870* (London, 1893), p. 41 (26th September, 1836).
5 Jules Janin, 'Mort de Madame Malibran', *Revue et gazette musicale*, 2.X.1836.
6 *Ibid.*
7 2.X.1836.
8 Lamartine, *Cours familier de littérature*, III, p. 465.
9 Legouvé, *Maria Malibran*, pp. 45–6.
10 Gautier, *Histoire de l'art dramatique en France*, 4ème série, p. 166.
11 Liszt to Madame de Bacheracht (Manchester, 4th December, 1840), *cit.* Marix-Spire, *George Sand*, pp. 621–2.
12 Gautier, *Histoire de l'art dramatique en France*, 2ème série, p. 282.

PART IV, CHAPTER 5

1 See p. 230.
2 Nathan, p. 63.
3 Teatro del Corso. Three-act *canzone: Il testamento di una donna di spirito, ossia l'Incontro della Malibran e di Bellini agli Elisi*, Trebbi, p. 75.
4 *Gazzetta privigeliata di Milano*, 28.X.1836.
5 Three examples, from many: *Worcester Journal*, 6.X.1836; *Gazzetta privilegiata di Milano*, 28.X.1836; Nathan, p. 1, quoting the *Morning Chronicle*.
6 Letter of 26.XI.1838, *cit.* Quicherat, p. 274.
7 See p. 115.
8 Henry Dwight Sedgwick, *Alfred de Musset* (Indianapolis, 1931), p. 279; his source is Louise Colet.
9 Arianna Stassinopoulos, *Maria* (London, 1980), pp. 27 and 241.
10 Photograph in Reparaz, *Maria Malibran*, (Madrid, 1976), p. 85. No details given.
11 The 1849 picture was in the collections of Baron Chassériau; the 1852 picture was sold at auction in April 1974. There appears to have been a number of such portraits.
12 Hermann-Maurice Cossman (1821–90). Musée de Bagnères (Hautes Pyrénées).
13 Lamartine, *Cours familier de littérature*, III, p. 460.
14 For example: *Memoirs of the public and private life of the celebrated Madame Malibran, with numerous anecdotes of persons of distinction.* Printed and published by J. Thompson, Gloucester Street, Lambeth. Eight pages, with a very bad portrait. No anecdotes, merely an account of La Malibran's death. Another includes a song, with music by La Malibran herself: 'Thou Art an Angel Now', *A Tribute to the Memory of the Late Madame Malibran de Bériot, the Music being one of the Most Recent Compositions of the Eminently Gifted Artiste, to which is Appended a Critical and Historical Memoir.* London, 2nd ed., n.d.
15 *Memoirs of . . . Malibran* (see note 14, above), p. 7.
16 See Part IV, Chapter 3, note 9.
17 *Cenni biografici di Madama Maria Garcia Malibran*, Venice, 1835.
18 Gaetano Barbieri, *Notizie biografiche di M-F. Malibran*, Milan, 1836. *Madama Malibran e il suo secolo*, Lucca, 1836.

19 Isaac Nathan, *Memoirs of Madame Malibran de Bériot*, London, 1836, trans. A. de Tseskow, Quedlinbourg, 1837.
20 Nathan, p. 1.
21 *Ibid*, p. 3.
22 Fétis, *Biographie universelle*, article on Malibran.
23 Nathan, p. 2.
24 Baptismal certificate, Diocese of Seville, Libro+32, Folio, 192.17.
25 Nathan, p. 2.
26 Battista Morganti, *Manuele storico universale*, Lucca, 1847, pp. 535–6, quoting *Madama Malibran e il suo secolo*, Lucca, 1836.
27 See p. 183.
28 Henri Malherbe, *La passion de la Malibran* (Paris, 1937), pp. 32–3.
29 *Ibid*, p. 219; Merlin, II, pp. 13–14.
30 A. de Pontmartin, *Souvenirs d'un vieux mélomane* (Paris, 1879), 'Le bain de Madame Malibran', pp. 1–15.
31 See, for example, Lorenzo di Bradi, *La brève et merveilleuse vie de la Malibran* (Paris, 1937). Bradi devotes a whole chapter to La Malibran's charitable acts — pp. 137–45: 'L'âme charitable et pieuse de La Malibran'.
32 Louis Viardot to Charles de Bériot, 28.VIII.1845. Ms. copy, Brussels Conservatoire.
33 Société des Concerts Malibran, printed prospectus, 1857. Bibliothèque de l'Opéra, Paris.
34 H. Fiérens-Gevaert, *La Malibran à Bruxelles*, *Le Magasin pittorésque* (Paris), 15.VI.1901.
35 Stassinopoulos, p. 157.

PART IV, CHAPTER 6
1 Philarète Chasles, *Caractères et paysages* (Paris, 1833), p. 259.
2 Florimo, *Bellini*, p. 6.
3 Sinclair, p. 96.
4 Wilson, pp. 9–10.
5 Wilson, pp. 11 and 41.
6 Gabrielle M. Spiegel. 'The cult of St Denis and the Capetian Kings', in Wilson, p. 143.
7 Florimo, *Bellini*, 'Translazione delle ceneri di Vincenzo Bellini', pp. 153–243.
8 *Ibid*, Appendice, pp. 247–58.

9 *Ibid*, p. 241.
10 Wilson, p. 19.
11 *Evening News*, 30.IV.1980.
12 Sinclair, p. 95.
13 Blaze de Bury, *cit.* Lafôret, p. 211. *Manchester Guardian*, 28.IX.1836, and other writers.
14 See pp. 92–3.
15 *Guardian*, 4.V.1984.
16 Wilson, p. 37.
17 *Ibid*, p. 38.
18 *Ibid*, p. 37.

THE LEGACY OF LA MALIBRAN

1 Chorley, p. 15.
2 See Part III, Chapter 7, note 6.
3 Meyerbeer, p. 138 and p. 591, n. 79.
4 See p. 218 and footnote.
5 Emilie Gretsch, *cit.* Eigeldinger, *Chopin vu par ses élèves*, 2nd ed. (Neuchâtel, 1979), p. 73.
6 See Winton Dean, *Bizet* (London, 1978), pp. 230–2, and Tiersot, 'Bizet and Spanish Music', *Musical Quarterly*, XIII, pp. 566–81 (first published in *Le Ménéstrel*, 1925.)
7 Pougin, pp. 272–4, gives a list of Maria Malibran's compositions.
8 V. Fleury, 'La romance', *L'Artiste*, III, pp. 186–9 (1832). See also Guichard, pp. 42–64.
9 Berlioz: 'Dernières pensées musicales de Marie Félicité Garcia de Bériot', *Revue et gazette musicale*, 2.VII.1837.
10 Schumann: Leon B. Plantiga, *Schumann as Critic* (London, 1967), p. 56.
11 Debussy: *Enciclopedia dello spettacolo* (article on M. Malibran). This was also told me by the late Edward Lockspeiser, the well-known authority on Debussy, but I do not know what his source of information was.
12 Wauwermans, p. 92. At one time this portrait was in the possession of the artist's son.
13 Séché, *Alfred de Musset*, II, p. 136, n. 1.
14 Reproduced in *Les Arts et les lettres*, 1889 (4), p. 91.
15 The bust is in the Brussels Conservatoire.
16 J-H. Belloc (Nantes, 1786 — Paris, 1866); the portrait was in the collection of Baron de la Frésnaye.

17 Was in Moreau-Chelson Collection.
18 Whereabouts not known; one of the last portraits of La Malibran.
19 For example, in the Victoria and Albert Museum, London.
20 Séché, *Alfred de Musset*, p. 136, n. 1. There is an undated ms. note from Bouchot to La Malibran, thanking her for sitting to him, in the Brussels Conservatoire.
21 Philarète Chasles, *cit.* Séchan, p. 192.
22 P. A. Fiorentino, obituary of La Malibran in *La Presse* (undated newspaper cutting, Bibliothèque de l'Arsenal, Paris).
23 R. de Beauvoir, *L'Ecolier de Cluny*, Paris, 1832, I, p. 20.
24 Legouvé, *Maria Malibran*, p. 7.
25 A. Ricard, *L'Ouvreuse des loges*, *cit.* Bailbé, p. 48, n. 47.
26 Lorenzo da Ponte, *Memorie*, II, p. 127.
27 Christine Alan, *Mort de Marie Malibran*, first published in *Prométhée*, May, 1977; reprinted in *La Bataille romantique*, by A. L. Sire and C. Brochard, (Paris, 1980).
28 For example: *New York American*, 17.IV.1826; the poem is in Italian, unsigned; and *New York American*, 31.I.1826; the poem is in French, signed E.L.
29 For example, in *La Peau de chagrin* and *Sarrazine*.
30 R. de Beauvoir, *L'Ecolier de Cluny*, Paris, 1832, I, p. 20, *cit.* Bailbé, p. 100. See also A. Luchet, *Le nom de famille* (1842), II, p. 144 and *Madame de Saint-Surin* (1837), p. 138.
31 Musset, prose: for example, 'Concert de Mlle. Garcia', *Revue des deux mondes*, 4.XI.1839, and 'Débuts de Mlle. Pauline Garcia', *Revue des deux mondes*, 1.XI.1839. Musset alludes to La Malibran in other articles, and in his *Stances à Madame Ristori*.
32 Lamartine, *Cours familier de littérature*, Entretien XVIII. The poem is on La Malibran's grave (see page 253, footnote).
33 Jules Sandeau, *Le Concert pour les pauvres*, *La Sylphide*, 19 and 26.II.1842.
34 H. C. Andersen, see Bushnell, pp. 157–8.
35 For example: Bernardo Bellini, Gian-Carlo di Negri, Girolamo Zappi, Dr Caméll Mirabèll (in the Bolognese dialect). In the English edition of Countess Merlin's biography (London, 1840) Vol. II, pp. 270–94, there are several examples of Italian poems. See also Pougin, pp. 274–5.
36 Trebbi, p. 75.
37 Memorial Cantata: In morte di M. F. Malibran De (sic) Bériot. Cantata . . . la poesia è del Sig.ʳ Ant.º Piazza, la musica dei Sig.ⁱ

Maestri ... G. Donizetti ... G. Pacini ... S. Mercadante ... P. A. Coppola ... N. Vaccai. [Vocal Score]. Riccordi, Milan [1837]. See: A. Weatherston, 'Lament for a dead nightingale', *Donizetti Society Journal*, 5, 1984, pp. 155–62.

38 Heine, *Sämtliche Schriften* (Munich 1968–76), Vol. VI/1, pp. 211–14, *Himmelfahrt*.

39 Villiers de l'Isle Adam, *L'Inconnue*.

40 T. de Banville, *Les Camées parisiens*, 1er série. Paris, 1866.

41 See Sire and Brochard, *La Bataille romantique*, Paris, 1980.

42 *Maria Malibran*, opera in three acts, music by Robert Russell Bennett, libretto by R. A. Simon. New York, 1935. And *La Malibran*, opera in three acts, music by Berthe de Vito-Delvaux, libretto by Nicholas and Jean de Sart. Liège, 1949.

43 For example, there is a typescript scenario, *La Malibran*, signed by Aurore Sand, undated; it is not clear if it is for a play or an opera (Le Cesne Collection). François Musseau, *La Malibran à Venise, Acte en vers*, Paris, 1891 (Bibliothèque de l'Arsenal, Paris). Gustave Grillet, *La Malibran*, play in 4 acts, Théâtre Sarah Bernhardt, Paris, 10.IV.1924. *La Malibran*, Théâtre Fontaine, Paris, June, 1983.

44 *Maria Malibran*, with Maria Cebotari and Gredo Brignoni, 1943. *Der Tod der Maria Malibran*, Director: Werner Schroeter, with Christine Kaufmann. Colour, 108 minutes. 1972.

45 Radio programme, Poste Parisien, 1936. *Maria Malibran*, by Sarah Badel; BBC Radio 4, 26.XII.1979. TV programmes: *La naissance de la Malibran*, (Le calendrier de l'histoire), 21.XI.1971. And *Maria Malibran, ou l'âme musicienne* par Eve Ruggieri (Musiques au cœur), 30.XI.1986.

46 In the series 'Les amours célèbres', text by Paul Gordeaux, drawings by J-A. Carlotti, in *France-Soir*, 17.V.–15.VI.1978.

47 Pougin, pp. 262–4.

48 Jan Morris, *Last Letters from Hav*. London, 1986, p. 40.

SELECT BIBLIOGRAPHY

A Note on Some Earlier Biographies of La Malibran
It has not been possible to make a complete bibliography of all the
many books on La Malibran which have been published. Several
early biographies which are known to exist are now extremely rare,
and were not available in libraries to which I had access. There are
countless articles, many incorrect, in reference books and books on
opera; Eugenio Gara's article in *l'Enciclopedia dello Spettacolo* is
by far the most accurate and informative. Until Howard Bushnell's
biography was published in 1979, Arthur Pougin's *Marie Malibran*
(1911) was still the best; and although Bushnell's book must now
be considered the standard work and contains much new material
which was not available to Pougin, *Marie Malibran* is still a very
sensitive account of the singer and her epoch. Pougin was a well-
known musicologist, and in his biography set out to print only
'rigorously controlled' facts; I have therefore sometimes preferred to
quote letters and other information from him, rather than from
Countess Merlin and other sources. All subsequent books rely
heavily on Countess Merlin and Pougin; many, such as Albert
Flament's *Une Étoile en 1830 — La Malibran* (Paris, 1928) and his
L'Enchanteresse errante — La Malibran (Paris, 1937), are romantic
fiction. Henri Malherbe's *La Passion de La Malibran* (Paris, 1937),
is faction. Malherbe, a well-known writer, had had access to some
then unpublished documents, which he wove into his book (with no
bibliographical references), which is, according to the publisher's
publicity leaflet (in my possession), a novel. This is not stated on
the book itself. *La Malibran — Pauline Viardot*, by S. Desternes
and H. Chandet, with the collaboration of Alice Viardot (Paris,
1969), is a different case. Many passages in this shoddy book were
taken, word for word, and without my knowledge or permission,
from my *The Price of Genius* (London, 1964). The Society of
Authors, on my behalf, proposed to sue the authors; but they,
acknowledging their plagiarism, preferred to settle out of court, and
paid me compensation. The publisher (Fayard) agreed to withdraw

the book from circulation, but has not done so; it is still on sale in many French bookshops. Finally, I must point out that I myself made several errors of fact concerning the Garcia family in my two earlier books; I was then unaware of certain information which I have only recently discovered.

❊   ❊   ❊

Manuscripts in: British Library, London
                  Bibliothèque Nationale, Paris
                  Bibliothèque de l'Opéra, Paris
                  Le Cesne Collection, Paris
                  Bibliothèque royale Albert 1er, Brussels
                  Conservatoire Royale, Brussels

Typescript: Wauwermans, Général Henri.
              Maria Félicia de Bériot — Garcia, (La Malibran). Mémoires inédites, d'après des correspondances inédites.
              Bruxelles, 1er janvier, 1902.
              Unpublished typescript. Brussels Conservatoire and Le Cesne Collection, Paris.

ANON. *Memoirs of the Public and Private Life of the Celebrated Madame Malibran, with Numerous Anecdotes of Persons of Distinction*, Lambeth, 1836. (8 pages, no anecdotes, merely an account of her death).

ANON. 'Madame Malibran's Marriage', *Temple Bar*, Vol. 65, 1882, pp. 38–43.

ABARINOVA, A. M. 'Vospominaniya', *Istoricheskiy Vestnik* (St Petersburg), LXXXIII, 1901.

ADAM, ADOLPHE. *Souvenirs d'un musicien*, Paris [n.d.,] 1901?

ADKINS, N. F. *Fitz-Greene Halleck, An Early Knickerbocker Wit and Poet*, London, 1930.

AGOULT, MARIE, COMTESSE D', [Daniel Stern]. *Mes souvenirs*, par Daniel Stern. Paris, 1877.

AMATEUR. *Memoirs Critical and Historical of Madame Malibran de Beriot (sic)*, London, [1836].

ARCHER-SHEE, WILLIAM. *My Contemporaries, 1830–1870*, London, 1893.

ASHBROOK, WILLIAM. *Donizetti and his Operas*, London, 1965 and 1982.

BAILBÉ, JOSEPH-MARC. *Le Roman et la musique en France sous la Monarchie de Juillet*, Paris, 1969.

— 'George Sand et la Malibran', *Cahiers Ivan Tourguénev, Pauline Viardot, Maria Malibran* (Paris), No. 3, Oct. 1979, pp. 19–24.

BARBIERI, GAETANO. *Notizie biografiche di M. F. Malibran*, Milan, 1836.

BARBIERI, RAFFAELO. *Vite ardente nel teatro*, Milan, 1931.

BARRETT, WILLIAM ALEXANDER. *Balfe: His Life and Work*, London, 1882.

BAUER, KAROLINE. *The Posthumous Memoirs of Karoline Bauer*, translated from the German. 4 vols., London, 1884–5.

BEACONSFIELD, LORD. *Home Letters Written by Lord Beaconsfield, 1830–1852*, London, 1928.

BEALE, WILLERT (pseudonym: Walter Maynard). *The Light of Other Days*, 2 vols., London, 1890.

BELLINI, VINCENZO. *Memorie e lettere*, a cura di Francesco Florimo. Florence, 1882.

— *Le lettere di Bellini (1819–1835)*, ed. Francesco Pastura, Catania, 1935.

— *Epistolario*, a cura di Luisa Cambi, Milan, 1943.

BERLIOZ, HECTOR. 'Les dernières pensées musicales de Marie Félicité Garcia de Bériot', *La Revue et gazette musicale*, 2nd July, 1837.

— *A travers chants*, Paris, 1862.

— *Mémoires*, 2 vols., Paris, 1969.

BERTRAND, J. *La Malibran. Anecdotes*, Paris, 1864.

BLAZE DE BURY, HENRI. *Meyerbeer et son temps*, Paris, 1865.

BORREN, CHARLES VAN DEN. 'Charles de Bériot', *Biographie Nationale de Belgique*, Vol. XXIX, Supplement, I. Brussels, 1957.

BOUILLY, JEAN-NICHOLAS. *Mes récapitulations*, 3 vols., Paris, 1836–7.

BRADI, LORENZO DI. *La Brève et Merveilleuse Vie de la Malibran*, Paris, 1937.

BULL, SARA C. *Ole Bull — A Memoir*, London, 1886.

BUNN, ALFRED. *The Stage: both before and behind the curtain*, 3 vols., London, 1840.

BUSHNELL, HOWARD. *Maria Malibran, A Biography of the Singer*, Pennsylvania State University Press, 1979.

CASTIL-BLAZE, F. H. J. *Théâtres Lyriques de Paris. L'Opéra Italien de 1548 à 1856*. Paris, 1856.

CHARLTON, D. G. (editor). *The French Romantics*, 2 vols., Cambridge, 1984.

CHASLES, PHILARÈTE. *Caractères et paysages*, Paris, 1833.

CHOPIN, F. *Korespondencja*, ed. B. E. Sydow. 2 vols., Warsaw, 1955.

CHORLEY, HENRY F. *Thirty Years' Musical Recollections*, 2 vols, London, 1862.

CLARKE, MARY COWDEN. *The Life and Labours of Vincent Novello*, London, 1864.

CORTE, ANDREA DELLA. *L'interpretazione musicale e gli interpreti*, Turin, 1951.

COTARELO Y MORI, EMILIO. *Estudias sobre la historia del arte escénico*, Vol. III, *Isidoro Maiquez*, Madrid, 1902.

COTTINET, EDMOND. *Maria Malibran et Alfred de Musset*, limited edition (not for sale), extract from *Les Lettres et les arts*, Paris 4, 1889.

COTTRAU, G. *Lettres d'un mélomane pour servir de document à l'histoire musicale de Naples de 1829 à 1847*. Naples, 1885.

CUVILLIER-FLEURY, A. A. *Journal intime*, publié avec une introduction par Ernest Bertin, 2 vols., Paris, 1900.

DA PONTE, LORENZO. *Memorie*, a cura di Giovanni Gambarin e Fausto Nicolini, 2 vols., Bari, 1918.

DAVIES, T. R. *French Romanticism and the Press: The Globe*, Cambridge, 1906.

DELACROIX, EUGÈNE. *Journal, 1822–1863*, Introduction et notes d'André Joubin, Paris, 1980.

DELÉCLUSE, ETIENNE-JEAN. *Journal 1824–1828*, ed. Robert Baschet, Paris, 1948.

— *Souvenirs de soixante années*, Paris, 1862.

DEVRIENT, EDOUARD. *My Recollections of Felix Mendelssohn-Bartholdy, and His Letters to Me*, trans. Natalia Macfarren, London, 1869.

Donizetti Society Journal, No. 3, London, 1977. (Number devoted to *Maria Stuarda*), and No. 5, London, 1984.

DUMAS, ALEXANDRE (*père*). *Mes Mémoires*, texte présenté et annoté par Pierre Jusserand, 5 vols., Paris, 1954.

DUPREZ, GILBERT. *Souvenirs d'un chanteur*, Paris, 1880.

EBERS, JOHN. *Seven Years of the King's Theatre*, London, 1828.

EDWARDES, H. S. See Sutherland Edwardes.

ELLA, JOHN. *Musical Sketches Abroad and At Home*, 2 vols., London, 1869.

ESCUDIER, MARIE ET LÉON. *Vie et aventures des cantatrices célèbres*, Paris, 1856.

ESTÈVE, EDMOND. 'De Shakespeare à Musset. Variations sur la romance du saule', *Revue d'histoire littéraire de la France*, XXIX, 1922, pp. 288–315.

FERRANTI-GIULINI, MARIA. *Giuditta Pasta e i suoi tempi*, Milan, 1935.

FÉTIS, F. J. *Biographie universelle des musiciens et bibliographie générale de la musique*, 2ème ed., Paris, 1863.

FITZLYON, APRIL. *Lorenzo da Ponte, A biography of Mozart's librettist*, London, 1955, 1982.

— *The Price of Genius, A biography of Pauline Viardot*, London, 1964.

FLORIMO, FRANCESCO. See Bellini, V.

FONTANEY, ANTOINE. *Journal intime*, publié avec une introduction et notes par René Jasinski. Paris, 1925.

FOUCHER, PAUL. 'La Malibran', *La Chronique musicale*, 1.XII.1873, 1.I., 1.II., 1.V., 1.VI., 1874.

FRANCIS, DR J. W. *Old New York*, New York, 1865.

GARA, EUGENIO. 'Maria Malibran', article in *Enciclopedia dello Spettacolo*, Rome, 1954–68.

GATTI, CARLO. *Il Teatro alla Scala nella storia e nell'arte, (1778–1963)*. Milan, 1964.

GAUTIER, THÉOPHILE. *Histoire de l'art dramatique en France depuis vingt-cinq ans.*, 6 vols., Paris, 1858, 1859.

— *Histoire du Romantisme*, 2ème ed., Paris, 1874.

GIORGI-RIGHETTI, GELTRUDE. *Cenni di una Donna cantante sopra il Maestro Rossini*, etc., Bologna, 1823.

GIULINI, MARIA. See Ferranti Giulini, Maria.

GOBBI, TITO. *My Life*, London, 1979.

GOUNOD, CHARLES. *Mémoires d'un artiste*, Paris, 1896.

GRONOW, CAPT. R. H. *Recollections and Anecdotes*, second series, London, 1863.

GUICHARD, LÉON. *La musique et les lettres au temps du Romantisme*, Paris, 1955.

HEINE, HEINRICH. *Sämtliche Schriften*, 6 vols., Munich 1968–76.

HENSEL, SEBASTIAN. *The Mendelssohn Family (1729–1847)*, trans. Carl Klingemann, 2 vols., London, 1881.

HÉRITTE-VIARDOT, LOUISE. *Memories and Adventures*, London, 1915.

— *Une Famille de grands musiciens*, Paris, 1923.

HERON-ALLEN, E. *A contribution towards an Accurate Biography of Charles Auguste de Bériot and Maria Felicita (sic) Malibran-Garcia, De Fidiculis Opusculum VI*, London, 1894.

HOGARTH, GEORGE. *Memoirs of the Musical Drama*, 2 vols., London, 1838.

HORSLEY, F. AND S. *Mendelssohn and His Friends in Kensington, Letters from Fanny and Sophy Horsley, written 1833–36*, ed. by Rosamund Brunel Gotch, London, 1936.

HUSK, WILLIAM. *Templeton and Malibran, Reminiscences of those renowned singers*, London [1880].

HUYS, BERNARD. *L'Ecole belge de violon*, catalogue of an exhibition at the Bibliothèque royale Albert 1er, Brussels, 1978.

JAUBERT, CAROLINE. *Souvenirs de Madame C. Jaubert*, 5ème ed., Paris [1881].

KARÉNINE, WLADIMIR (i.e. V. Komarova-Stasova). *George Sand, sa vie et ses oeuvres*, 4 vols., Paris, 1899–1926.

KENNEY, CHARLES LAMB. *A Memoir of Michael William Balfe*, London, 1875.

LAFORET, CLAUDE. *La Vie musicale au temps romantique*, Paris, 1929.

LAMARTINE, ALPHONSE DE. *Cours familier de littérature, Entretien XVIII* (Alfred de Musset), Vol. III. Paris, 1857.

LAMARTINE, MME. VALENTINE DE. *Lettres à Lamartine, 1818–1865*, publiées par Mme Valentine de Lamartine, Paris, 1892.

LANQUINE, CLÉMENT. *La Malibran*, Paris [1911].

LARIONOFF, P. AND PESTELLINI, F. *Maria Malibran e i suoi tempi*, Florence, 1935.

LEGOUVÉ, ERNEST. *Max*, Paris, 1833.

— *La Croix d'Honneur et les comédiens*, Paris, 1863.

— *Maria Malibran*, Paris [1880].

— *La Question des femmes*, Paris, 1881.

— *Soixante ans de souvenirs*, 2 vols., Paris, 1886–7.

— *Epis et bluets, Souvenirs biographiques*, Paris, 1893.

LENNOX, LORD WILLIAM PITT. *Fifty Years' Biographical Reminiscences*, 2 vols., London, 1863.

— *My Recollections from 1806–1873*, 2 vols., London, 1874.

LESURE, FRANÇOIS (editor), *La Musique à Paris en 1830–1831*. Enquête [. . .] sous la direction de François Lesure. Paris (Bibliothèque Nationale), 1983.

LISZT, F. *Correspondance de Liszt et de la Comtesse d'Agoult, 1833–40*. 2 vols., Paris [1937].

— *Pages romantiques*, publiées avec une introduction et des notes par Jean Chantavoine, Paris, 1912.

LUCAS-DUBRETON, J. *La Restauration et la Monarchie de Juillet*, Paris, 1926.

LUMLEY, BENJAMIN. *Reminiscences of the Opera*, London, 1864.

MACKENZIE-GRIEVE, AVRIL. *Clara Novello, 1818–1908*, London, 1955.

MACKINLAY, M. S. *Garcia the Centenarian and His Times*, Edinburgh and London, 1908.

MACREADY, WILLIAM CHARLES. *Diaries, 1833–1851*, ed. William Toynbee, 2 vols., London, 1912.

MAIGRON, LOUIS. *Le Romantisme et les moeurs, Essai d'étude historique et sociale*, Paris, 1910.

— *Le Romantisme et la mode*, d'après des documents inédits, Paris, 1911.

MALHERBE, HENRI. *La Passion de la Malibran*, Paris, 1937.

MALIBRAN, LE DOCTEUR (de Menton), 'La névrose de la Malibran', *La Chronique Médicale*, 1er fév., 1913, pp. 65–71.

— 'La légende imaginée par La Malibran', *La Chronique Médicale*, 1er juin, 1924, pp. 165–71.

MARIX-SPIRE, THÉRÈSE. *Les Romantiques et la musique. Le cas George Sand, 1804–38*, Paris, 1954.

MAUGRAS, GASTON. *Les Comédiens hors la loi*, 2ème édition, Paris, 1887.

MENDELSSOHN-BARTHOLDY, F. *Letters from Italy and Switzerland*, trans. from the German by Lady Wallace, London, 1862.

MÉRIMÉE, PROSPER. *Lettres de Mérimée à Ludovic Vitet*, publiées avec une introduction et des notes par Maurice Parturier, Paris [1934].

— *Correspondance générale*, annotée par Maurice Parturier, 17 vols., Paris, 1941–64.

MERLIN, MARIA DE LOS MERCEDES DE JARUCO, COMTESSE. *Les Loisirs d'une femme du monde*, Paris, 1838, Leipzig, 1839.

— *Madame Malibran*, 2 vols., Brussels, 1838. (The edition used in this book).

— *Memoirs of Madame Malibran*, 2 vols., London, 1840 and 1844.

— *Memoirs and Letters of Madame Malibran*, 2 vols., Philadelphia, 1840.

MEYERBEER, GIACOMO. *Briefwechsel und Tagebücher*, ed. Heinz Becker, Band 2, 1825–36. Berlin [1970].

MICHOTTE, EDMOND. *Richard Wagner's visit to Rossini (Paris 1860) and An Evening at Rossini's at Beau Séjour (Passy), 1858.* Trans. from the French and annotated, with an introduction and appendix by Herbert Weinstock, Chicago, 1968.

MILAČIĆ, D. *Marija Malibran*, Belgrade, 1954.

MONALDI, GINO. *Cantanti celebri del secolo XIX*, Rome [1907].

— *Le prime rappresentazioni celebri*, Milan, 1910.

MORGULIS, G. 'La Malibran en Italie', *La Revue de littérature comparée*, April, 1936.

MOSCHELES, CHARLOTTE. *Life of Moscheles*, adapted from the original German by A. D. Coleridge, 2 vols., London, 1873.

MOUNT EDGCUMBE, EARL OF. *Musical Reminiscences*, London, 1834.

MUSSET, ALFRED DE. *Oeuvres complètes*, 11 vols., Paris, 1866.

NATHAN, ISAAC. *Memoirs of Madame Malibran de Bériot*, 3rd ed., London, 1836.

NICOLAI, OTTO. *Tagebücher nebst Biographischen Ergänzungen*, herausgeben von B. Schröder, Leipzig, 1892.

— *Briefe an seinem Vater*, Regensburg, 1924.

NOVELLO, MARY SABILLA. 'The Last Days of Malibran', *Morning Post* and *Manchester Guardian*, 15.X.1836, and other papers.

ODELL, GEORGE C. D. *Annals of the New York Stage*, Vol. III [1821–1834], New York, 1928.

OLIVIER, JUSTE. *Paris en 1830*, Lausanne, 1951.

OWEN, ROBERT DALE. *Threading my Way*, London, 1874.

PACINI, GIOVANNI. *Le mie memorie artistiche*, Florence, 1865.

PARRY, JOHN ORLANDO. *Victorian Swansdown*, Extracts from the early travel diaries of John Orlando Parry, ed. by G. B. Andrews and J. A. Orr-Ewing, London, 1935.

PASTURA, FRANCESCO. *Bellini secondo la storia*, Parma, 1959.

PONTMARTIN, A. DE. *Souvenirs d'un vieux mélomane*, Paris, 1878.

POUGIN, ARTHUR. *Bellini, sa vie et ses oeuvres*, Paris, 1868.

— *Marie Malibran, Histoire d'une cantatrice*, Paris, 1911, reprint Geneva, 1973.

— *Marie Malibran, The Story of a Great Singer*, London, 1911.

PROD'HOMME, J. G. 'La Fayette and Maria-Felicia Malibran' (after unpublished letters), *The Chesterian*, Sept., 1919, pp. 17–20.

— 'The Baron de Trémont. Souvenirs of Beethoven and other contemporaries', *Musical Quarterly*, July, 1920, pp. 366–91.

PULVER, JEFFREY. *Paganini, The Romantic Virtuoso*, London, 1936.

QUICHERAT, L. *Adolphe Nourrit*, 3 vols., Paris, 1867.

RADICIOTTI, GIUSEPPE. *Gioacchino Rossini:Vita documentata, opere ed influenza su l'arte*, 3 vols., Tivoli, 1927–9.

RAYNOR, HENRY. *Music and Society since 1815*, London, 1976.

REPARAZ, CARMEN DE. *Maria Malibran*, Madrid, 1976. French translation, Paris, 1979.

ROGNONI, LUIGI. *Gioacchino Rossini*, Turin, 1977.

ROSENTHAL, HAROLD. *Two Centuries of Opera at Covent Garden*, London, 1958.

ROSSELLI, JOHN. *The Opera Industry in Italy from Cimarosa to Verdi*, Cambridge, 1984.

SAND, GEORGE. *Correspondance*, ed. Georges Lubin, I, Paris, 1964. II, 1966.

— *Lettres inédites de George Sand et de Pauline Viardot, 1839–1849*, ed. T. Marix-Spire, Paris, 1959.

SÉCHAN, CHARLES. *Souvenirs d'un homme de théâtre*, Paris, 1883.

SÉCHÉ, LÉON. *Etudes d'histoire romantique: Lamartine de 1816 à 1830*, Paris, 1905.

— *Alfred de Musset*, 2 vols., Paris, 1908.

SINCLAIR, MARIANNE. *Those who died young*, London, 1979.

SMART, SIR GEORGE. *Leaves from the journals of Sir George Smart*, ed. H. B. and C. E. E. Cox. London, 1907.

SOUBIES, ALBERT. *Le Théâtre Italien de 1801 à 1913*, Paris, 1913.

STASSINOPOULOS, ARIANNA. *Maria* [Callas], London, 1980.

STEINMETZ, JEAN-LUC (ed.) *La France frénétique de 1830, choix de textes*, Paris, 1978.

STENDHAL (Henri Beyle), *Correspondance*, édition établie et annotée par Henri Martineau et V. del Litto, 3 vols. [Paris], 1962–8.

— *Oeuvres intimes*, Paris, 1966.

— *Life of Rossini*, trans. and ed. by Richard N. Coe, 2nd ed., London, 1970.

STERLING-MACKINLAY, M. see Mackinlay.

STERN, DANIEL. See Marie d'Agoult.

SUBIRÁ, JOSÉ. 'El operetista Manuel García en la Biblioteca Municipal de Madrid', *Revista de la Biblioteca Archivo y Museo Ayuntamiento di Madrid*, Año XII, Abril, 1935, Numéro 46.

SUTHERLAND EDWARDES, H. *The Prima Donna*, 2 vols., London, 1882.

TENEO, MARTIAL. 'La Malibran d'après des documents inédits', *Sammelbände der Internationalen Musikgesellschaft*, Jahrgang VII, pp. 437–82, Leipzig, 1906.

TIERSOT, JULIEN. *Lettres de musiciens écrites en français du XVème au XXème siècle*, 2 vols., Paris, Turin, 1924, 1936.

— *La Musique aux temps romantique*, Paris, 1930.

TINTORI, GIAMPIERO. (ed.) *La Scala: Cronologia completa degli spettacoli e dei concerti*, Milan, 1964.

TISSOT, ERNEST. 'Le premier mariage de Madame Marie Malibran', *La Revue des revues*, Vol. 102 (July–August), 1913, pp. 506–24.

TREBBI, ORESTE. *Nella vecchia Bologna; Cronache e riccordi*, Bologna, 1924.

VACCAI, G. *Vita di Nicola Vaccai, scritto del figlio Giulio.* Bologna, 1882.

VERDI, G. *Verdi intimo, carteggio di Giuseppe Verdi con il conte Opprandino Arrivabene*, ed. A. Alberti, Verona, 1931.

VÉRON, DR L. *Mémoires d'un bourgeois de Paris*, 6 vols., Paris, 1853–5.

VIARDOT, PAULINE. 'Letters to Julius Rietz', *Musical Quarterly*, Vol. I, 1915, pp. 350–80, 526–59. Vol. II, 1916, pp. 32–60. For her correspondence with George Sand see under Sand, G.

VICTORIA, QUEEN OF ENGLAND. *The Girlhood of Queen Victoria*, A selection from Her Majesty's Diaries between the years 1832 and 1840, ed. Viscount Esher, 2 vols., London, 1912.

VIGNY, ALFRED DE. *Correspondance*, ed. Léon Séché, I, 1822–1849, Paris, n.d.

VILLIERS, ANDRÉ. *La Psychologie du comédien*, Paris, 1942.

— *Prostitution de l'acteur*, Paris, 1946.

— *La Psychologie de l'art dramatique*, Paris, 1951.

— *Le Cloître et la scène*, Paris, 1961.

WEINSTOCK, HERBERT. *Donizetti and the world of opera in Italy, Paris and Vienna in the first half of the nineteenth century*, London, 1963.

— *Bellini, his life and his operas*, London, 1972.

— *Rossini, a biography*, London, 1968.

WILLIS, N. P. *Pencillings by the Way*, 3 vols., New York, 1855.

WILSON, STEPHEN (editor, introduction and annotated bibliography), *Saints and Their Cults, Studies in Religious Sociology, Folklore and History*, Cambridge, 1983.

ZAVADINI, GUIDO. *Donizetti: Vita, musiche, Epistolario.* Bergamo, 1948.

NEWSPAPERS
British
Bath Journal and General Advertiser, Manchester Guardian,

Manchester Chronicle, Manchester and Salford Advertiser, Morning Post, The Times, Worcester Herald, etc.

French

Le Globe, La Revue des deux mondes, Le Journal des débats, Le Figaro, La Chronique musicale, La Revue et gazette musicale, etc.

Italian

Il giornale delle Due Sicilie, La gazetta privilegiata di Milano, etc.

American

American, New York American, New York Review, Albion, National Gazette and Literary Register (Philadelphia), etc.

Index

Page numbers in bold type indicate main references

composer, second husband of
La Malibran

life and career: family 102; birth
102; character 103–4, 170,
172, 195, 203; physical
appearance 104; as violinist
103, 115, 141–2, 155, 170–1,
220, 242n; as composer 171,
264n, 242n; first marriage
199–200; 'secret marriage'
109–12, 170, 173, 180;
second marriage 242n; and
Naples 193, 194

relationship with: Sontag 101–2;
sister 106 and n, 107, 142,
147, 231, 235, 237; Maria
Malibran 101–2 and n, 108–9,
116, 117, 118, 125, 143, 146,
148, 156, 160, 168, 173, 180,
195–7, 211, 212, 213, 219,
241; mother-in-law 167, 237;
Bellini 191; Thalberg 199n,
242n

and La Malibran's death: her last
illness 222, 224, 225, 226,
227; Dr Belluomini 225, 231,
237; her death 227, 229, 230
and n; instructions for her
funeral in Manchester 228;
decision to have her buried in
Belgium 235, 237, 238;
exhumation 238–9; burial of
La Malibran in Belgium
241–2, 243 and n; relics of La
Malibran, 249, 265;
constructs shrine at Laeken
253; opinion of him in
Manchester 229, 231, 238,
239, 240, 245; as seen by
posterity, 268

children: unidentified child, 157
and n; Charles Wilfrid 169,
172, 199, 242n; Franz Charles
157n, 242n

Bériot, Charles Wilfrid de, b1833,

Brussels, d1914, Paris. Son of
La Malibran and Charles de
Bériot, Belgian pianist 169,
172–3, 175, 196, 199, 242n

Bériot, Constance de—*see*
Francquen, C. de

Bériot, Franz Charles, 1841–63.
Son of Charles de Bériot and
his second wife 157n, 242n

Bériot, Maria Felicia—*see*
Malibran, M.F.

Bériot, Marie de (*née* Hueber),
1822–58. Second wife of
Charles de Bériot 242 and n

Berlioz, Hector, 1803–69. French
composer 60, 62, 68, 70, 76,
115, 132, 139, 162, 264
La mort de Sardanapole (*Prix de
Rome* cantata, 1830) 114

Bernhardt, Sarah, 1844–1923.
French actress, 93

Berry, Marie-Caroline de Bourbon
Sicilie, Duchesse de,
1798–1870 67

Bertin de Veaux, Mme Sophie.
Friend of La Malibran 217n

Beyle, Henri—*see* Stendhal

Bishop, Anna, 1810–84. English
soprano 220

Bishop, Henry (later Sir),
1786–1855. English composer
and conductor, first husband
of Anna Bishop, *q.v.* 178, 179

Bizet, Georges, 1838–75. French
composer
Carmen (1875) 264

Blargnies. Belgian lawyer, uncle of
Charles de Bériot 109–10

Boieldieu, François Adrien,
1775–1834. French composer
67
Jean de Paris (1812) 52

Bologna 182, 183, 185, 188, 194,
199n, 232, 250, 265

1796–1864. French engineer, one of the founders of Saint-Simonism **155**

Fairbanks, Douglas (senior), 1883–1939. American film star 256
Ferdinand II, 1815–59. King of the Two Sicilies from 1830 159, **182–3**
Fétis, François-Joseph, 1784–1871. Belgian musicologist, journalist and professor of music in Brussels and Paris 15, 70, **72**, 78, **101–2 and n**, **159**, 241n, 243, 252
Feydeau, Ernest, 1821–73. French novelist
Le Mari de la danseuse 231
Fidelio—*see* Beethoven, L. van
Fiennes, Monsieur de. Belgian lawyer, cousin of Charles de Bériot **238**, 240, 241
Figaro, Le. French newspaper 133
Figlia dell'arciere, La—*see* Coccia, C.
Figlia dell'aria, La—*see* Garcia, Manuel, snr
Fille d'Albano, La—*see* Sand, George
Flint, Lady. Friend of La Malibran 107
Florimo, Francesco, 1800–88. Italian librarian, musicologist, teacher and composer **179n**, **188 and n.**, 189, 190, 192, 205
Fontaney, Antoine-Etienne, 1803–37. French writer and diplomat 151
Francis, Dr. La Malibran's doctor in New York 91
Francquen, Angélique-Antoinette de—*see* Wauwermans, A. A.
Francquen, Constance de, 1799–?.

Charles de Bériot's sister 103, 104, **106–7**, 108, **109–12**, 142, 147–8, 156, 169, 172, 231, 235, 237, 239, 243 **and n.**
Francquen, Joseph de. Belgian cavalry officer, C. de Bériot's brother-in-law 107, **142**
Frederick-William III, 1770–1840. King of Prussia 128
Freischütz, Der—*see* Weber, C. M. von
Frith, The Rev Randolph. Roman Catholic priest in Manchester **235**

Galli, Filippo, 1783–1853. Italian bass (originally tenor) 68, 69, 100
Gallo, Giovanni. Theatre director in Venice 128n, **200**
Garcia family 25, 26, 30, 34, 35, 40, 104, 110, 139, 172
Garcia, Joaquina, 1780–1864. Spanish singer, mother of La Malibran 23, **25–7**, 29, 31, 35, 36, 40, 51, 123, 137, **152**, 167, 237, **239–41 and n**, 242
Garcia, Josepha—*see* Ruiz-Garcia, J.
Garcia, Manuel de el Pópulo Vicente Rodriguez, b Seville 1775 d Paris 1832. Spanish tenor, father of La Malibran
life and career: origins and childhood 23–4, 252; career in Spain, 24–5; first marriage 25; second (bigamous) marriage 26; character 24, 33, 167; leaves Spain 27; first appearance in Paris 25; association with Rossini 29; goes to New York 34; New York seasons 35–8, **46–7**; goes to Mexico 47; returns